Judy Harden
Marcia Hill
Editors

Breaking the Rules: Women in Prison and Feminist Therapy

Breaking the Rules: Women in Prison and Feminist Therapy has been co-published simultaneously as *Women & Therapy*, Volume 20, Number 4 1997 and Volume 21, Number 1 1998.

Pre-publication
REVIEWS,
COMMENTARIES,
EVALUATIONS . . .

"**W**omen behind bars are among the most silenced, poorly understood, and undersupported people among us. Their numbers are exploding . . . when services and programs for all prisoners have suffered drastic cuts. In this book the authors describe several prison programs that have created very caring communities where women have been able to gain a voice, a sense of self, and become more connected to each other, their families, and their communities. It is a marvel that such programs can evolve even in highly authoritarian and punitive systems designed to keep prisoners isolated, powerless, shamed, and dependent."

Mary Field Belenky, EdD
co-author of Women's Ways of Knowing *and, most recently,* A Tradition That Has No Name: Nurturing the Development of People, Families, and Communities

Breaking the Rules: Women in Prison and Feminist Therapy

Breaking the Rules: Women in Prison and Feminist Therapy has been co-published simultaneously as *Women & Therapy,* Volume 20, Number 4 1997, and Volume 21, Number 1 1998.

Breaking the Rules:
Women in Prison
and Feminist Therapy

Judy Harden, PhD
Marcia Hill, EdD
Editors

Breaking the Rules: Women in Prison and Feminist Therapy, edited by Judy Harden and Marcia Hill, was simultaneously issued by The Haworth Press, Inc., under the same title, as special issues of the journal *Women & Therapy,* Volume 20, Number 4 1997 and Volume 21, Number 1 1998, Marcia Hill and Esther D. Rothblum, Editors.

The Harrington Park Press
An Imprint of
The Haworth Press, Inc.
New York • London

1-56023-107-6

Published by

The Harrington Park Press, 10 Alice Street, Binghamton, NY 13904-1580 USA

The Harrington Park Press is an imprint of The Haworth Press, Inc., 10 Alice Street, Binghamton, NY 13904-1580 USA.

Breaking the Rules: Women in Prison and Feminist Therapy has been co-published simultaneously as *Women & Therapy,* Volume 20, Number 4 1997 and Volume 21, Number 1 1998.

Cover design by Thomas J. Mayshock Jr.
Cover illustration by Beth Merriam

Library of Congress Cataloging-in-Publication Data

Breaking the rules : women in prison and feminist therapy / Judy Harden, Marcia Hill, editors.
    p. cm.
    "Co-published simultaneously as Women & therapy, volume 20, number 4, 1997, and volume 21, number 1 1998."
    Includes bibliographical references and index.
    ISBN 0-7890-0365-1 (alk. paper). – ISBN 1-56023-107-6 (alk. paper)
    1. Women prisoners–Mental health–United States. 2. Women prisoners–Counseling of–United States. 3. Feminist therapy–United States. I. Harden, Judy. II. Hill, Marcia.
RC451.4.P68B74 1997
362.2'086'927–dc21
                                                97-45550
                                                 CIP

INDEXING & ABSTRACTING

Contributions to this publication are selectively indexed or abstracted in print, electronic, online, or CD-ROM version(s) of the reference tools and information services listed below. This list is current as of the copyright date of this publication. See the end of this section for additional notes.

- *Abstracts of Research in Pastoral Care & Counseling*, Loyola College, 7135 Minstrel Way, Suite 101, Columbia, MD 21045

- *Academic Abstracts/CD-ROM*, EBSCO Publishing Editorial Department, P.O. Box 590, Ipswich, MA 01938-0590

- *Academic Index (on-line)*, Information Access Company, 362 Lakeside Drive, Foster City, CA 94404

- *Alternative Press Index*, Alternative Press Center, Inc., P.O. Box 33109, Baltimore, MD 21218-0401

- *Behavioral Medicine Abstracts*, University of Washington, Department of Social Work & Speech & Hearing Sciences, Box 354900, Seattle, WA 98195

- *CNPIEC Reference Guide: Chinese National Directory of Foreign Periodicals*, P.O. Box 88, Beijing, People's Republic of China

- *Current Contents: Clinical Medicine/Life Sciences (CC: CM/LS) (weekly Table of Contents Service), and Social Science Citation Index. Articles also searchable through Social SciSearch, ISI's online database and in ISI's Research Alert current awareness service*, Institute for Scientific Information, 3501 Market Street, Philadelphia, PA 19104-3302 (USA)

- *Digest of Neurology and Psychiatry*, The Institute of Living, 400 Washington Street, Hartford, CT 06106

- *Expanded Academic Index,* Information Access Company, 362 Lakeside Drive, Forest City, CA 94404

- *Family Studies Database (online and CD/ROM)*, National Information Services Corporation, 306 East Baltimore Pike, 2nd Floor, Media, PA 19063

- *Family Violence & Sexual Assault Bulletin*, Family Violence & Sexual Assault Institute, 1121 E. South East Loop 323, Suite 130, Tyler, TX 75701

- *Feminist Periodicals: A Current Listing of Contents*, Women's Studies Librarian-at-Large, 728 State Street, 430 Memorial Library, Madison, WI 53706

- *Health Source: Indexing & Abstracting of 160 selected health related journals, updated monthly:* EBSCO Publishing, 83 Pine Street, Peabody, MA 01960

(continued)

- *Health Source Plus: expanded version of "Health Source" to be released shortly:* EBSCO Publishing, 83 Pine Street, Peabody, MA 01960
- *Higher Education Abstracts*, Claremont Graduate School, 231 East Tenth Street, Claremont, CA 91711
- *IBZ International Bibliography of Periodical Literature*, Zeller Verlag GmbH & Co., P.O.B. 1949, d-49009, Osnabruck, Germany
- *Index to Periodical Articles Related to Law*, University of Texas, 727 East 26th Street, Austin, TX 78705
- *INTERNET ACCESS (& additional networks) Bulletin Board for Libraries ("BUBL") coverage of information resources on INTERNET, JANET, and other networks.*
  - <URL:http://bubl.ac.uk/>
  - The new locations will be found under <URL:http://bubl.ac. uk/link/>.
  - Any existing BUBL users who have problems finding information on the new service should contact the BUBL help line by sending e-mail to <bubl@bubl.ac.uk>.
  The Andersonian Library, Curran Building, 101 St. James Road, Glasgow G4 0NS, Scotland
- *Mental Health Abstracts (online through DIALOG)*, IFI/Plenum Data Company, 3202 Kirkwood Highway, Wilmington, DE 19808
- *ONS Nursing Scan in Oncology-NAACOG's Women's Health Nursing Scan*, NURSECOM, Inc., 1211 Locust Street, Philadelphia, PA 19107
- *PASCAL, % Institute de L'Information Scientifique et Technique. Cross-disciplinary electronic database covering the fields of science, technology & medicine.* Also available on CD-ROM, and can generate customized retrospective searches. For more information: INIST, Customer Desk, 2, allee du Parc de Brabois, F-54514 Vandoeuvre Cedex, France; http//www.inist.fr
- *Periodical Abstracts, Research I* (general & basic reference indexing & abstracting data-base from University Microfilms International (UMI), 300 North Zeeb Road, P.O. Box 1346, Ann Arbor, MI 48106-1346), UMI Data Courier, P.O. Box 32770, Louisville, KY 40232-2770
- *Periodical Abstracts, Research II* (broad coverage indexing & abstracting data-base from University Microfilms International (UMI), 300 North Zeeb Road, P.O. Box 1346, Ann Arbor, MI 48106-1346), UMI Data Courier, P.O. Box 32770, Louisville, KY 40232-2770
- *Psychological Abstracts (PsycINFO)*, American Psychological Association, P.O. Box 91600, Washington, DC 20090-1600
- *Published International Literature on Traumatic Stress (The PILOTS Database)*, National Center for Post-Traumatic Stress Disorder (116 D), VA Medical Center, White River Junction, VT 05009
- *Sage Family Studies Abstracts (SFSA)*, Sage Publications, Inc., 2455 Teller Road, Newbury Park, CA 91320

(continued)

- *Social Work Abstracts*, National Association of Social Workers, 750 First Street NW, 8th Floor, Washington, DC 20002

- *Sociological Abstracts (SA)*, Sociological Abstracts, Inc., P.O. Box 22206, San Diego, CA 92192-0206

- *Studies on Women Abstracts*, Carfax Publishing Company, P.O. Box 25, Abingdon, Oxon OX14 3UE, United Kingdom

- *Violence and Abuse Abstracts: A Review of Current Literature on Interpersonal Violence (VAA)*, Sage Publications, Inc., 2455 Teller Road, Newbury Park, CA 91320

- *Women Studies Abstracts*, Rush Publishing Company, P.O. Box 1, Rush, NY 14543

- *Women's Studies Index (indexed comprehensively)*, G. K. Hall & Co., P.O. Box 159, Thorndike, ME 04986

SPECIAL BIBLIOGRAPHIC NOTES

related to special journal issues (separates)
and indexing/abstracting

❏ indexing/abstracting services in this list will also cover material in any "separate" that is co-published simultaneously with Haworth's special thematic journal issue or DocuSerial. Indexing/abstracting usually covers material at the article/chapter level.

❏ monographic co-editions are intended for either non-subscribers or libraries which intend to purchase a second copy for their circulating collections.

❏ monographic co-editions are reported to all jobbers/wholesalers/approval plans. The source journal is listed as the "series" to assist the prevention of duplicate purchasing in the same manner utilized for books-in-series.

❏ to facilitate user/access services all indexing/abstracting services are encouraged to utilize the co-indexing entry note indicated at the bottom of the first page of each article/chapter/contribution.

❏ this is intended to assist a library user of any reference tool (whether print, electronic, online, or CD-ROM) to locate the monographic version if the library has purchased this version but not a subscription to the source journal.

❏ individual articles/chapters in any Haworth publication are also available through the Haworth Document Delivery Service (HDDS).

CONTENTS

Preface   xiii

Women Prisoners: A Contextual Framework   1
    Susan D. Phillips
    Nancy J. Harm

The Experiences of Women in Prison: Implications
    for Services and Prevention   11
    Cynthia García Coll
    Jean Baker Miller
    Jacqueline P. Fields
    Betsy Mathews

An Analysis of the Impact of Prison on Women Survivors
    of Childhood Sexual Abuse   29
    Jan Heney
    Connie M. Kristiansen

Comparison Study of Women Who Have and Have Not
    Murdered Their Abusive Partners   45
    Gloria Hamilton
    Tammy Sutterfield

Managing Motherhood in Prison: The Impact of Race
    and Ethnicity on Child Placements   57
    Sandra Enos

Restricted Love   75
    Dominik Morgan

Children Without Childhoods: A Feminist Intervention
    Strategy Utilizing Systems Theory and Restorative Justice
    in Treating Female Adolescent Offenders   85
    Carol Lee O'Hara Pepi

Lessons from a Mother's Program in Prison: A Psychosocial
   Approach Supports Women and Their Children   103
     Kathy Boudin

Girls in Jail   127
     Verna J. Tuesday

Women in Prison: Approaches in the Treatment
   of Our Most Invisible Population   141
     Stephanie S. Covington

To Find a Voice: Art Therapy in a Women's Prison   157
     Beth Merriam

A Feminist Examination of Boot Camp Prison Programs
   for Women   173
     Susan T. Marcus-Mendoza
     Jody Klein-Saffran
     Faith Lutze

Index   187

ABOUT THE EDITORS

Judy Harden, PhD, teaches psychology and feminist studies at Goddard College in Vermont. She has taught courses about women and the criminal justice system that have involved community service work in the local prison for women. Her interests include projects involving collaboration among academics, human services organizations, and the Vermont state legislature. Dr. Harden is becoming more involved with policy and program development for the justice system in Vermont.

Marcia Hill, EdD, is a psychologist who has spent over 20 years practicing psychotherapy. She is Co-Editor of the journal *Women & Therapy* and a member and past Chair of the Feminist Therapy Institute. In addition to therapy, Dr. Hill does occasional teaching, writing, and consulting in the areas of feminist therapy theory and practice. The Editor of *More than a Mirror: How Clients Influence Therapists' Lives* (The Haworth Press, Inc., 1997), she has co-edited three other Haworth books: *Classism and Feminist Therapy: Counting Costs* (1996); *Couples Therapy: Feminist Perspectives* (1996); and *Children's Rights, Therapists' Responsibilities: Feminist Commentaries* (1997). She is currently in private practice in Montpelier, Vermont.

Preface

The unruly woman is the undisciplined woman. She is a renegade from the disciplinary practices which would mold her as a gendered being. She is the defiant woman who rejects authority which would subjugate her and render her docile. She is the offensive woman who acts in her own self interests. She is the unmanageable woman who claims her own body, the whore, the wanton woman, the wild woman out of control. She is the woman who cannot be silenced. She is a rebel. She is trouble. . . . The "bad girl" of cultural stereo-typing is the product of class-biased, racist and heterosexist myths. Historically and to the present, her appearance, actions and attitudes have been offensive to the dominant discourses which define, classi-fy, regulate and set penalties for deviance. (Faith, 1993, p. 1)

My (JH) first experience inside a prison, one for men that also housed some 34 women, haunted me for a long time; I found few words to articulate my experience, but I was permeated with the sound of large, heavy, metal doors clanging shut over and over again. There was some-thing incongruous about the strength and impenetrability of the fortress in which I sat and the ordinariness and vulnerability of the eight or nine young women prisoners sitting in a circle talking about their families and their lives. The walls, keys, bars, guards, fences, electronic surveillance devices all served to protect "us" from "them," and also made it difficult to see who these women were, ways in which we were connected, how they got there, where they might go next, and what they might need in order to get there. The physical isolation and seclusion and inaccessibility of these women was graphic and horrifying. These women seemed to me

[Haworth co-indexing entry note]: "Preface." Harden, Judy, and Marcia Hill. Co-published simul-taneously in *Women & Therapy* (The Haworth Press, Inc.) Vol. 20, No. 4, 1997, pp. xv-xx; and: *Breaking the Rules: Women in Prison and Feminist Therapy* (ed: Judy Harden, and Marcia Hill) The Haworth Press, Inc., 1998, pp. xiii-xviii; and: *Breaking the Rules: Women in Prison and Feminist Therapy* (ed: Judy Harden, and Marcia Hill) The Harrington Park Press, an imprint of The Haworth Press, Inc., 1998, pp. xiii-xviii. Single or multiple copies of this article are available for a fee from The Haworth Document Delivery Service [1-800-342-9678, 9:00 a.m. - 5:00 p.m. (EST). E-mail address: getinfo@haworth.com].

xiii

immensely vulnerable both personally and socioculturally; it was hard at first to see the strength and power suggested in the quote above.

My personal interest in this area stems from a lifelong pattern of rebellion and defiance, but always within limits; I found relatively safe ways to challenge, to push, to defy, to be bad. I was able to do this partly because of a fair amount of social and economic privilege that muffled and protected me from ever getting too close to official societal responses, such as incarceration. This privilege also meant that there was a lot I didn't have to fight for, or against; I was not propelled by conditions of my life to take more defiant personal risks. I did not have a strongly developed social conscience that might have led me in those years to more outrageous (and dangerous) acts. If I thought about women "criminals" at all in my younger years, I probably thought of them in the same category as Women Who Pierced Their Ears–Not Like Me, Other.

After that first visit to the prison, I was sharply aware both of my connection with the women, and of much that separated us. After more visits, and more reading and talking, my sense of connection with the women grew, and I began to think about how crime is defined and who defines it. Karlene Faith (1993) quotes Freda Adler as saying, "Stripped of ethical rationalizations and philosophical pretensions, a crime is anything that a group in power chooses to prohibit" (p. 64). I had a pretty clear idea about which group has been defining what is criminal, in need of "correction," so it didn't take long to start making more connections with feminism. I could see how we have conveniently split off our most needy and rowdy women and locked them up.

In editing this collection, we began to wonder how psychology had participated in defining crime through its propensity to pathologize, and to " . . . flatten, depoliticize, and individualize" (Fine, 1992, p. 14), and conversely, what "interruptive questions" (Fine, 1992, p. 16) we might raise about women in prison. How do definitions of crime reflect current values and assumptions about women? As the authors here point out, many women in prison are there for "crimes" that are in fact unsolved social problems: drug use, retaliation against an abuser, prostitution. What social problems are deflected or camouflaged through incarceration of "problem" people, "problem" women? And what would we do about these matters if prison were not an option? Prison allows us to tidy up the consequences of oppression and distorted economic priorities, to put the results of our failures as a society somewhere out of sight. We call this "making the streets safe," and the implied beneficiary of this safety is, of course, those of us with enough privilege to have escaped entrapment in these very problems. In a culture with prisons, we are all living in a gated community.

Psychologically, the threat of jail is often seen as a deterrent to crime, but the existence of prisons has psychological functions for obedient citizens as well. Prison represents the defense of splitting, of emotional separation from the other, the "not me." Melinda Garcia (1995) describes how white women's self-concept as "nice" prevents us from integrating information about our own racism and thus from making alliances with women of color. Similarly, to integrate information about our own complicity in creating and sustaining the conditions which necessitate prisons, and to make alliances with those inside prisons, we would have to stop defining ourselves as nice, as "law-abiding citizens." Prison allows us to make "other" of those among us who are most injured and most without resources, thus protecting us from the dangerous knowledge that access to resources and protection from injury is actually arbitrary. And prison allows us to deny and split off the part of each of us that is bad, unruly. How defiant, offensive, unmanageable, wild, and rebellious can we be without being incarcerated? What are the conditions that protect some of us, and not others of us? How can we retain this energy and direct it towards transforming the conditions that put women behind bars in the first place?

Sociocultural problems are not abstract influences but personally felt and lived, part of the individual and her sense of possibilities. Behind each problem–violence or poverty or drug use–stands a multitude of individuals, each with a personal history of narrowing options. We need to know more about who is in prison, for what transgressions, against whom. The conditions of class, race, family life, and working life from which these women come must be understood, as well as the relationship of these conditions to the nature of their crimes. We need to know more about the kinds of resources available to women in prison, and especially, the kinds that are still needed. What do women "inside" want us to know about who they are and how they live?

Finally, an important consideration for feminist therapists is the role we are playing in the lives of women prisoners, and the ways in which this role might be strengthened, expanded. In this Preface, we have emphasized the sociocultural and political factors associated with incarceration, but there are individual factors operating as well, individual choices within a variety of social contexts. As Kathy Boudin puts it in a reflective part of her writing, " . . . if we define problems as overwhelmingly rooted in the social structure, how can we avoid leaving people feeling passive and unable to change their lives?" How can feminist therapists help women in prison explore their past and the choices they have made in such a way that they can learn about their own complexities, come to feel a sense of responsibility for their lives that will be empowering rather than crippling? Several authors underline the importance of helping women within these authoritarian, controlling fortresses develop autonomy, self-reliance, and skills to become self-supporting.

The collection of writings we have put together includes some that address theoretical frameworks within which to look at some of these questions, as well as those that describe experiences behind the prison walls. All include suggestions for therapists in working with women in prison. Some themes that emerge persistently in many of the articles are the rapid and higher rate of increase of incarceration of women as compared to men, the high proportion of these women who are mothers, and the lack of programs geared specifically to women's needs. Susan Phillips and Nancy Harm provide a good overview of these concerns and a contextual framework for understanding some of the issues facing women in prison and their children, as well as implications for direct practice. Cynthia García-Coll and her colleagues continue the exploration of these themes while looking at the needs of women prisoners from a variety of theoretical perspectives: relational, diversity, and developmental. Their work with incarcerated women reveals histories of high-risk conditions and early trauma, which becomes another theme that percolates throughout many of the articles included herein.

Jan Heney and Connie Kristiansen explore the impact of prison on women survivors of childhood abuse, and the powerlessness that is consequently re-evoked, as well as old strategies of coping which emerge, like substance abuse, violence, suicide. Means of coping with domestic abuse is the focus of the work of Gloria Hamilton and Tammy Sutterfield; they compared histories of abuse among women who have murdered their partners with women who have not, the kinds of help they sought, the responses they received (or didn't).

The following three works, while continuing the themes described above, focus more specifically on particular factors affecting the experience of women in prison. Sandra Enos discusses the impact of race and ethnicity on patterns of mothering and caretaking of children of women prisoners; this work directly addresses some of the issues faced by mothers in prison by describing options available for women in placing their children, maintaining contact, and maintaining place in families. Lesbian relationships among women in prison, written from the perspective of a woman prisoner, Dominik Morgan, are described in a way that challenges stereotypes of women prisoners: a more complex, and by now in the collection, familiar, view of them as "mothers, non-violent offenders, and victims of abuse." The intersection of adolescence and gender is the focus of Carol Pepi's presentation of feminist theory in relation to the treatment of girls who have broken the law; she addresses the important question of gender bias in the detention of girls–in the rates of their arrests, the kinds of crimes for which they are arrested, and sentencing and program options, as well as implications for treatment.

In the following essays, the emphasis is on specific intervention strategies. The article by prisoner Kathy Boudin describes prisoner-led support groups for mothers from the perspective of a psychosocial group model; this work " . . . illustrates that when a mother works on her own emotional issues, this process can also improve her ability to parent her children . . . " A different kind of group work in prison, consciousness-raising discussion groups focusing on internalized sexism among girls in a juvenile detention facility, is described by Verna Tuesday.

Stephanie Covington tackles the ubiquitous problem of the increase in drug-related convictions and mandatory sentences for these offenses in some states coupled with the dearth of treatment opportunities for addicted women prisoners; she describes a "relational model of treatment that incorporates the multiple issues involved in women's recovery." Women with histories of traumatic experiences (sexual abuse, parental death at an early age, living on the streets, prostitution, substance abuse, etc.) are the focus of Beth Merriam's art therapy; she uses case histories to show how this relatively non-verbal approach can enable the women to "reconnect with disowned thoughts, feelings, and fantasies in a safe way." Finally, Susan Marcus-Mendoza and her colleagues look at "correctional boot camp" practices within the context of feminist therapy practices; these programs are critiqued as an example of a low-cost, short-term alternative to traditional prison programming.

We wanted to work on bringing together this collection of writings in part to bring some of the questions and issues described earlier to the table, to learn about who among us is thinking about these questions and others, but most of all, to make a connection with women in prison. We wanted to show how women behind bars are us–minus privilege, caution, luck; we are them, just not despairing enough or defiant enough to have come to the attention of the law. We wanted to look at prisons and prisoners through the lens of feminism, which sees women in the context of patriarchal rules and women's choices in relation to those rules. Karlene Faith (1993) describes this link:

> There are important connections between women who are selectively labeled criminal for random or impulsive illegal rebellions, and unruly

women whose legal defiances signify deliberate rejection of the values that sustain existing hierarchical power relations. Whether an action is considered a crime or deviancy, or a behavior is socially tolerated, depends entirely on the historical and cultural contexts and the particular configurations of power which issue formal and informal judgements. Whether or not they are labeled "criminal," unruly women do what ordinary women do. They feel love and fear; they try to make a living or find someone to support them; if they are mothers they care for their children the best they can; they get lost in dreams of how life might be, if only . . . And along the way, if they are truly unruly women, they get into trouble. Most female rebels have been victimized in some way, and most victims have the capacity to resist and to become active players in social transformation. (p. 8)

Questioning the assumptions associated with the existence of prisons and the definition of prisoners is unruly behavior, feminist behavior. We invite you to break the rules by asking these and other questions for yourselves, in alliance with the women behind bars.

Judy Harden
Marcia Hill

REFERENCES

Faith, Karlene (1993). *Unruly women: The politics of confinement and resistance.* Vancouver: Press Gang Publishers.

Fine, Michelle (1992). *Disruptive voices: The possibilities of feminist research.* Ann Arbor: University of Michigan.

Garcia, Melinda (1995, November). *Talking for real and playing innocent: Issues in intercultural dialogue.* Paper presented at the Fourteenth Advanced Feminist Therapy Institute, Albuquerque, NM.

Women Prisoners:
A Contextual Framework

Susan D. Phillips
Nancy J. Harm

SUMMARY. As a consequence of "the war on drugs" and "take a bite out of crime" policies, the prison population in the United States has increased dramatically. One of the seldom discussed consequences of these policies is their impact on women. Between 1980 and 1994 the population of women inmates increased 386% compared to a 214% increase in the male prison population. The majority of these women are mothers who were living with minor children before being sent to prison. This article provides a contextual framework for understanding the issues facing women in prison and their children. *[Article copies available for a fee from The Haworth Document Delivery Service: 1-800-342-9678. E-mail address: getinfo@haworth.com]*

The prison population in the U.S. began a dramatic upward turn in the 1970s. A frequently overlooked consequence of the criminal justice poli-

---

Susan Phillips, LMSW, is Community Resource Development Coordinator for the Parenting from Prison program at Centers for Youth and Families in Little Rock, AR. She is also a member of the Ad Hoc Committee on Women Inmates and the Arkansas steering committee for Mothers in Prison, Children in Crisis Campaign 1996. Nancy Harm, PhD, is Professor at the University of Arkansas Graduate School of Social Work in Little Rock, AR. Nancy is a former corrections administrator and has worked extensively in the area of domestic violence.

Address correspondence to: Susan Phillips, LMSW, The Parent Center, 5905 Forest Place, Suite 205, Little Rock, AR 72207.

[Haworth co-indexing entry note]: "Women Prisoners: A Contextual Framework." Phillips, Susan D., and Nancy J. Harm. Co-published simultaneously in *Women & Therapy* (The Haworth Press, Inc.) Vol. 20, No. 4, 1997, pp. 1-9; and: *Breaking the Rules: Women in Prison and Feminist Therapy* (ed: Judy Harden, and Marcia Hill) The Haworth Press, Inc., 1998, pp. 1-9; and: *Breaking the Rules: Women in Prison and Feminist Therapy* (ed: Judy Harden, and Marcia Hill) The Harrington Park Press, an imprint of The Haworth Press, Inc., 1998, pp. 1-9. Single or multiple copies of this article are available for a fee from The Haworth Document Delivery Service [1-800-342-9678, 9:00 a.m. - 5:00 p.m. (EST). E-mail address: getinfo@haworth.com].

1

cies underlying the expansion of the prison population is their impact on women and the children they leave behind while they serve their prison sentences. The number of women in correctional facilities has grown at a significantly faster rate than the population of male inmates. Between 1980 and 1994, the number of women in State prisons increased by 386%, compared to a 214% increase in the male population (Department of Justice, 1995). More than ever before professionals are encountering women who have been imprisoned, children who have experienced separation from their mothers because of incarceration, and grandparents and other relatives caring for children who have a mother in prison.

IN THE SHADOW OF MEN

The needs of women inmates have been largely overshadowed by preoccupation with the predominantly male prison population. Historically, the corrections system's response to women offenders has been based on stereotypes of women as incapable of rehabilitation, as needing training only in typically female occupations, and as being too great a risk to men's moral integrity to allow them access to the same programs (Harm, 1992). Within the history of women in correctional institutions, women have been viewed as totally corrupt and utterly depraved and thus, not worth the effort of rehabilitation. Alternately, during the Progressive Era, women were treated as children who had gone astray. With the criminalization of abortion, illegitimacy and other "moral" crimes, many young new immigrants were placed in "reformatories." These were constructed in the same architectural style as juvenile facilities. To teach women to conform with middle-class values and standards, these women were trained solely in domestic sciences.

While the rate of increase in the number of women in prison is staggering, male inmates continue to constitute the majority (94.3%) of prisoners (Department of Justice, 1993). The fact that women inmates account for only a fragment of the total prison population has been used to excuse the system's failure to meet the needs of women inmates. However, in a 1979 class-action lawsuit in Michigan (*Glover v. Johnson*), the judge ruled that "parity" required that women have access to the same rehabilitation opportunities provided male inmates (Van Ochten, 1993). Other states have also faced litigation regarding the issue of parity in programming for female inmates.

Not only have the needs of women inmates historically been overlooked in prison programming, but differences between men and women are also ignored in debates that shape criminal justice policy. In mainstream discussions of crime, criminologists argue whether crime rates are being influenced by incarceration, shifting demographics, changes in the reporting of crime statistics, or new policing policies (Edna McConnell Clark Foundation [EMCF], 1995). Missing from that debate are distinctions between the crimes committed by women and men and the context in which those crimes and imprisonment occur.

Violent Crime

One of the factors that has fueled the increase in the prison population is public concern about violent crime–particularly random violence. According to the Bureau of Justice Statistics (Department of Justice, 1993), 4 out of 10 women in prison in 1991 were serving a sentence for a violent crime compared to 6 out of 10 men. In real numbers there are appreciably fewer women than men in prison for violent crimes since women represent only 5.7% of the total prison population (Department of Justice, 1993).

The argument that harsher sentences will protect communities from violent criminals omits the context in which many women commit violent crimes. Thirty-six percent of the women in prison for a violent crime committed a violent act against an *intimate* (spouse, ex-spouse, or boyfriend) or other relative. In comparison, only 16% of the men in prison for a violent crime are serving time for a crime involving a spouse, ex-spouse, girlfriend or other relative. Half the men serving time for violent crimes were sent to prison for a crime against a stranger (Department of Justice, 1993).

Women serving time for violent crimes are the most likely to report having been physically or sexually abused (Department of Justice, 1994). This group of women is the most likely to report having been victimized by a spouse, ex-spouse, boyfriend or other relative.

Drug-Related Crimes

Tougher laws and lengthy mandatory sentences in response to drug abuse and drug-related crime have contributed substantially to the growth in the prison population (EMCF, 1995). Between 1986 and 1991 there was a *432%* increase in the number of women serving time for drug offenses in State prisons compared to a 281% increase in men (Department of Justice, 1994). These offenders are primarily low-level, non-violent offenders with no substantial role in drug trafficking (EMCF, 1995).

A 1993 report by The Sentencing Project discussed in "Seeking Justice: Crime and Punishment in America" (EMCF, 1995) explains that although many deaths occur each year as a result of drunk driving, "the majority of drunk drivers are white males who, unless their crimes cause substantial harm, are generally charged as misdemeanants and typically receive sentences involving fines, license suspension, community service and alcohol treatment." In comparison, low-income and African-American or Hispanic defendants arrested for drug possession are typically charged with felonies and frequently sent to prison (EMCF, 1995).

While drug treatment is considered effective in treating addiction, drug treatment programs that address the needs of women with minor children are the exception rather than the norm. Drug abuse treatment is primarily available for middle-class users and is in short supply for low-income offenders (EMCF, 1995). Consequently, low-income women and women of color are imprisoned for drug offenses yet lack access to adequate drug treatment options in the community.

While serving time, the availability of drugs inside prisons allows many women to continue their addiction (EMCF, 1995). Further, insufficient space in drug treatment programs in prisons precludes many women from receiving treatment while incarcerated. Although 54% of women in prison report using drugs during the month before their arrest, only 38% of these inmates report participating in any type of a drug treatment program after incarceration (Department of Justice, 1994).

The Children of Women Prisoners

Nearly 80% of the women in prison are parents compared to 59.6% of men. A significantly larger percentage of mothers (78%) than fathers (50.5%) lived with their children before entering prison (Department of Justice, 1994). When fathers are sent to prison, 88.5% of their children remain with their natural mothers; however, only 22.1% of the children of women sent to prison remain with their fathers. Grandparents (53.1%), particularly grandmothers, are the most common caregivers for children during a mother's incarceration (Department of Justice, 1994).

Since 1980 there has been a 44% increase in children living in homes maintained by their grandparents and great-grandparents (Mullens, 1995). A 1993 study by Margaret Platt Jendrek found that 34.4% of the grandparents studied had assumed responsibility for the care of a grandchild because of the mother "being in trouble with the law." Grandparents frequently assume custody after increasingly lengthy periods of informal care.

Relatives who assume the role of caregiver face tremendous challenges. Tasks as seemingly simple as enrolling children in school, obtaining medical care, and housing children can be riddled with obstacles. Existing public benefit programs were not designed for children who live with someone other than their parent. Complex and inconsistent eligibility requirements often make it difficult for relatives to obtain services and support (Mullens, 1995).

Enduring Trauma

In a study of mothers in jail, 11.4% of the children of women participating in the survey had been arrested and 10% had been incarcerated (Johnston, 1991). A survey of youth in custody in long-term, state-run institutions found that 51.8% of these youth had at some point had a parent in prison (Department of Justice, 1988). It has been postulated that incarcerated parents and their children who become involved in the criminal justice system have histories of *enduring trauma* in common. "Enduring trauma" refers to recurrent episodes of multiple types of trauma throughout at least one stage of a child's development. The traumas that children of women prisoners may experience include abuse, neglect, molestation, witnessing violence, grief, parent-child separation, multiple placements, and changes in caregivers (Johnston, n.d.).

Lack of assistance and support for caregivers assuming responsibility may create levels of stress that will hinder caregivers' capacity to assist children in resolving traumas that occurred prior to the mother's incarceration (McFarlane, 1987). Disregard for the needs of these families also increases the likelihood that children of female inmates will continue to experience traumatic events while separated from their mothers. As many as 75% of children with a mother in prison have been reported to experience a change in caregiver during their mother's prison term (Hadley, 1981; Zalba, 1964). Also, up to 50% of the children of women studied experienced separation from siblings while their mother was incarcerated (Baunach, 1979; Zalba, 1964).

CURRENT ISSUES

Community-Based Sanctions

There are alternatives to sending women to prison. Where flexibility in sentencing exists, judges have discretion in selecting punishments to fit the circumstances of individual offenders (EMCF, 1995). Community-based sanctions such as probation, work release, electronic monitoring, community service, and treatment programs are potentially less disruptive to the lives of children whose mothers are involved in the criminal justice system. These alternatives are also less costly than prisons. One survey of community punishment programs found the average annual per participant cost of probation to be $869 compared to $14,363 for jail and $17,794 for prison (EMCF, 1995).

There was an effort at the level of federal government to address the issues of parents involved in the criminal justice system and the impact that separation during incarceration has on children. Family Unity Demonstration Projects authorized under the Violent Crime Control and Law Enforcement Act of 1994 (P.L. 103-322) would have allowed states to undertake community corrections demonstration programs in which parents convicted of nonviolent crimes could live in residential facilities with their children under age 7. Funding for these demonstration projects, however, was not subsequently appropriated.

At the grassroots level there is a growing movement advocating for alternatives to prison as the sentencing standard for women offenders with dependent children. The national *Mothers in Prison, Children in Crisis Campaign* began in New York City in 1992. Sponsored by JusticeWorks Community, this annual Mother's Day campaign involved activists in 14 major cities in 1995. Campaign activities give formerly incarcerated women and family members a forum to participate in organized efforts to change the criminal justice system's response to women.

Welfare Reform

The Personal Responsibility and Work Opportunity Reconciliation Act of 1996 (Conference Agreement for H.R. 3734) contains provisions which directly and indirectly affect women prisoners. One provision requires states to permanently deny Title IV-A cash assistance and food stamp benefits to individuals convicted of a felony drug charge for the possession, use, or distribution of drugs. States have the option of passing legislation that would circumvent this prohibition or limit the period of the prohibition. Given the disproportionate increase in the number of women serving time for drug offenses and the fact that a larger percentage of women (85.2%) than men (51.9%) plan to live with their minor children following release from prison (Department of Justice, 1994), this prohibition appears particularly punitive with respect to the children of women prisoners.

Not only do more women plan to reunite with their children after release from prison, but their capacity to support their children is different from that of a father being released from prison. First, women who serve time in prison generally have less work experience to begin with than male inmates–only 5 out of 10 women in prison were working prior to entering prison compared with 7 out of 10 men (Department of Justice, 1993).

After they serve their sentence, mothers must find adequate employment to support their children in an economic environment where the median income of women is significantly less than the median income of men. Mothers are also handicapped by Federal restrictions that make public housing inaccessible to a person with a criminal history. This adds to a mother's difficulty in providing a safe and affordable place for her children to live.

There is no evidence that unilaterally denying economic assistance to a mother will decrease the risk of her relapsing or recidivating, or improve the outcomes for her children. To the contrary, poverty is associated with increased rates of every type of trauma that children suffer and is in part responsible for the high levels of stress that prevent parents from providing adequate care and support for children.

IMPLICATIONS FOR DIRECT PRACTICE

How do these policies affect the direct service practitioner? First, therapists must recognize the sociopolitical context in which the incarceration of unprecedented numbers of women is occurring. Incarcerated women are oppressed women. They are predominantly poor, addicted, and survivors of abuse. They are women who have learned a variety of survival skills, some of which have resulted in imprisonment and loss of their children. In order for them to establish a different kind of life, these women need to develop marketable educational and vocational skills, support systems, and a perception of themselves that gives credit to their resources and strengths.

Lessons from the Battered Women's Movement

Strategies for empowering women similar to those used in the battered women's movement have applicability to incarcerated women and female ex-offenders. For instance, through education women can come to make the connection between what has happened in their personal lives and the structure of power in society. This strategy allowed many battered women to free themselves of self-blame and begin to take steps toward control over their own lives. The support, encouragement and connectedness found in shelters and support groups gave women the courage to risk stepping into new worlds. These same strategies need to be used with women while they are in prison and after they return to the community.

Increased Availability of Drug Treatment for Women

Increasing the number of beds available in community-based drug treatment programs for women is critical for the prevention of relapse and potential recidivism. A growing body of research and literature indicates that the treatment needs of women addicts are different than those of men. Issues of relationship, particularly with families and children, and gender-specific issues of physical and sexual abuse, rape, and incest are necessary components in the recovery of women (Carten, 1996; Department of Health and Human Services, 1994; Finklestein & Piedade, 1993; Goldberg, 1995).

Family-Centered Intervention

The majority of women in prison plan to be with their children when they are released from prison. If family issues are not addressed during incarceration, the family system remains trapped in pre-incarceration dynamics. Problems in the family system don't just go away during the mother's absence from the system; in fact, incarceration often adds new insults to the system. All members of the system have issues to be addressed: caregiver's anger at the mother who has made so many promises in the past only to relapse or return to prison; the guilt of the mother who was separated from her children; the hopes and anxieties of children when faced with reunification with their mother. Therapists must be willing to confront and resolve these issues within the context of the family system if the mother is to be adequately reintegrated into that system.

In order to address the issues that women in prison face, the direct service practitioner must engage in collaborative strategies that challenge the status quo of programs and support available to women inmates, female ex-offenders, their children and families. A comprehensive system of care for women prisoners must include advocacy, support, education, trauma resolution, substance abuse treatment, and family counseling. These services should be focused on strengths rather than deficits and should be grounded in principles of empowerment.

REFERENCES

Baunach, P.J. (1979). *Mothering from behind prison walls.* Paper presented at the meeting of the American Society of Criminology, Philadelphia, PA.

Carten, A.F. (1996). Mothers in recovery: Rebuilding families in the aftermath of addiction. *Social Work, 41,* 214-223.

Department of Health and Human Services. (1994). *Practical approaches in the treatment of women who abuse alcohol and other drugs.* Rockville, MD: Center for Substance Abuse Treatment.

Department of Justice. (1988). *Survey of youth in custody, 1987* (NCJ-113365). Washington, DC: Bureau of Justice Statistics.

Department of Justice. (1993). *Survey of state prison inmates* (NCJ-136949). Washington, DC: Bureau of Justice Statistics.

Department of Justice. (1994). *Women in prison* (NCJ-145321). Washington, DC: Bureau of Justice Statistics.

Department of Justice. (1995). *Prisoners in 1994* (NCJ-151654). Washington, DC: Bureau of Justice Statistics.

Edna McConnell Clark Foundation [EMCF]. (1995). *Seeking justice: Crime and punishment in America.* New York: Edna McConnell Clark Foundation.

Finkelstein, N. & Piedade, E. (1993). The relational model and the treatment of addicted women. *The Counselor,* May/June, 8-12.

Goldberg, M.E. (1995). Substance-abusing women: False stereotypes and real needs. *Social Work, 40,* 789-798.

Hadley, J.G. (1981). *Georgia women's prison inmates and their families.* Atlanta, GA: Department of Offender Rehabilitation.

Harm, N.J. (1992). Social policy on women prisoners: A historical analysis. *Affilia, 7* (1), 90-108.

Jendrek, M.P. (1993). *Grandparents who parent their grandchildren: Findings and policy implications.* Oxford, OH: Miami University.

Johnston, D. (n.d.). *Effects of parental incarceration.* Pasadena, CA: Pacific Oaks Center for Children of Incarcerated Parents.

Johnston, D. (1991). *Jailed mothers.* Pasadena, CA: Pacific Oaks Center for Children of Incarcerated Parents.

McFarlane, A.C. (1987). Post traumatic phenomena in a longitudinal study of children following a national disaster. *Journal of the American Academy of Child and Adolescent Psychiatry, 26 (5),* 764-769.

Mullens, F. (1995). *A tangled web: Public benefits, grandparents, and grandchildren.* Washington, DC: Public Policy Institute, American Association of Retired Persons.

Van Ochten, M. (1993). Legal issues and the female offender. In American Correctional Association (Eds.), *Female offenders: meeting needs of a neglected population* (pp. 31-36). Laurel, MD: American Correctional Association.

Zalba, S. (1964). *Women prisoners and their families.* Sacramento, CA: Department of Social Welfare and Department of Corrections.

The Experiences of Women in Prison: Implications for Services and Prevention

Cynthia García Coll
Jean Baker Miller
Jacqueline P. Fields
Betsy Mathews

SUMMARY. Women in prison represent a neglected population. The facilities and the services offered to female inmates are based primarily on models derived from male inmates. The need for this approach to change is increasingly recognized because the number

---

Cynthia García Coll, PhD, is Professor of Education, Psychology, and Pediatrics at Brown University. Jean Baker Miller, MD, is Clinical Professor of Psychiatry at Boston University School of Medicine, Lecturer at Harvard Medical School, and Director of Education at the Stone Center. Jacqueline Fields, PhD, is Senior Research Associate at the Stone College Center for Research on Women. Betsy Mathews, BA, was a research assistant on the Stone Center's Women in Prison project as an undergraduate at Wellesley College.

This study was made possible by the support of the Massachusetts Committee on Criminal Justice, The Massachusetts Department of Correction and the Stone Center for Developmental Services and Studies at Wellesley College. Special thanks need to be given to the women who participated as volunteers in the study. We also want to acknowledge the contribution of Sandra Yarne, Erika Stewart, Julia Perez, Yvonne Jenkins, Jan Surrey, Margaret Potter, Joey Fox and Heidie A. Vázquez García on the conceptualization and conduct of the study.

Address correspondence to: Cynthia García Coll, Education Department, Box 1938, Brown University, Providence, RI 02912. Email (cgc@brownvm.brown.edu).

[Haworth co-indexing entry note]: "The Experiences of Women in Prison: Implications for Services and Prevention." García Coll, Cynthia et al. Co-published simultaneously in *Women & Therapy* (The Haworth Press, Inc.) Vol. 20, No. 4, 1997, pp. 11-28; and: *Breaking the Rules: Women in Prison and Feminist Therapy* (ed: Judy Harden, and Marcia Hill) The Haworth Press, Inc., 1998, pp. 11-28; and: *Breaking the Rules: Women in Prison and Feminist Therapy* (ed: Judy Harden, and Marcia Hill) The Harrington Park Press, an imprint of The Haworth Press, Inc., 1998, pp. 11-28. Single or multiple copies of this article are available for a fee from The Haworth Document Delivery Service [1-800-342-9678, 9:00 a.m. - 5:00 p.m. (EST). E-mail address: getinfo@haworth.com].

11

of women in the correctional system is increasing at an alarming rate, the criminal profile of female inmates is distinct, and independently because the racial and ethnic composition of the female prisoners is shifting. In the present study, the needs of women prisoners were studied from a variety of theoretical perspectives: relational, diversity, and developmental. Focus groups and questionnaires were conducted with 54 women incarcerated in a minimum security correctional facility for men and women in a Northeastern state. The women's developmental histories reflected high-risk conditions and early trauma. From the ease with which these women responded to questions about their main relationships (i.e., closeness and mutuality) with visitors and other inmates, it is clear that they are struggling but maintaining a relational context in their lives despite being incarcerated. Most women had children, and retained custody of their children, which has strong implications for their children's development. The findings suggested a number of important policy and service implications which differed for ethnic/racial groups. *[Article copies available for a fee from The Haworth Document Delivery Service: 1-800-342-9678. E-mail address: getinfo@haworth.com]*

Women in prison represent a neglected population. For example, the health problems and health care needs of incarcerated women have been rarely studied (Ingram-Fogel, 1991). It has been observed that male inmates receive most of the programs and services, including medical and dental, recreational, educational and vocational (Arditi, Goldberg, Hartle, Peters & Phelps, 1973; Clement, 1993; Goetting, 1985). Moreover, while the treatment of women in prison has reflected a process of increasingly recognizing the need to differentiate male and female inmates, the facilities that have been created and the services offered to female inmates are based primarily on models derived from male inmates (Rafter, 1992). More recently, models for mental health services in correctional facilities (i.e., Hilkey, 1988) do not include gender considerations. As a reflection of society at large, the correctional system responds to women's needs and experiences within frameworks that represent male perspectives.

However, the need for this approach to change is increasingly recognized (Benedict, 1993; Gondles, 1993). The failure to address the needs of female inmates in a systematic and appropriate way has been justified in the past as well as in the present by the fact that women constitute a significantly smaller proportion of the incarcerated population. But the number of women in the correctional system is increasing at an alarming rate (Kline, 1992). For example, between the years 1984 and 1992 the number of women in the Federal and State inmate populations went from

20,853 to 50,409 (Bureau of Justice Statistics, 1988, 1991, 1992). In other words, the number of women in prison more than doubled in the space of eight years.

An additional reason for concentrating on women is that within the inmate population, female offenders present a different profile than their male counterparts. For example, there is a greater proportion of women compared to men who are serving time for non-violent offenses (i.e., property, drug and public offenses) as opposed to violent crimes (Bureau of Justice Statistics, 1991). Moreover, not only are the reasons for incarceration different but their behavioral profile within the institutions is also distinct (Turnbo, 1992). In general, in comparison to male prisoners, incarcerated women report more often a history of physical and sexual abuse and suicidal thoughts. They present a different pattern of interaction with the staff: more verbal, more frequent and with a wider range of emotional display. Family and children's issues are more important since a higher percentage of them are the primary caregivers. They also report more health concerns, including their reproductive health needs, that have not been met. Finally, their job skills, work histories and educational attainments are lower than those reported by male prisoners. In short, the female inmates present a distinct pattern of characteristics that can have a profound impact on their management within a correctional facility.

In addition, there is a whole body of knowledge generated primarily in the last thirty years that points out the existence of gender differences in behavioral, cognitive, moral and psychological characteristics that should have implications for the supervision and management of female inmates. For example, males are five times more likely to engage in aggressive and violent behaviors, and these findings have been replicated cross-culturally (Maccoby & Jacklin, 1980; Parke & Slaby, 1983; Whiting & Whiting, 1975). In terms of thought processes, women tend to attribute failure to their own incompetence more often than men (Crandall, 1969; Dweck, Goetz & Strauss, 1980), but they are more easily influenced, especially in perceived supportive contexts (Eagly, 1987), and they take personal relationships more into consideration when confronted with a moral dilemma (Gilligan, 1982; Lyons, 1988). In addition, there is a well-developed theoretical and clinical perspective that documents how women's psychological growth occurs mostly within relationships (Gilligan, 1982; Jordan, Kaplan, Miller, Stiver & Surrey, 1991; Miller, 1976). The application of this knowledge to how women learn, operate, change their behaviors and grow should be used to address what Rafter (1992) refers to as the need for a new model for treatment of women in prison by taking gender differences into account.

It is clear from the dramatic increase in the female incarcerated population and the theoretical knowledge about their growth and development that female prisoners merit special attention. However, this change is also accompanied by a shift in demographic composition. Although the number of women in State and Federal prisons has increased across all ethnic groups, the increase in the African American and Hispanic populations has been higher. Thus, even if all groups increased, the number of women of color is now much larger than the number of Caucasians. This diversity has tremendous implications for understanding this new prison population and the appropriateness of existing services (Chin, De La Cancela & Jenkins, 1993; Comas-Díaz & Greene, 1994; García Coll, 1992; Rogler, Cortes & Malgady, 1991).

Further impetus for rethinking treatment plans for women prisoners is provided by the recent body of scholarly work which critiques gender difference work for its tendency to essentialize gender and overlook the role of race and ethnicity in constructing the identities and behavior of women of color (Collins, 1990; Comas-Díaz & Greene, 1994; Dugger, 1991; Reid & Kelly, 1994). These scholars argue that the socioemotional development and behavior of women from diverse racial, ethnic, and socioeconomic backgrounds differs qualitatively from both Caucasian women's and men of color's development and behavior (Reid & Comas Díaz, 1990). Moreover, they underscore the ways in which these differences have been marginalized by those who have sought to uncover gender based differences, largely by excluding women with diverse racial and ethnic backgrounds from their research (Collins, 1990; Reid & Kelly, 1994). The assertion that women of color are culturally and emotionally distinct from Caucasian women as well as from men of color, and that these significant differences have been marginalized in the past, lends further credence to the notion that the assumptions on which prison treatment plans have been based require reexamination.

The purpose of the present pilot study was to document the experience of women in prison from a psychosocial perspective using a variety of theoretical frameworks. A starting point was provided by relational theory, which holds that psychological well-being, growth and development of women is the product of mutual empathic relationships (see Jordan et al., 1991; Miller, 1976). Within this framework, optimal human growth and development is seen as occurring through and toward relationships. Similarly, recovering from early trauma, abandoning substance abuse, raising self-esteem, increasing ability to cope or becoming less depressed or angry is also conceived as a function of relational empowerment. A basic question of the study was: How can women build an empowering relational context within a prison system that tends to discourage connections among inmates and staff and places serious limitations on accessibility to other relationships outside the prison?

A second framework was provided by recent theory and research on how diversity affects human development: the main question here was how do women of different racial/ethnic backgrounds experience incarceration and describe their relationships? Race, ethnicity and social class are seen as fundamental influences on human experience and developmental outcome as well as response to treatment (Chin et al., 1993; Comas-Díaz & Greene, 1994; García Coll, 1992; Rogler et al., 1991). Since minority women in prison perceive more racial discrimination than white women (Kruttschnitt, 1983), a main goal was to compare the experience of women in prison as a function of ethnicity and race.

The third framework is a developmental and preventive framework, which guides us to inquire about the developmental histories of these women (see Miller, 1991; Sameroff & Fiese, 1990; Institute of Medicine, 1994). This area of inquiry can lead us to identify possible antecedents to incarceration (to help formulate universal, selective and indicated prevention programs) as well as to identify these women's present needs so as to inform treatment and maintenance programs to reduce recidivism and intergenerational transmission of criminal behavior. The main questions here pertain to the woman's prior developmental history, her children's current conditions and her perceived needs.

METHOD

Setting

This pilot study was conducted in a minimum security correctional facility for men and women in a northeast state. The study was conducted in April and May, 1994. At the time of the study there were 82 women incarcerated in this facility. The women were housed in different buildings that were adjacent to the men's facilities.

Sample

The total sample consisted of 54 women (which constitutes 66% of the population housed at this facility). Table 1 shows the demographic characteristics of the sample by ethnic group. There were significant differences

TABLE 1. Sample Characteristics

	Anglo-American (n = 27)	African-American (n = 12)	Hispanic/Latina (n = 12)	$p \leq$
Marital Status				
Not married	13	10	10	
Married	14	2	2	.05
Place of Birth				
Born in U.S.	26	12	2	.001
Age				
Average age	37.48	35.58	37.50	n.s.
Education				
Less than High School	9	5	7	n.s.
High School graduate	6	2	1	n.s.
More than High School	12	5	4	n.s.
Parenting Status				
Number of mothers	22	9	10	n.s.
Number of mothers with children who are minors	17	6	6	n.s.
Percentage of First Time Offenders				
First time incarceration	21	9	9	n.s.
Type of Offenses by Percentage				
Drug-related	50	41.7	83.3	n.s.
Violent/manslaughter	23.1	33.3	16.7	n.s.
Theft/larceny	7.7	8.3	0	n.s.
Arson	7.7	0	0	n.s.
Prostitution	3.8	0	0	n.s.
Other	9.4	16.7	0	n.s.

between the groups in marital status and place of birth, although the groups were of a similar age. Anglo-European mothers were more likely to be married or have been married than African-American or Latina women ($X^2 = 6.9$, p < .05). Latina women were more likely to have been born outside the U.S. than African-American and Anglo-European ($X^2 = 39.58$, p < .001). The sample in this study is demographically similar to descriptions of females in federal prisons and in the state prison (Kline, 1992; Massachusetts Department of Correction, 1992). Seventy-six percent of these women were incarcerated for the first time; 56% percent for drug-related offenses, which are also similar to national and statewide statistics.

Procedure

This study was approved by the Institutional Review Boards of the Department of Corrections and Wellesley College. Data was collected through focus groups and questionnaires.

Potential participants were contacted during two house meetings where the inmates were informed of the purpose and procedures of the study, and were asked to sign up if interested in participating. Informed consent was obtained prior to any data collection. Two different methodologies were employed in the present study. First, focus groups were conducted with the women at the correctional facility. A total of eleven different focus groups were conducted with the number of participants ranging from two to seven. Each focus group met three times for ninety minutes each time and was designed to provide answers and discussion to six different questions. The focus groups were tape recorded and later transcribed by professional transcribers (and translated back to English, for the one focus group conducted in Spanish). Second, structured questionnaires were administered in groups or individually at the end of the third focus group session.

In order to ensure confidentiality, at no time were correction officers or other prison personnel present during the focus groups and the administration of the questionnaires. The focus groups and interviews were conducted by a multi-ethnic, all female research team, including two bilingual interviewers (Spanish/English). Each subject was assigned a number; all data were recorded using this number.

Measures

For this report, answers to the two following questions from each of the focus groups were analyzed: (1) What do you think are the most important needs of women in prison? and (2) What do women need in order to make it on the outside and to stay out? Two research assistants went over the transcripts and extracted each statement that included responses to each of these two questions. These statements were subsequently organized thematically. Two of the co-investigators independently examined these statements and content-analyzed them for emerging themes among the women about their perceptions of their present and future needs.

The questionnaires that were administered included questions about demographic characteristics, developmental histories (i.e., prior experience of child/adult abuse, age at leaving home), substance abuse history, and experienced life events preceding incarceration. In regard to the present situation, we asked about children's characteristics and current caregiving situations and about their current relationships and visitors. The questionnaires were filled out independently or with the assistance of one of the researchers if there were reading or comprehension difficulties.

We used several methods to assess the relational context. First we recorded frequency of visits while in prison and the relationship to every visitor (i.e., husband/boyfriend, mother, other relative, friend, child, etc.). Then we asked the women to place, within a series of concentric circles, all of the important current relationships in their lives and identify if they were friends or relatives and if friends were inside or outside the prison setting. The position in the circles provided a rating of how close the woman felt to that particular person. This methodology has been success-fully used in other studies of social support networks (i.e., Crockenberg, 1987). Next we asked them to choose their closest relationship inside and outside the prison, and to fill out an adaptation of the Mutual Psychologi-cal Development Questionnaire (MPDQ: Genero, Miller & Surrey, 1992; Genero, Miller, Surrey & Baldwin, 1992) to describe each of these rela-tionships. The MPDQ is a recently developed questionnaire that measures perceived mutuality in close relationships. A recent validation study re-vealed that the MPDQ has good internal consistency, test-retest reliability and is negatively correlated with depression. All of the instruments were translated and back translated into Spanish and inmates who self-identi-fied as Hispanics were given the option of responding to the question-naires in either English or Spanish.

RESULTS

Developmental Histories

What do these women bring into their prison experience? As informed by prevention and developmental theoretical frameworks, an important area of inquiry is their life course. Their childhood experiences reflect high-risk conditions and early trauma: 37% of these women lived with somebody different than their parents as a child; 70% report being sexual-ly and/or physically abused as a child, and 55% left home at age 16 or younger. No differences were observed between the three ethnic groups in the incidence of any of these factors. As in other populations where early trauma has been associated with substance abuse and battering, 70% of the sample also reported being abused as an adult and over a third reported a history of substance abuse (41% to drugs and 30% to alcohol). Actually, 79% of women who reported being abused as a child reported being in an abusive relationship as an adult, yielding a significant association between abuse as a child and as an adult ($X^2 = 4.3$, $p < .05$). No ethnic differences were observed in these two variables. However, several ethnic differences were observed in patterns of alcohol and drug use. Although there were no differences in the number of women that reported being *addicted* to drugs and alcohol, more Anglo-European women reported alcohol (85%) and drug use (78%) than African-American (58% and 50%, respectively) and Latina women (46% and 27%) prior to incarceration (for alcohol, $X^2 = 6.9$, $p < .03$; for drug use, $X^2 = 9$, $p < .01$). This ethnic difference in self-reported alcohol and drug use merits further investigation.

Relational Context

Given that psychological well-being and growth are conceptualized within a relational context, we were very interested in documenting the relationships that these women were maintaining at the present time. Some of the main questions were: What were their main relationships inside and outside prison? How were these relationships described in terms of closeness and mutuality? How often did they have visitors, in general: Who were these visitors and how frequently did they visit? Our purpose was to assess the women's perspectives of their main relationships as well as with their extended network.

Most of these women, even if they had established relationships inside the prison, cited relatives and friends outside the prison as their main relationship partners. The following percentages were observed from the placement of the relationships in the inner circle (i.e., closest to them): 56% had at least one parent placed in the inner circle; 69% placed at least one child; 64% had at least one relative other than parent, and 45% placed at least one friend. Sixty-seven percent of married women placed their husband in the inner circle. No ethnic differences were observed in these patterns of main relationships.

However, when asked to choose an important relationship inside the prison and outside the prison and describe them in terms of mutuality, 46 out of the 54 women had no problem describing an important relationship within the prison. Most women spoke of another female inmate of similar age. Outside the prison, they chose male friends (including boyfriends or lover, 24%) over female friends (10%) and when they chose relatives (42%), these were twice as likely to be females (mothers 33% and daughters 24%), in comparison to males (fathers 5% and sons 5%). What is striking about these women's description of their relationships in terms of mutuality is that their ratings are very similar for relationships inside the prison (mean mutuality score = 4.6 ± 7.6) and outside the prison (mean score = 4.65 ± 7.5). Thus, even if they do not consider the relationships developed in prison as close as those outside prison, their reports on how these relationships operate are similar. Moreover, these women's mutuality scores for a relationship inside the prison are moderately correlated with their mutuality scores for the relationship outside the prison (r = .40, p < .01), suggesting that the relationships that women develop inside the prison reflect some continuity in perceived mutuality with other relationships in these women's lives. Surprisingly, no ethnic differences were observed in any of these parameters, except for the fact that a higher percentage of African-Americans knew their current friend in prison before this incarceration, compared to Latinas or Anglo-Europeans ($X^2 = 15$, p < .001).

Finally, we asked these women to tell us about their visitors: who visits, how they are related (relative, friend, etc.), and the frequency of visits. Our purpose was to assess how the connections with outside relationships were maintained by a regular visitation pattern. Ninety-one percent of the women said they receive regular visits: 33% weekly, 45% monthly. A striking ethnic difference was found: only 67% of African-American in comparison to 100% of Anglo-European and 92% of Latinas reported regular visitors ($X^2 = 10.5$, p < .01). Male friends (including boyfriends) were the most frequent visitors (63%), followed by female friends (45%) and then relatives for all ethnic groups. However, Latina women reported different members of the extended family more often, including brothers ($X^2 = 7.2$, p < .05) and sister- and brother-in-laws ($X^2 = 6.2$, p < .05 and $X^2 = 10.7$, p < .01) compared to Anglo-European and African-American women.

Children

Because of the high percentage of women with children within the incarcerated population (82% in this sample), and the implications of incarceration for both mother and child, we asked several questions about their children. How many women have minor children? If minors, who has custody? How often do they visit? Who is bringing them? Are they having problems with the law?

Sixty-six percent of these women had minor children, for a total of 67 children, since most women had one or two children. These figures suggest that there are tremendous implications for the impact of incarceration on these children. Fourteen percent of the women reported that the Department of Social Services had custody of their children; 10% reported that they were in foster homes; 2% reported that their children had been legally adopted. Thus, most of these women are retaining custody or might regain custody of their children, which also has tremendous implications for these women's parenting role during and after incarceration.

Most of these children were currently living with their father (24%) or other relatives (34% with the maternal grandmother, aunt or other female relative). However, most of the children (66%) had not only been separated from their mothers, but appeared to be separated from their siblings as well, since their mothers reported that they were not living together. The only ethnic difference observed was the fact that none of the Hispanic children lived with their fathers compared with 50% of African-American and 76% of Anglo-European ($X^2 = 6.2$, $p < .05$) children. Most of the children were brought to the visits by their maternal grandmother or an aunt (48%).

Needs Assessment

Finally, because of an interest in informing policy and services we asked the women about their most important needs. What are their needs while in prison and after release? Do they have release plans? Do they need housing, substance abuse treatment, etc.? Are there ethnic differences in the expressed needs? These data were gathered through the focus group discussions and specific items in the questionnaire.

For the purpose of this report we will refer to the inmates' responses to two general questions during the focus groups: (1) What do you think are the most important needs of women in prison? and, (2) What does a woman need in order to make it on the outside and stay out of prison?

While the focus group format followed a prescribed set of questions and encouraged individuals to respond to the structured set of questions, a central theme response was sought rather than a 1:1 response tally. There were numerous responses to each question, but six overarching and recurring aggregate themes emerged that clearly identified the most important things that the women found as most needed in prison. The six themes were as follows:

Respect from Correctional Officers

Inmates reported that being respected as people with dignity was one of the most important components for survival in prison. Inmates stated that it appeared that correctional officers did not understand that many women in prison were addicts and alcoholics and not criminals, and they questioned what type of training correctional officers had to prepare them to deal with the issues of substance abusers as well as women incarcerated for other crimes. They provided numerous examples of how correctional officers' disrespect toward the inmates was demeaning and demoralizing. One inmate said that she "had seen it a lot with people just starting to feel good about themselves. I've seen people willing to go into a program and they're torn down by a correctional officer and they back off. When an inmate is working to build up her self-esteem, a disrespectful correctional officer can tear it down." Other female inmates described gross disrespect by the entire correctional system when the women were subjected to a general punitive prison edict because one man across the road at the men's prison was guilty of a serious punishable behavior; "When the men get into trouble, they bear down on the women."

Education for Women in Prison

The inmates in this study mentioned the need for more basic education. Female offenders are generally poorly educated. Nearly one third of the women in the study never completed high school (Bureau of Justice Statistics, 1992). The high school completion rate of the women in this pilot study (n = 54) was 18%. The range of educational programs needed to meet the needs of women in prison goes from the lowest literacy levels to GED and college courses. Of significant importance in meeting these educational needs is the sequencing and scheduling of classes for the orderly completion of courses. In addition to basic education, the inmates expressed that they needed and wanted other learning opportunities while in prison. These opportunities referred to as "women's health" issues include such topics as AIDS education, CPR and first aid training.

Sources of Motivation

Inmates in the study commented that having a job that pays a salary is a powerful motivator in prison. They also mentioned that the opportunity to earn "good time" by attending programs and counseling sessions that reduce an inmate's sentence, and the earning of certificates for their participation in programs were high motivators. Finally, inmates mentioned education opportunities (e.g., GED classes) as another motivator in prison.

Counseling–Learning About the Self

Inmates mentioned a variety of individual experiences regarding psychological counseling. Inmates expressed how counseling helps them deal with the source of their problems, what happens and why things are going on. Inmates with substance abuse problems found such counselors especially helpful.

Additional Resources in Prison

Women in prison said that they needed a variety of resources that presently do not exist for them in prison. The needed resources ranged from desks and notebooks for their class work to recreational resources, better medical attention, opportunities to speak to a lawyer, access to the law library and an office for social service assistance.

Employment and Job Training While in Prison

Employment, for pay, while in prison was expressed as a distinct need by the inmates who were allowed to work. While the amount of stable jobs for women in prison is inadequate, and the erratic nature of the work schedules is problematic, inmates expressed a need for job training in order for them to learn how to reintegrate themselves into society upon leaving prison.

While the inmates articulated similar needs, there were some ethnic differences in the needs expressed. More Hispanic (67%) and African-American (75%) women reported their ability to speak English only as good or fair and not excellent, in comparison to the Anglo-European women (33%), indicating the need for English instruction and English as a second language or perhaps improvement of accent or speaking ability ($X^2 = 13.7$, p < .01). Housing needs after release also seem to differ as a function of race/ethnicity. One hundred percent of Latina women compared to only 63% of Anglo-Europeans and 50% of African-Americans expect to be living in another person's house (primarily a member of the extended family) when released ($X^2 = 7.3$, p < .05). The lack of housing after release for African-American women is also reflected by the trend observed in their responses about shelters: 25% of African-American women reported that they would be going to shelters after release compared to 4% of Anglo-American and 0% of Latinas ($X^2 = 5.6$, p < .055). These ethnic differences merit further investigation.

DISCUSSION

The purpose of this study was to document the experiences of women in prison, to inform our understanding of these women's life course and their present and future needs. Several theoretical frameworks guided the present study and informed our inquiry as well as our interpretation of the findings. One was the importance of relationships in women's lives and well-being. From the ease with which these women responded to questions about their main relationships (i.e., closeness and mutuality) and their visitors, it is clear that they are struggling but maintaining a relational context in their lives despite being incarcerated. It was our impression that maintaining these relationships was a way for these women to cope with the sense of loss and separation from loved ones, especially their children.

The implications of these findings are many. Are the policies for visitation at correctional facilities for women supportive of maintaining relationships with significant others outside the correctional setting and of developing supportive relationships within? In other words, how much are policies toward women inmates geared toward punishment vs. rehabilitation? If punishment is the driving force, making the ability to establish and maintain connections difficult might be indicated; if rehabilitation is the driving force, maintaining these connections especially with significant others outside of prison might be an important component of programming within prisons. These patterns of connections might contribute to growth and self-reflection during incarceration, might make the transition into the outside world somewhat easier as well as might provide the necessary supports to establish a crime-free life after release and contribute to the reduction of recidivism.

Maintaining relationships with children is also extremely important. One of the main concerns that these women expressed was the well-being of their children and the example that they were setting for them. As indicated by our data, most of these women were retaining custody of their minor children (only 2% had given their children up for legal adoption and 13% were in the custody of the state). The remaining minor children were living with the father or other relatives, and regaining their custody was a driving force for some of these women as expressed in the following quote:

> I will feel tremendous happiness because I will be with my children again and I have a son who needs me because he has strayed. And he needs that I be with him. And now what I dream about is getting out in order to go and find my son, and have him nearby and that he learns that he has a mother that supports him, that he is not alone.

Of course the children's ages at the time of incarceration have clear implications for the impact on both mother and child. During infancy and the pre-school years, separation from the mother can have tremendous

impact on the patterns of attachment that the child can develop and therefore lifelong implications for the development of relationships as an adult
(Bretherton & Waters, 1985). Incarceration during school age, although
possibly less traumatic because of increasing understanding of the tran-
sient nature of the loss (she is gone forever) and less egocentric thought
(she left because of me), can also be traumatic because of change in
residences, school, neighborhoods, family composition (most children
were living now in different households), etc. Moreover, during this stage
and the adolescent years, the beginnings of high-risk, antisocial and criminal behavior is observed, and thus, parental monitoring and investment is
crucial. Finally, as adults, these women's children become a major source
of support as expressed by the high number of women who placed their
adult children in the inner circle (69%) of their relational diagram.

A second framework was that provided by recent work that stresses the
importance of race and ethnicity in explaining women's experiences.
Within the present population, we found similarities as well as differences
as a function of race/ethnicity, which might have important implications
for services for women in prisons, in preparation for release, and in transi-
tioning out into the community. For all women it seems that educational
and vocational programs are desperately needed. As reported by Turnbo
(1992), female prisoners have lower educational and job skills than men.
In the present sample, although there was a wide range of educational
levels, most of the women reported a great desire to pursue their educa-
tional/vocational training further. Some expressed the irony about the fact
that this was the first time that they were by themselves, not having to take
care of anybody else, and thus conceptualizing it as an opportunity to
invest in furthering their own development. Others wanted to prove to the
outside world that they had learned their lesson and that they had actually
made the best of their time served for their crimes:

> For me, taking my GED motivates me because when I get out of
> here, I want to get an education so that I can show my children that
> mother has not wasted her time, that mother wants to be somebody,
> be somebody so that they may feel proud of me.

However, the eagerness to improve their educational and occupational
status is being curbed by the recent federal cuts for educational and occupational programs for prisoners.

Our findings suggest that there are other program needs that are more
crucial for some ethnic/racial groups than for others. For the Anglo-Europeans, substance abuse prevention programs seem to be indicated by the
fact that a larger percentage of these women report drug and alcohol use

before incarceration. For Latina women, programs in English as a second language and accessibility of other services that are linguistically and culturally appropriate are indicated. For African-American women, the lack of regular visitors and appropriate housing after release might indicate a breakdown in important primary support systems that needs to be addressed prior to release. Since a growing body of literature suggests that programs that are geared to the specific needs of women and ethnic minorities are more successful (i.e., Chin et al., 1993; Rogler et al., 1991), we recommend integrating relational and diversity approaches into the management, care and treatment of incarcerated women.

Moreover, our data suggest that use of knowledge about psychology of women (particularly Relational Theory) and the effects of diversity on women, should be incorporated into models of prevention. Specifically, several factors were present in these women's lives prior to incarceration: leaving home relatively early, history of abuse as a child, exposure to violence as an adult. The presence of these factors might place women at risk for substance abuse which can lead to criminal behavior, problems with the law and ultimately incarceration. For example, prevention programs can be targeted to youth at risk or first time offenders that would address their developmental histories from a relational and diversity perspective.

Although suggestive, our findings are limited by the small sample size, which may not allow enough power to detect small effect sizes and can place serious limitations on the generalizability of the findings. Also, our findings may only be representative of populations in minimal security correctional facilities. Despite the limitations, this pilot study should guide further large scale investigations of the experience of this growing and neglected population.

REFERENCES

Arditi, R. R., Goldberg, F., Hartle, M. M., Peters, J. H., & Phelps, W. R. (1973). The sexual segregation of American prisons. *The Yale Law Journal, 82(6),* 1229-1273.

Benedict, M. (January, 1993). Report of the special House committee to investigate the conditions and treatment of females in the criminal justice system. Commonwealth of Massachusetts, House of Representatives, Per House order, No. 3489.

Bretherton, I., & Waters, E. (Eds.) (1985). *Growing points of attachment theory and research. Monographs of the Society for Research in Child Development,* Serial No. 209, 50(1-2).

Bureau of Justice Statistics. (1988). *Source book of Criminal Justice Statistics, 1987.* Washington, DC: Government Printing Office.

Bureau of Justice Statistics. (1991). *Women in prison.* Special Report (March). Washington, DC: Government Printing Office.

Bureau of Justice Statistics. (1992). *Prisoners in 1991.* Special Report (May). Washington, DC: Government Printing Office.

Chin, J. L., De La Cancela, V., & Jenkins, Y. M. (1993). *Diversity in psychotherapy: The politics of race, gender, and ethnicity.* Westport, CT: Praeger.

Clement, M. J. (1993). Parenting in prison: A national survey of programs for incarcerated women. *Journal of Offender Rehabilitation, 19(1/2),* 89-100.

Collins, P. H. (1990). *Black feminist thought.* New York: Unwin Hyman.

Comas-Díaz, L., & Greene, B. (Eds.) (1994). *Women of color: Integrating ethnic and gender identities in psychotherapy.* New York: Guilford Press.

Crandall, V. C. (1969). Sex differences in expectancy of intellectual and academic reinforcement. In C. P. Smith (Ed.), *Achievement-related motives in children.* New York: Russel Sage.

Crockenberg, S. (1987). Predictors and correlates of anger toward and punitive control of toddlers by adolescent mothers. *Child Development, 58,* 964-975.

Dugger, K. (1991). Race differences in the determination for legalized abortion. *Social Science Quarterly, 72(3),* 570-587.

Dweck, C.S., Goetz, T.E., & Strauss, N.L. (1980). Sex differences in learned helplessness: An experimental and naturalistic study of failure generalization and its mediators. *Journal of Personality and Social Psychology, 38,* 441-452.

Eagly, A. H. (1987). *Sex differences in social behavior: A social role interpretation.* Hillsdale, NJ: Erlbaum.

García Coll, C. T. (1992). Cultural diversity: Implications for theory and practice. Work in Progress #59, *Working Papers,* Wellesley, MA: Stone Center, Wellesley College.

Genero, N. P., Miller, J. B., & Surrey, J. (1992). *The Mutual Psychological Development Questionnaire* (Research Project Rep. No. 1). Wellesley, MA: Stone Center, Wellesley College.

Genero, N. P., Miller, J. B., Surrey, J., & Baldwin, L. M. (1992). Measuring perceived mutuality in close relationships: Validation of the Mutual Psychological Development Questionnaire. *Journal of Family Psychology, 6(1),* 36-48.

Gilligan, C. (1982). *In a different voice: Psychological theory and women's development.* Cambridge: Harvard University Press.

Goetting, A. (1985). Racism, sexism, and ageism in the prison community. *Federal Probation, 49,* 10-22.

Gondles, J. A. (1993). Foreword. *Female offenders: Meeting the needs of a neglected population.* Baltimore: United Book Press.

Hilkey, J. H. (1988). A theoretical model for assessment of delivery of mental health services in the correctional facility. *Psychiatric Annals, 18(12),* 676-679.

Ingram-Fogel, C. (1991). Health problems and needs of incarcerated women. *Journal of Prison & Jail Health, 10(1),* 43-57.

Institute of Medicine. (1994). *Reducing risks for mental disorders: Frontiers for preventive intervention research.* Washington, DC: National Academy Press.

Jordan, J. V., Kaplan, A. G., Miller, J. B., Stiver, I. P., & Surrey, J. L. (1991). *Women's growth in connection.* New York: Guilford Press.

Kline, S. (1992). A profile of female offenders in state and federal prisons. Federal Bureau of Prisons' Spring 1992 *Federal Prisons Journal.*

Kruttschnitt, C. (1983). Race relations and the female inmate. *Crime & Delinquency, 29,* 577-592.

Lyons, N. (1988). Two perspectives on self, relationships, and morality. In C. Gilligan, J. V. Ward, J. M. Taylor, & B. Bardige (Eds.), *Mapping the moral domain: A contribution to women's thinking to psychological theory* (pp. 21-48). Cambridge, MA: Harvard University Press.

Maccoby, E. E., & Jacklin, C. N. (1980). Sex differences in aggression: A rejoinder and reprise. *Child Development, 51,* 964-980.

Massachusetts Department of Correction. (1992). *Female offenders in Massachusetts: Statistical descriptions, trends, and population projections.* Research Division, Massachusetts Department of Correction, November 25, 1992.

Miller, J. B. (1976). *Toward a new psychology of women.* Boston: Beacon Press.

Miller, J. B. (1991). The development of women's sense of self. In J. V. Jordan, A. G. Kaplan, J. B. Miller, I. P. Stiver, & J. L. Surrey (Eds.), *Women's growth in connection* (pp. 11-26). New York: Guilford Press.

Parke, R. D., & Slaby, R. G. (1983). The development of aggression. In E. M. Hetherington & P. H. Mussen (Vol. Eds.), *Handbook of child psychology: Socialization, personality and social development, Volume 4* (pp. 547-641). New York: Wiley.

Rafter, N. H. (1992). Equality or difference? Federal Bureau of Prisons, Spring 1992. *Federal Prisons Journal.*

Reid, P. T., & Comas Díaz, L. (1990). Gender and ethnicity: Perspectives on dual status. *Sex Roles, 22(7/8),* 397-408.

Reid, P. T., & Kelly, E. (1994). Research on women of color: From ignorance to awareness. *Psychology of Women Quarterly, 18,* 477-486.

Rogler, L. H., Cortes, D. E., & Malgady, R. G. (1991). Acculturation and mental health status among Hispanics. *American Psychologist, 46(6),* 585-597.

Sameroff, A. J., & Fiese, B. H. (1990). Transactional regulation and early intervention. In S. J. Meisels & J. P. Shonkoff (Eds.), *Handbook of early childhood intervention* (pp. 119-191). New York: Cambridge University Press.

Turnbo, C. (1992). Differences that make a difference: Managing a women's correctional institution. Federal Bureau of Prisons, Spring 1992 *Federal Prisons Journal.*

Whiting, B. B., & Whiting, J. W. M. (1975). *Children of six cultures: A Psychocultural analysis.* Cambridge: Harvard University Press.

An Analysis of the Impact of Prison on Women Survivors of Childhood Sexual Abuse

Jan Heney
Connie M. Kristiansen

SUMMARY. The prevalence of child abuse histories among incarcerated women has fundamental implications for understanding women's well-being during incarceration. This review of the literature on child sexual abuse and women in prison suggests that incarcerated survivors are likely to be frequently reexposed to the powerful traumatizing processes associated with their early abuse, including traumatic sexualization, powerlessness, stigmatization, and betrayal (Finkelhor & Browne, 1985). Reexposure to these traumagenic dynamics has the potential to trigger traumatic relivings of imprisoned

Jan Heney, PhD, is a consultant and therapist at the Kingston Prison for Women. She also conducts workshops and seminars on women in conflict with the law and on adult survivors of childhood sexual abuse. Connie Kristiansen, PhD, is Associate Professor of Psychology at Carleton University in Canada. Her current research concerns violence toward women and children and the nature of traumatic memory.

The authors would like to thank Judy Harden, Marcia Hill, and Wendy Hovdestad for their helpful comments on an earlier version of this paper.

Address correspondence to: Jan Heney, Psychology Department, Kingston Prison for Women, P.O. Box 515, Kingston, Ontario, Canada K7L 4W7, or Connie M. Kristiansen, Department of Psychology, Carleton University, Ottawa, Ontario, Canada K1S 5B6.

[Haworth co-indexing entry note]: "An Analysis of the Impact of Prison on Women Survivors of Childhood Sexual Abuse." Heney, Jan, and Connie M. Kristiansen. Co-published simultaneously in *Women & Therapy* (The Haworth Press, Inc.) Vol. 20, No. 4, 1997, pp. 29-44; and: *Breaking the Rules: Women in Prison and Feminist Therapy* (ed: Judy Harden, and Marcia Hill) The Haworth Press, Inc., 1998, pp. 29-44; and: *Breaking the Rules: Women in Prison and Feminist Therapy* (ed: Judy Harden, and Marcia Hill) The Harrington Park Press, an imprint of The Haworth Press, Inc., 1998, pp. 29-44. Single or multiple copies of this article are available for a fee from The Haworth Document Delivery Service [1-800-342-9678, 9:00 a.m. - 5:00 p.m. (EST). E-mail address: getinfo@haworth.com].

survivors' pasts, to which survivors respond with a variety of coping strategies often seen in prison, including substance abuse, violence, self-injury, and suicide. The implications of these dynamics and women's responses to them for those who work with incarcerated women, for prison policy, and for research are discussed. *[Article copies available for a fee from The Haworth Document Delivery Service: 1-800-342-9678. E-mail address: getinfo@haworth.com]*

INTRODUCTION

Consistent with the claim that understanding women's offending is facilitated by knowledge of women's own victimization (Faith, 1993; Kruttschnitt, 1993), the aftereffects of child abuse appear to bring some women into conflict with the law. In a prospective study, for example, Widom (1989) observed that abused girls were more likely than girls who had not been abused to become delinquents and criminals. In another study, Lake (1993, p. 41) reported that "early physical abuse was associated with earlier entry into crime, and with more diverse criminal activity" among 83 women inmates. Given such findings, it is not surprising that, compared to the general population where about 30% of women are sexually assaulted before the age of 18 (Berliner & Elliott, 1996), over 50% of the women in Canada's Federal Prison for Women (P4W) are survivors of child sexual abuse (Arbour, 1996; Heney, 1990, 1996; Shaw, 1991, 1992; Task Force on Federally Sentenced Women, 1990) and at least 75% have experienced either sexual or physical abuse during their childhoods (Heney, 1990; Task Force on Federally Sentenced Women, 1990). Adding insult to injury, imprisoned women often come from families characterized by attributes known to exacerbate the effects of child abuse (Berliner & Elliott, 1996), including parental divorce, violence, criminality, substance abuse, and neglect (Arbour, 1996; Faith, 1993; Flowers, 1995; Heney, 1996; Shaw, 1991, 1992; Task Force on Federally Sentenced Women, 1990). Further, in Canada, both child abuse and stressful family backgrounds are more typical of Native than non-Native women (Arbour, 1996; Grossman, 1992; Sugar & Fox, 1989-1990), a disproportionate number of whom are imprisoned (Arbour, 1996; Faith, 1993; Shaw, 1991, 1992).

The prevalence of child abuse among incarcerated women raises a consortium of concerns regarding women's well-being during incarceration. The ways that prison replicates survivors' experiences of child abuse, for example, have fundamental implications for understanding the effects of prison life on survivors because once these feelings are triggered, a woman "experiences the emotional intensity of the original trauma without conscious awareness of the historical reference" (Janoff-Bulman, 1992, p. 103). Further, just as "the healthy, normal, emotionally resilient child will learn to accommodate to the reality of continuing sexual abuse" (Summit, 1983, p. 184), an incarcerated survivor may try to adapt to the reassertion of these dynamics in prison using the coping skills she learned as a child. We therefore examine how prison replicates the four key traumagenic processes underlying child abuse and its diverse aftereffects, as outlined in Finkelhor and Browne's (1985; Finkelhor, 1988) Traumagenic Model of Child Sexual Abuse. These trauma-inducing dynamics include traumatic sexualization, betrayal, powerlessness and stigmatization.

Traumatic Sexualization

Traumatic sexualization "refers to the conditions in sexual abuse under which a child's sexuality is shaped in developmentally inappropriate and interpersonally dysfunctional ways" (Finkelhor, 1988, p. 69). A sexually abused child may develop misconceptions about sexual behavior, aggression and morality, and a child who is rewarded for complying with the abuse may come to believe that her sexuality is her only value. Given these aftereffects, it is not surprising that survivors are more likely to become sex-trade workers (Chesney-Lind & Rodriguez, 1983; Earls & David, 1990; Finkelhor, 1988), which may bring them before the gaze of the law.

In prison, survivors' traumatic sexualization is replicated in the form of "institutionalized assaults by line staff on prisoner's bodies which are conducted in the name of security" (Faith, 1993, p. 229). Incarcerated women's bodies are "patted down" on a daily basis. Strip searches also occur, during which "the woman prisoner stands naked before uniformed guards with keys–the literal and symbolic tools of her control" (Eaton, 1993, p. 240). Internal searches, although less frequent, are conducted when prison staff have reason to believe a woman is concealing drugs or weapons within her body. Although the woman must give her consent, because this permission is often obtained by presenting her with the option of submitting or being placed in segregation, this process is coercive at best.

More extreme violations of women's bodies can also occur in prison. In April 1994, for example, an Emergency Response Team entered P4W to quell a disturbance among six women in the segregation unit. These women were forcibly stripped, handcuffed and shackled by male officers in full riot gear, and "two inmates who testified [to the government inquiry] spoke of their fear, humiliation, and the painful reliving of earlier memories of abuse" (Arbour, 1996, p. 86). Further, in institutions with male officers, survivors may literally reexperience their childhood rape (Faith, 1993). While extreme violations may be relatively infrequent, other aspects of incarceration, including the lack of privacy and the use of harassment, force, restraint, and confinement, have the potential to retraumatize women on a regular basis.

Although women in prison may traumatize each other, women inmates are less violent than imprisoned men (Faith, 1993). Further, unlike men who more frequently rape their fellow inmates, most sexual contact between women prisoners occurs within a loving relationship (Faith, 1993). Thus, incarcerated survivors are more likely to be sexually retraumatized at the hands of prison staff or by the inherent nature of prison control and surveillance than by their peers (Zupan, 1992).

Powerlessness

The structural distinction between the powerful and the powerless is perhaps the most fundamental dynamic underlying both child abuse (Briere, 1989; Finkelhor, 1988; Finkelhor & Browne, 1985; Summit, 1983) and incarceration (Arbour, 1996; Faith, 1993; Heney, 1996; Sommers, 1995; Task Force on Federally Sentenced Women, 1990). This dynamic is inherent in the structure of many institutions. As Fromuth and Burkhart (1992, p. 84) noted in regard to survivors' psychiatric hospitalization, "contributing to the feelings of powerlessness is the inherent power differential between staff and patient which mirrors the power differential between adults and children." This power differential is likely greater in prison than in psychiatric facilities because, in addition to their legitimized power over inmates, prison officers have the prerogative and the duty to punish women who do not accept their control. Moreover, this control extends to virtually every aspect of an inmate's life, including when she eats, when she sleeps, when she socializes, and even what she wears (Eaton, 1993; Faith, 1993; Jose-Kampfner, 1990; Kendall, 1993; Padel & Stevenson, 1988). Further, as described above, an incarcerated woman loses her right to determine how her body will be touched and by whom. As a result, all women prisoners are routinely reminded of their powerlessness and, hence, those who are survivors are often exposed to situations reminiscent of their childhoods.

In order to perpetrate the abuse and maintain its secrecy, abusers often undermine a child's perceptions and feelings by blaming the child for the abuse, describing the abuse as love, or even denying it altogether (Summit, 1983). The child is further disempowered if her credibility is challenged upon disclosure. This process is also evident in many institutions. Psychiatric hospitals often replicate this aspect of women's earlier experiences because the status of psychiatric inpatient reduces their credibility. So, for example, "a patient's complaint against a staff member may be viewed as a reflection of the patient's psychopathology, and a patient's anger over hospitalization may be viewed as 'resistance' or 'transference' " (Fromuth & Burkhart, 1992, pp. 84-85). Comparable disempowerment occurs in prison where women, by virtue of their criminal status, have little credibility. Indeed, women in prison "have been persecuted in the name of 'discipline' for reporting offences against themselves" (Faith, 1993, p. 249).

In Finkelhor and Browne's (1985) scheme, survivors have two seemingly contradictory ways of coping with their feelings of powerlessness, namely by helplessness and by an exaggerated need for control. Continually frustrated attempts at self-protection may induce feelings of helplessness that translate into "learning problems, school difficulties, employment difficulties, running away, and more generalized despair and depression" (Finkelhor, 1988, p. 76), problems that are also common among incarcerated women (Arbour, 1996; Shaw, 1991, 1992; Sommers, 1995).

Although some researchers appeal to the concept of learned helplessness to account for these aftereffects, especially the depression frequently experienced by survivors, the suggestion that survivors act as if they are helpless is difficult to reconcile with their often exaggerated need for control (Finkelhor, 1988; Herman, 1992a; van der Kolk, 1996). These control issues may stem from the self-blame associated with sexual abuse: by believing that the abuse is her fault, the child preserves the hope that it is within her power to stop the abuse. Although this sense of control is illusory because it involves the behavior of another more powerful person (the abuser), it has important survival value. As Taylor and Brown (1988, p. 201) noted, "evidence from converging sources suggests that positive illusions about the self, one's control, and the future may be especially apparent and adaptive under circumstances of adversity, that is, circumstances that might be expected to produce depression or lack of motivation." One might speculate that the more survivors feel helpless, the more they will try to control their immediate reality, and thereby preserve their psychic survival. If so, the more incarceration increases women's feelings of helplessness, the more incarceration is likely to trigger survivors' control issues.

Consistent with this perspective, Finkelhor (1988, p. 76) noted that survivors may try to cope with the traumagenic dynamic of powerlessness through "a compensatory reaction, an unusual need to control or dominate." Externalized in this way, survivors' powerlessness may manifest as "aggressive and delinquent behavior . . . stemming from the desire to be powerful and even fearsome to compensate for past powerlessness" (Finkelhor, 1988, p. 76). Sommers (1995, p. 100) documented this process in her interviews with 14 incarcerated women:

> Their visible expression of anger brought these women into conflict with the law. Their actions, although extreme, should be seen as an expression of their hurt, depression, loneliness, confusion and fear. When viewed as a secondary emotion that reflects the intensity of the underlying primary emotions, their anger gives evidence of the extreme pain that lay at the root of their actions.

In line with this, some imprisoned women adopt the facade of being aggressive and invulnerable to alleviate their feelings of powerlessness (Darke, 1987).

Survivors' need for control may also account for Heney's (1996) finding that incarcerated survivors reported more suicidal ideation when in prison than on the street. Because prisons are socially sanctioned to have power over inmates, survivors are likely to encounter many situations in which they are powerless and have few coping options. This increases the probability that an incarcerated survivor may resort to the only control she believes she has left: control over life and death. As Herman (1992a, p. 85) put it, "the stance of suicide is active; it preserves an inner sense of control." Perhaps, then, both the aggressive and suicidal behaviors of incarcerated women involve desperate attempts to regain control. Indeed, this commonality may account for the positive relation between incarcerated women's histories of suicide and violence (Heney, 1996).

Finally, it should be noted that the price that survivors pay to maintain an illusion of control is, paradoxically, dependency. Rather than trying to control their responses to external events, survivors try to control the events themselves (Summit, 1983). As a result, external events become master of the survivor; her well-being a slave to circumstance. Thus, survivors' efforts to regain control may do little more than exacerbate their feelings of powerlessness.

Betrayal

The third traumagenic dynamic contributing to the aftereffects of child abuse is the sense of betrayal that comes from the fact that a trusted person, often a significant other on whom the child depends, has violated and harmed the child. An abused child is further betrayed by those who failed to intervene or disbelieved her disclosure (Finkelhor & Browne, 1985; Summit, 1983). Likewise, many incarcerated women regard prison as a form of victimization and believe that they have been betrayed by society on at least two occasions: first when no one came to their rescue as children, and second when their potential rescuers became their persecutors (Heney, 1996).

Like powerlessness, betrayal promotes two distinct patterns of response. The first pattern involves antisocial behaviors that provide a way of retaliating for past betrayals and avoiding future ones. As Finkelhor (1988, p. 75) explained, "anger and hostility may be a primitive way victims try to protect themselves from future betrayals. . . . And antisocial behavior may be a form of retaliation for betrayal." The second response to betrayal involves extreme dependency and impaired judgment about other people's trustworthiness. As Finkelhor (1988) noted, the latter pattern may underlie survivors' tendency to be revictimized, be it by rape or partner abuse (Berliner & Elliott, 1996; Herman, 1992a, 1992b; Lake, 1993; van der Kolk, 1996). Incarcerated women may be at greater risk for revictimization because of their criminal lifestyle which increases their risk for victimization (e.g., by the company they keep or the locations they frequent; Lake, 1993). Further, because of their feelings of betrayal and the difficulty they have trusting and maintaining adaptive beliefs about life, including the notion that the world is just and fair (Herman, 1992a, 1992b; Janoff-Bulman, 1992; van der Kolk, 1996), survivors may be reluctant to turn to traditional methods for resolving personal difficulties. They may, for example, prefer to resolve domestic disputes on their own rather than calling in the police and this may lead to conflict with the law. In line with this possibility, Shaw (1992, p. 19) reported that "women who are assaulted by their partners are more likely to use violence against others."

Stigmatization

In the Traumagenic Model, stigmatization "refers to the negative messages about the self–evilness, worthlessness, shamefulness, guilt–that are communicated to the child around the experience" (Finkelhor, 1988, p. 70), be it from the perpetrator or society (Summit, 1983). As a result, "victims often feel isolated and gravitate to stigmatized levels of society–for example, among drug abusers, into criminal subcultures, or into prostitution" (Finkelhor, 1988, pp. 75-76). It is, therefore, not surprising that drug-related crimes often bring women into prison. In Canada, for example, 21% of female prisoners have committed a serious drug offense (Solicitor General Canada, 1995).

Like child sexual abuse (Finkelhor, 1988; Finkelhor & Browne, 1985; Herman, 1992a, 1992b; Summit, 1983; van der Kolk, 1996) and psychiatric hospitalization (Fromuth & Burkhart, 1992), being labeled a criminal marks a woman for life, be it interpersonally through social discrimination or intrapersonally through shame. And while psychiatric institutions label women "mad," and reinforce survivors' beliefs that they are "crazy or unable to cope" (Fromuth & Burkhart, 1992, p. 87), penal institutions teach women that they are "bad," thereby confirming survivors' self-loathing (Faith, 1993; Finkelhor, 1988; Finkelhor & Browne, 1985; Herman, 1992a, 1992b; Summit, 1983; van der Kolk, 1996). These total institutions may also reinforce survivors' feelings of badness or craziness by stigmatizing their symptoms (Summit, 1983), symptoms that include substance abuse, self-injury, suicide attempts, and other behaviors that prison staff find difficult to control.

Survivors of childhood sexual abuse (Summit, 1983) and incarcerated women (Heney, 1996) also experience the stigmatization that stems from secrecy. The secrecy of child abuse is typically enforced by the abuser's threats and/or the child's fear that she will be disbelieved or blamed if she discloses. The child is also silenced by the knowledge that disclosing may have profound consequences: her parents may separate, her father may be sent away, she may be sent away. Similarly, in prison the inmate code dictates that inmates remain silent about abuse by other inmates and, like the veil of silence that cloaks child abuse, this silence is enforced by threats and/or the fear that there will be practical and emotional consequences if the silence is broken. Breaches in the inmate code can result in a woman being identified as a "rat" which, in turn, may result in her being abused by other inmates or being segregated from the rest of the prison population. Also, like the secrecy of child abuse, it is the abuser who ultimately benefits from the inmate code, while the survivor is "stigmatized with a sense of badness and danger from the pervasive secrecy" (Summit, 1983, p. 181).

Not only does the stigmatization of child abuse make it more likely that women will come into conflict with the law and exacerbate their experience of incarceration, it is also likely to affect women as they attempt to reenter society following their release. Just as abused children may be regarded as "damaged goods" (Finkelhor, 1988; Finkelhor & Browne, 1985; Summit, 1983), "people who have come into conflict with the law and who have been separated from other people by imprisonment . . . are often considered different in the sense of being anomalous, abnormal, to be feared, and to be ostracized from society" (Sommers, 1995, p. 15). If a woman released from prison tries to hide her prison record to avoid such social discrimination, she runs the risk of triggering her experience of child abuse where "the secrecy makes it clear to the child that this is something bad and dangerous. The secrecy is both the source of fear and the promise of safety" (Summit, 1983, p. 181). Further, because incarcerated women often come from dysfunctional and disadvantaged families (Arbour, 1996; Flowers, 1995; Shaw, 1991, 1992), they are likely to have few social resources to help them cope with such ostracism. Hence, a survivor may experience the full, unmitigated force of her stigmatization and come to regard it as yet another betrayal. She had, after all, "paid for her crime with her time." To the extent that a survivor's experience following her release recreates the traumagenic dynamics of stigmatization and betrayal, then, society itself is likely to frustrate a survivor's efforts to reintegrate into society and thereby revictimize rather than rehabilitate her.

Conclusion

Because women's experiences in prison in many ways parallel their experiences of child sexual abuse, an incarcerated survivor will be inundated with situations that have the potential to recapitulate her abuse experience, including the traumatic violation of physical and sexual boundaries, the dichotomy of the powerful and the powerless, stigmatization and devaluation, and issues of trust and betrayal. Reinstating these dynamics may propel an imprisoned woman toward any number of coping strategies, including substance abuse, self-injury, or violence. Taken to the extreme, reliving these dynamics may make it more likely that a survivor will pay for her crime, and the crimes of others, with her life. Just as the child abuse accommodation syndrome is based on a constellation of behaviors "which allows for [the] immediate survival of the child within the family but which tends to isolate the child from eventual acceptance, credibility or empathy within the larger society" (Summit, 1983, p. 179), it seems that imprisoned survivors respond to their comparable circumstances with comparable behaviors. That is, they respond with behaviors that facilitate their survival within the prison while alienating them from a society that already condemns them.

THERAPY, POLICY AND RESEARCH IMPLICATIONS

The rate of child abuse among incarcerated women (Arbour, 1996; Heney, 1990, 1996; Shaw, 1991, 1992; Task Force on Federally Sentenced Women, 1990), the likelihood that prison recapitulates the traumagenic dynamics of child sexual abuse (Finkelhor, 1988; Finkelhor & Browne, 1985), and survivors' neurologically-based hypersensitivity to such dynamics (van der Kolk, 1996), together make it imperative that prison staff, policy makers and researchers be sensitive to issues that stem from child abuse. In effect, people who work with prisoners "are faced with the task of both processing the reality of the . . . [imprisonment] . . . while understanding the . . . [inmate's] current behavior, feelings and perceptions in the context of this history" (Fromuth & Burkhart, 1992, p. 89).

Therapy Implications

As Fromuth and Burkhart (1992, p. 93) noted, it is important that therapists who "work within the constraints of a poor milieu . . . [where a survivor's] . . . perceptions of revictimization, unfortunately, may be quite accurate," validate the reality of a survivor's perceptions of revictimization. Because survivors are chronically sensitive to traumagenic dynamics (van der Kolk, 1996), counselors might usefully explain how these dynamics operate within prison. Although prison reinstates all four of the traumagenic processes of child sexual abuse, the patriarchal structure of prison mandates that particular attention be devoted to survivors' sensitivity to powerlessness. Hence, counselors should be cognizant of the dynamics of powerlessness and skilled in strategies that can help a survivor move to a position of power from which she tries to control her own responses to external events rather than the events themselves. Therapists can also work to anticipate crises that might instigate feelings of powerlessness (Fromuth & Burkhart, 1992), as might occur when women are involuntarily segregated because they are deemed dangerous to themselves or others. In order for an inmate to retain a sense of control over her own experience, and to avoid authoritarian, revictimizing actions that "are likely to result in a variety of 'negative' survivor behaviors, such as manipulation [sic.], rage or 'acting out' " (Briere, 1989, p. 58), it is preferable to negotiate noncoercive contracts for safety in advance. More generally, by working through the traumagenic factors common to child abuse and prison life "the therapist might mitigate the harm to the . . . [inmate]. Indeed, the therapist who is aware of these dynamics may be able to use these reawakened memories and feelings to process the abuse" (Fromuth & Burkhart, 1992, p. 93).

Because substance abuse, self-harm and suicidal behaviors are common among incarcerated survivors (Faith, 1993; Heney, 1990, 1996; Sommers, 1995), the traumagenic dynamics addressed by these coping strategies merit special attention. For example, drug treatment programs specifically designed for survivors of childhood abuse should be readily available to incarcerated women. Indeed, giving up substance abuse is typically regarded as one of the first tasks of recovery (Herman, 1992a). Because substance abuse is in itself a coping mechanism, however, "exposing motivational tiers is also important in working with women who are drug addicted so that areas of vulnerability can be identified and appropriate coping mechanisms developed" (Sommers, 1995, p. 133).

Perhaps the most helpful resources for dealing with substance abuse, self-injury and suicide are the incarcerated survivors themselves. As Root (1992, p. 245) noted,

> having at least one companion victim with whom one can talk about traumatic experiences decreases the likelihood of feeling uniquely vulnerable, increases the likelihood that one can refuse blame for the traumata, and provides a unique type of social support . . . The companionship of other victims allows for the possibility of absolving oneself of blame by absolving the other person(s).

In accordance with this and drawing on the informal network of support that emerges among incarcerated women (Heney, 1990), a Peer Support Team was developed at P4W consisting of volunteers of diverse backgrounds trained to provide women-centered support and crisis intervention to other prisoners. Team members completed a six-week training program covering various topics such as socialization, racism, homophobia, classism, violence against women and children, women's anger, self-injury, substance abuse, suicide intervention, and counseling skills. Based on interviews with over 50 women at P4W, Pollack (1993) found that:

> 32% had used a peer counselor, seeking assistance primarily for depression and the urge to self-harm. Over 80% of these women felt significantly assisted by the counseling: they felt "less alone," "less depressed," "more optimistic," and "less angry." [Further], the peer counselors were themselves assisted by their involvement in the program. (Faith, 1993, p. 245; see also Kendall, 1993)

Given the strategies that survivors are likely to call upon in their efforts to cope with incarceration (e.g., substance abuse, self-injury, suicidal behavior, aggression), many of these women might be diagnosed as suffering from Borderline Personality Disorder (BPD). Because BPD provides a vehicle through which women can be labeled *both* "bad and mad," this psychiatric diagnosis might be especially appealing to those in corrections in view of their tradition of explaining women's criminality as stemming from women being "bad" *or* "mad" (Kendall, 1993). This perspective, however, may do little to help imprisoned survivors given that there is little evidence for the validity of BPD as a diagnostic entity (Brown, 1992) and much evidence for its harm (e.g., Herman, 1992a). Traditional conceptualizations of BPD also ignore findings that most women with BPD have histories of severe child abuse (Berliner & Elliott, 1996; Brown, 1992; Harney, 1992; Herman, 1992a; Herman, 1992b; Root, 1992; van der Kolk, 1996). As a result, "these explanations become entities reified in a diagnostic system that often blames the 'wounded' persons for their inability to reorganize their lives after horrible experiences" (Root, 1992, p. 230). In so doing, a diagnosis of BPD allows society to deny responsibility for child abuse by attributing survivors' problems to their allegedly flawed personalities (Brown, 1992; Herman, 1992a; Root, 1992; Summit, 1983). This, in turn, obviates the need for social change.

The diagnosis of BPD is also problematic because it fails to acknowledge the symptoms of Posttraumatic Stress Disorder (PTSD) that typically accompany it (Brown, 1992; Herman, 1992a, 1992b; van der Kolk, 1996). A study of Australian female prisoners, for example, "demonstrated that PTSD and a history of abuse were almost ubiquitous in these women, and that these factors contributed significantly to their criminal histories (Raeside, Shaw & McFarlane, 1995)" (McFarlane & Yehuda, 1996, p. 168). More recent conceptualizations consider both the characterological changes and symptoms of PTSD that follow chronic trauma such as child abuse (Herman, 1992a, 1992b; Linehan, 1993; van der Kolk, 1996). To avoid further stigmatizing survivors, and to acknowledge the etiology of these women's problems, some of these researchers suggest that the label BPD be replaced by terms such as Complex Posttraumatic Stress Disorder (Herman 1992a, 1992b) or Disorder of Extreme Stress Not Otherwise Specified (DESNOS; van der Kolk, 1996). Nevertheless, because these conceptualizations "continue to describe . . . [survivors'] responses as pathological" (Brown, 1992, p. 220), they ultimately blame the victim and thereby have the potential to rekindle the traumagenic dynamics of child abuse.

Policy Implications

Incarcerated women's histories of child abuse have implications for prison staffing policies. Correctional officers should be trained to act in ways that minimize the dynamics common to both prison and child abuse. For example, treating women with respect may avoid stigmatizing them, and decreasing the frequency of invasive search procedures may reduce feelings of powerlessness. As Axon (1989, p. 13) noted in her international review of programs for female inmates, "measures which appear to, from the inmates' point of view, . . . deny inmates opportunities to exercise self-control and self-determination are clearly counterindicated."

Sommers (1995, p. 131) suggested that, "by conceptualizing their tasks around a core of empathy, compassion, and the power to effect positive change, the officers as well as the women might become empowered to feel more effective in their worlds." Such a policy, however, may be difficult to enact because it requires officers to empower those whom they are expected to have power over. In this regard, Hannah-Moffat (1995, p. 153) stated, "it is difficult to envision the development of meaningful, respectful, and supportive relationships when guards continue to perform strip searches, open women's mail, monitor their relations with others within and outside the institution, and at times punish the prisoners." Further, the inherent power imbalance in the officer-inmate relationship may, because of its similarity to past abuse, overshadow the impact of guards' efforts to treat survivors respectfully. Indeed, combining these roles may recreate the dynamic whereby a child was violated by the person on whom she depended, making this approach especially harmful to survivors. As Sommers (1995, p. 131) commented, then, "research and education efforts would wisely be spent on the exploration and piloting of projects in which correctional officers can develop new perceptions of their purpose and their method of operation."

In effect, prison policies should strive to reduce any dynamics that might retraumatize survivors. This includes hiring female officers because "the hiring of male staff for such positions could interfere with the healing process for those who have survived physical, sexual and/or psychological abuse" (Task Force on Federally Sentenced Women, 1990, p. 89). Grievance procedures and other checks that increase officers' accountability, including a zero tolerance policy with respect to harassment and abuse, should be in place to increase survivors' power and reduce the likelihood of sexual retraumatization (Arbour, 1996). Women's privacy needs should also be met, for example, by using devices that impair visual access to toilet facilities or pairing male with female officers (Arbour, 1996).

Attention must also be given to the issues that women face when their incarceration ends. In this regard, correctional services might usefully identify the nature of women's needs following incarceration and implement programs and provide resources to fulfill these needs. Correctional services might also develop public education strategies to address the social stigmatization that haunts previously incarcerated women.

Research Implications

The incidence of child abuse among incarcerated women draws attention to a number of empirical questions. In particular, research might usefully examine the extent to which prison recapitulates the traumagenic dynamics of child abuse, the degree to which these dynamics affect incarcerated survivors, and the mechanisms by which women cope with these dynamics. It would also be worthwhile to know whether these traumagenic processes affect incarcerated women who are not survivors, and how other forms of oppression, such as that suffered by women of Native ancestry, exacerbate the traumatic impact of incarceration. Similarly, it would be useful to evaluate the efficacy of programs designed to overcome the traumagenic dynamics of women's experiences before, during, and after their incarceration.

CONCLUDING COMMENTS

Sommers (1995, p. 130) argued that women must "be freed of the burden of victimization, or they will continue to come into conflict with the law." In addition, it seems that women might be less likely to reoffend if society also freed them of their revictimization during their incarceration and following their release. Consistent with the claim that opened this paper, then, understanding women offenders has again been facilitated by knowledge of women's own victimization (Faith, 1993; Heney, 1990, 1996; Kruttschnitt, 1993; Lake, 1993; Widom, 1989). It is imperative that this understanding be used to ensure incarceration does not constitute cruel and unusual punishment for survivors of childhood sexual abuse. The extent to which prison officials are willing to consider the implications of this understanding for prison staffing, policy, and research, and thereby act upon this understanding, however, remains to be seen.

REFERENCES

Arbour, L. (1996). *Commission of inquiry into certain events at the prison for women in Kingston.* Ottawa: Canada Communication Group.

Axon, L. (1989). *Model and exemplary programs for female inmates: An international review.* Ottawa: Ministry of the Solicitor General.

Berliner, L., & Elliott, D. M. (1996). Sexual abuse of children. In J. Briere, L. Berliner, J. A. Bulkley, C. Jenny, & T. Reid (Eds.), *APSAC handbook on child maltreatment* (pp. 51-71). Thousand Oaks, CA: Sage.

Briere, J. (1989). *Therapy for adults molested as children: Beyond survival.* New York: Springer.

Brown, L. S. (1992). A feminist critique of the personality disorders. In L.S. Brown & M. Ballou (Eds.), *Personality and psychopathology: Feminist reappraisals* (pp. 206-228). New York: Guilford Press.

Chesney-Lind, M., & Rodriguez, N. (1983). Women under lock and key. *Prison Journal, 63,* 47-85.

Darke, J. (1987). The violent female offender. In J. Maclatchie (Ed.), *Violence in contemporary Canadian society* (pp. 140-145). Ottawa: John Howard Society of Canada.

Earls, C. M., & David, H. (1990). Early family and sexual experiences of male and female prostitutes. *Canada's Mental Health, 38,* 7-11.

Eaton, M. (1993). *Women after prison.* Buckingham: Open University Press.

Faith, K. (1993). *Unruly women: The politics of confinement and resistance.* Vancouver: Press Gang Publishers.

Finkelhor, D. (1988).The trauma of child sexual abuse: Two models. In G. E. Wyatt & G. J. Powell (Eds.), *Lasting effects of child sexual abuse* (pp. 61-82). Newbury Park, CA: Sage Publications.

Finkelhor, D., & Browne, A. (1985). The traumatic impact of child sexual abuse: A conceptualization. *The American Journal of Orthopsychiatry, 55,* 530-541.

Flowers, R. B. (1995). *Female crime, criminals and cellmates: An exploration of female criminality and delinquency.* London: McFarland & Company Inc.

Fromuth, M., & Burkhart, B. (1992). Recovery or recapitulation? An analysis of the impact of psychiatric hospitalization of the child sexual abuse survivor. *Women & Therapy, 12,* 81-95.

Grossman, M. G. (1992). Two perspectives on aboriginal female suicides in custody. *Canadian Journal of Criminology, 34,* 403-416.

Hannah-Moffat, K. (1995). Feminine fortresses: Woman-centered prisons? *The Prison Journal, 75,* 135-164.

Harney, P. A. (1992). The role of incest in developmental theory and treatment of women diagnosed with borderline personality disorder. *Women & Therapy, 12,* 39-57.

Heney, J. (1990). *Report on self-injurious behavior in the Kingston Prison for Women.* Ottawa: Ministry of the Solicitor General, Corrections Branch.

Heney, J. (1996). *Dying on the inside: Suicide and suicidal feelings among federally incarcerated women.* Unpublished doctoral dissertation, Carleton University, Ottawa, Canada.

Herman, J. L. (1992a). *Trauma and recovery.* New York: Basic Books.

Herman, J. L. (1992b). Complex PTSD: A syndrome in survivors of prolonged and repeated trauma. *Journal of Traumatic Stress, 5,* 377-391.

Janoff-Bulman, R. (1992). *Shattered assumptions: Towards a new psychology of trauma.* New York: Free Press.

Jose-Kampfner, C. (1990). Coming to terms with existential death: An analysis of women's adaptation to life in prison. *Social Justice, 17,* 110-125.

Kendall, K. (1993). *Literature review of therapeutic services for women in prison.* Ottawa: Correctional Service of Canada.

Kruttschnitt, C. (1993). Violence by and against women: A comparative and cross-national analysis. *Violence and Victims, 8,* 253-270.

Lake, E. S. (1993). An exploration of the violent victim experiences of female offenders. *Violence and Victims, 8,* 41-51.

Linehan, M. M. (1993). *Cognitive-behavioral treatment of borderline personality disorder.* New York: Guilford Press.

McFarlane, A. C., & Yehuda, R. (1996). Resilience vulnerability, and the course of posttraumatic reactions. In B.A. van der Kolk, A.C. McFarlane & L. Weisaeth (Eds.), *Traumatic stress: The effects of overwhelming experience on mind, body, and society* (pp. 155-181). New York: Guilford Press.

Padel, U., & Stevenson, P. (1988). *Insiders: Women's experience of prison.* London: Virago Press.

Pollack, S. (1993). *Opening the window on a very dark day: A program evaluation of the Peer Support Team at the Kingston Prison for Women.* Unpublished Masters Thesis, Carleton University, Ottawa.

Raeside, C. W. J., Shaw, J. J., & McFarlane, A. C. (1995). *Posttraumatic stress disorder (PTSD) in perpetrators of violent crime.* Manuscript submitted for publication.

Root, M. P. P. (1992). Reconstructing the impact of trauma on personality. In L.S. Brown & M. Ballou (Eds.), *Personality and psychopathology: Feminist reappraisals* (pp. 229-265). New York: Guilford Press.

Shaw, M. (1991). *Survey of Federally sentenced women: Report to the Task Force on Federally Sentenced Women.* Ottawa: Ministry of the Solicitor General of Canada, Corrections Branch.

Shaw, M. (1992). *Paying the price: Federally sentenced women in context.* Ottawa: Ministry of the Solicitor General of Canada, Corrections Branch.

Solicitor General Canada. (1995). *Basic facts about corrections in Canada. 1994 edition.* Ottawa: Ministry of Supply and Services Canada.

Sommers, E. K. (1995). *Voices from within: Women who have broken the law.* Toronto: University of Toronto Press.

Sugar, F., & Fox, L. (1989-1990). Nistum Peyako Séht'wawin Iskwewak': Breaking chains. *Canadian Journal of Women and the Law, 3,* 465-482.

Summit, R. C. (1983). Child sexual abuse accommodation syndrome. *Child Abuse and Neglect, 7,* 177-193.

Task Force on Federally Sentenced Women. (1990). *Creating choices.* Ottawa: Ministry of the Solicitor General.

Taylor, S., & Brown, J. (1988). Illusion and well-being: A social psychological perspective on mental health. *Psychological Bulletin, 103,* 193-210.

van der Kolk, B. A. (1996). Complexity of adaptation to trauma: Self-regulation, stimulus discrimination, and characterological development. In B.A. van der Kolk, A.C. McFarlane & L. Weisaeth (Eds.), *Traumatic stress: The effects of overwhelming experience on mind, body, and society* (pp. 182-213). New York: Guilford Press.

Widom, C. S. (1989). The cycle of violence. *Science, 244,* 160-166.

Zupan, L. (1992). Men guarding women: An analysis of the employment of male correctional officers in prisons for women. *Journal of Criminal Justice, 20,* 297-309.

Comparison Study of Women Who Have and Have Not Murdered Their Abusive Partners

Gloria Hamilton
Tammy Sutterfield

SUMMARY. This study compared histories of domestic violence and help-seeking behavior of two groups of women, women who had been imprisoned for killing their abusers and women who had received assistance from women's shelters. Of the 49 participants in this study, 20 had been incarcerated for homicide of their abusive partner. The remaining 29 had received services from shelters for battered women. Questionnaires about their personal experiences of violence were administered to all 49 participants. Differences were found on historical factors such as whether or not community resources, including police assistance, were available during as well as subsequent to the domestic violence episodes. *[Article copies available for a fee from The Haworth Document Delivery Service: 1-800-342-9678. E-mail address: getinfo@haworth.com]*

When a female victim of domestic violence murders the abuser, her act stops the cycle of private domestic violence and moves her into the

Gloria Hamilton, PhD, Clinical Psychologist, is Associate Professor of Psychology at Middle Tennessee State University. Tammy Sutterfield, MA, works with the Family Center in Denton, TX.

Address correspondence to: Gloria Hamilton, PhD, Box 97, Middle Tennessee State University, Murfreesboro, TN 37132.

[Haworth co-indexing entry note]: "Comparison Study of Women Who Have and Have Not Murdered Their Abusive Partners." Hamilton, Gloria, and Tammy Sutterfield. Co-published simultaneously in *Women & Therapy* (The Haworth Press, Inc.) Vol. 20, No. 4, 1997, pp. 45-55; and: *Breaking the Rules: Women in Prison and Feminist Therapy* (ed: Judy Harden, and Marcia Hill) The Haworth Press, Inc., 1998, pp. 45-55; and: *Breaking the Rules: Women in Prison and Feminist Therapy* (ed: Judy Harden, and Marcia Hill) The Harrington Park Press, an imprint of The Haworth Press, Inc., 1998, pp. 45-55. Single or multiple copies of this article are available for a fee from The Haworth Document Delivery Service [1-800-342-9678, 9:00 a.m. - 5:00 p.m. (EST). E-mail address: getinfo@haworth.com].

45

arena of public accountability. The violence now becomes the concern of society at large and the battered woman, charged with homicide, becomes visible. This study was designed to focus on events prior to the homicide: the woman's attempts to escape the violence while the abuser was still alive and the responses of those to whom she turned for help. Data were analyzed to determine the differences between help-seeking experiences of two populations of battered women, those who were able successfully to leave situations of domestic violence, including leaving the abuser, and those who resorted to homicide as a solution to the violence. The intent of this study is delineation of the factors that were present for the women who were able to escape domestic violence as well as determination of the factors that were operating to increase the risk of homicide in domestic violence situations. To decrease homicide, it is important to determine which variables increase the risk of lethality in situations of domestic violence. This study investigated help-seeking behaviors of female victims of abuse and their ratings of the helpfulness of responses to their calls for help. Two groups of battered women were selected for inclusion in this study, women incarcerated for murdering their abusers and women who had received assistance from battered women's shelters.

A common assumption by the general public is that battered women don't want to leave the abuser. Walker (1979) found that many battered women experience a state of fear that leads them to believe that escape is not possible. Walker observed patterns of behavior, psychological factors, and perceptions that are characteristic of women who have survived repeated physical abuse by their partners. The victims' feelings of guilt and shame, in combination with the abusers' possessive and controlling behaviors, lead to emotional, psychological, and physical isolation from friends and families. Economic and social factors further ensure entrapment in the violence. The battered woman's financial and emotional dependence on the abuser, traditional societal views that emphasize the importance of marriage to women's identity, and the insufficiency of existing legal and societal remedies to end domestic violence combine to explain battered women's difficulties in safely escaping domestic violence.

Studies demonstrate that battered women do reach out to formal and informal help sources for assistance. Gelles and Strauss (1988) found that approximately 50% of the women in their study who experienced minor violence and nearly 70% of those who experienced severe domestic abuse actively attempted to secure outside help. A study by Frank and Houghton (1981) led them to conclude that an important determinant of whether a battered woman actively attempts to leave the abusive partner is her perception of whether she will receive community support and assistance from community agencies.

Battered women have relied on their own resourcefulness in creating strategies to mitigate the violence. Based on interviews with battered women, Bowker (1983) identified seven common strategies used by battered women in their attempts to end marital violence: (1) attempting to talk the batterer out of the abusive behavior, (2) attempting to extract a promise from the batterer to stop the abuse, (3) threatening nonviolent actions such as contacting the police or suing for a divorce, (4) hiding from the batterer, (5) attempting to reduce the physical damage by using passive self-defense, (6) aggressively fighting back, and (7) avoiding the abusive partner prior to the eruption of overt aggression. Of these strategies, the third most commonly reported is that of leaving and/or hiding. In-depth interviews revealed that 7 out of 10 battered women had left their abusive partners during the preceding year. Approximately half of those who had left their abusive partner felt that the strategy had been very effective. Almost half reported that leaving had not proven to be effective and 13% stated that leaving had made their situations worse (Bowker, 1983).

Data show that the woman is usually the partner who dies when violence escalates in the home to the point of murder (Browne, 1987). Less typically the woman may end the battering by killing the batterer. Factors predictive for homicide of the batterer include a sharp escalation in the severity of the incidents and life-threatening and/or severe violence or injuries on the first occasion of domestic violence (Walker, 1984). Browne (1987) found no significant differences in total number of battering episodes experienced by battered women who committed homicide when compared to those who had not. She did find that more serious injuries were experienced by the women who had been convicted of spousal homicide. Walker (1989) studied battered women who murdered their abusers and concluded that the women believed that their lives could or would be ended by the abuser. Ewing (1987) found that 33% of spousal homicides by women occurred during a battery episode. Researchers Browne and Williams (1989) concluded that battered women who killed their violent partners experienced the brunt of the violence just prior to the homicide and reacted out of self-defense. Campbell (1986) found that females convicted of spousal homicide were far more likely than males convicted of spousal homicide to be responding to rather than initiating violence. The factor common to these studies of battered women who murdered their abusers is the intensity of the physical and psychological immediacy of that final episode of domestic violence.

Foster, Veale, and Fogel (1989) interviewed women imprisoned for killing their abusive male partners and concluded that three factors were present in most of these relationships: threats by the abuser to kill the woman, daily use of alcohol by the abuser, and a firearm in the home. Jurik and Winn (1990) analyzed the patterns of homicides committed by women and men and found that women more frequently killed in response to physical aggression initiated by the batterer. Walker (1984) asserted that battered women killed their abusers as a last resort in their attempts to end the violence. These findings lend support to a self-protection model of homicides by battered women.

In a 1984 study of women who murdered their batterers, Walker found that all of the women reported having suffered repeated assaults by their partners. Many of the women stated that they could not have escaped danger even by leaving the batterers. More than one third of these women had attempted suicide, believing that others did not take them seriously and could not be depended on for protection. Studies have shown that the psychological abuse of battered women who killed their batterers differed qualitatively from that experienced by battered women who have not killed, and is perhaps best explained by noting the variables that correlate with likelihood of homicide of the abuser. The likelihood of homicide positively correlates with threats of retaliation by the abuser and with social isolation of the victim. Indeed, the risk for homicide of the batterer was proportional to the extent of social isolation of the wife by the batterer.

This study compared histories of domestic violence of two groups who had reported spouse abuse, women incarcerated for murdering their abusers and women receiving services from battered women's shelters. Questionnaires were constructed to focus on help-seeking behaviors employed by the women at the time of battering and the responses the women received. Given the findings in the literature of the high incidence of help-seeking behavior from victims of domestic violence, the researchers predicted findings of no differences between the groups in help-seeking contacts with police, the courts, health resources (mental health professional, medical professional), co-worker/friend, or private resources (family member, minister/priest). It was predicted that there would be significant differences between the groups on whether the responses of those contacted were rated as helpful in stopping the abuse.

METHOD

Participants

This study involved 49 women who reported that they had experienced domestic violence. The first group consisted of 20 women (17 Caucasian, 2 African-American, and 1 Hispanic-American) who were convicted of murdering their domestic partners and had been sentenced to prison for the homicide. The second group consisted of 29 women (28 Caucasian and 1 African-American) who had received assistance from a shelter for battered women. Such assistance included previous or current residence at the shelter and/or participation in a shelter-sponsored weekly support group for battered women. Both groups reported a modal education level equivalent to a high school diploma.

Measures

Two-part questionnaire. The questionnaire administered to both groups of participants consisted of questions pertaining to demographics (age, race, education, occupation), histories of domestic violence, and experiences with formal and informal resources for victims of domestic abuse. Participants were asked whether they had contacted the following resources: courts, police, women's shelter, mental health professional, medical professional, co-worker/friend, family member, minister/priest. Participants were asked to rate the helpfulness of responses given by agencies and persons contacted on a scale with options of: 1 = Very Helpful, 2 = Somewhat Helpful, 3 = Not at all Helpful. Helpfulness ratings were individually determined by the participants in the study. For the women who had been found guilty of murder, a separate part of the questionnaire was designed to collect data regarding their offense and sentencing. The version of the questionnaire administered to participants residing in the shelters did not include questions about criminal offense and sentencing.

Procedures

Participants were obtained by contacting the directors of battered women's shelters and Department of Corrections officials in the same southeastern state. They were informed of the purpose of the research and were asked to distribute informational packets to battered women in their facilities. Each informational packet contained an Informed Consent document, information concerning the purposes and procedures of the study, and contact information. No indication of whether all women who received an informational packet agreed to participate was provided by the officials who had distributed the initial materials. On return of the Informed Consent document, questionnaires were given to each participant to complete in private.

RESULTS

The following information was determined by descriptive statistics for the two groups that were included in this study. With regard to ethnicity, the majority were Caucasian (85% in the prisons and 97% in the shelters); 2 in the prison group were African-American and 1 was Hispanic-American while 1 in the shelter group was African-American. At the time of the domestic violence, 50% of the subjects in the prison group and 66% of the women in the shelter group considered themselves to be "battered women." Those percentages had risen to 70% in the prison group and 83% in the shelter group at the time that the interviews were conducted.

Spouses accounted for 70% of the batterers of the prison sample and 93% of the shelter sample. Violence most frequently occurred in the home for both groups. In their attempts to deal with the abuse, 65% of the women in the prison group and 59% of the women in the shelter group had left their home at least one time previous to the last violent episode. Of the participants in this study who had left the abuser on a previous occasion, 38% of those in the prison group and 18% of those in the shelter group reported that the abuser had tracked them and pressured them into returning. Typical resources to which the women fled were family, cited by 18% of the shelter sample and 23% of the prison sample, and a women's shelter. While none of the women in the prison group had gone to a shelter for assistance, 5 of the women in the shelter group had resided at a shelter prior to their participation in this study.

Both groups of battered women (60% of the prison sample and 90% of the shelter sample) reported that they had turned to a co-worker or a friend for help. For the shelter group, 86% of the sample initiated help-seeking contacts with friends and 21% of the sample solicited help from co-workers. For the prison sample, 55% of the women initiated help-seeking contacts with friends and 40% approached co-workers for help. While every woman in the shelter sample reported having asked for and received help, a total of 7 women in the prison sample (35%) stated that they had told no one of the abuse. Of the women in the prison sample who had called a shelter to obtain help in escaping the abuse, 5 of 6 rated the shelter staff as Not At All Helpful, while 4 of 6 rated their help-seeking contacts with a minister as Not At All Helpful. The shelter sample rated mental health professionals as Not At All Helpful by the largest percentage (28%) for resources contacted by this sample. The resource rated Not At All Helpful by the largest percentage (45%) of the prison sample was the police.

The police had been called by or for 60% of the women in the prisons and 65% of the women at the shelters. Further, 45% of the subjects in the prison group and 55% of the women in the shelter group had called the police on more than one occasion. "Warnings" and "nothing" were the most common police responses reported by the battered women who were later incarcerated for homicide. Arrest of their partners was the most common form of police assistance reported by the women in the shelter group, accounting for 31% of police interventions in this group; only 5% of the women in the prison group reported that their partners were arrested at the time of the assault. None of the women in the homicide group reported that the police had assisted by transporting them to a women's shelter. One of the women in the shelter group had been taken to the shelter as a result of a 911 call to the police.

In attempting to stop spousal abuse, 15% of women in the prison sample and 62% of women in the shelter sample had contacted the judicial system for help. Of the women in the shelter sample who petitioned the courts for assistance, 12 sought (and were granted) divorce, 8 requested a Restraining Order, 7 requested an Order of Protection, 3 sought a Legal Separation, 1 filed a Peace Bond, and 1 asked for (but did not receive) Victim's Compensation. Four women in the shelter group expressed outrage that the system "had not kept him (the abuser) in jail." Among the women in the prison sample, one had received an Order of Protection and one had been granted both an Order of Protection and a Restraining Order, subsequently violated by the batterer.

Hypothesis one predicted findings of no differences between the groups in help-seeking contacts with police, the courts, health resources, private resources, and personal contacts such as a friend or co-worker. Inferential statistics in the form of *t* tests and one-way analysis of variance were used to test for differences between group means on sources contacted for assistance and ratings of helpfulness of responses. One-way analysis of variance found no differences between groups in help-seeking behavior directed toward health resources (medical professional, mental health professional) or private resources (family member, minister). A *t* test found no significant difference between the groups on frequency of contacts with the police. Significant differences between group help-seeking behavior were found on the following: a greater percentage of women in the shelter sample solicited the courts, t (19,28) = 2.98, p < .005, and friends, t (19,28) = 2.56, p < .014, for help. Hypothesis one was partially supported.

Hypothesis two predicted there would be significant differences between groups on whether the responses of those contacted were rated as helpful in stopping the abuse. A one-way analysis of variance found no differences between groups on ratings of helpfulness by contact with health resources (medical professional, mental health professional) or with private resources (family member, minister/priest). A t test found no significant difference between group ratings of helpfulness of the courts. Differences were found between group ratings of helpfulness of friends, t (19,28) = 3.75, p < .0006, and helpfulness of the police, t (19,28) = 2.33, p < .028, with the shelter group rating both as significantly more helpful than the prison group. Hypothesis two was partially supported.

DISCUSSION

This study investigated whether there were significant differences between the abuse histories of battered women incarcerated for murder of their abusers and battered women receiving services from a shelter for battered women. Abuse histories, help-seeking behaviors, and ratings of helpfulness of the resources that were contacted at the time of the abuse were compared. The purposes of the study were: (1) to identify resources that were rated as helpful by the shelter group in helping them escape domestic violence, and (2) to identify those resources that received low or nil ratings of helpfulness by the prison group who had been convicted of homicide of their abusers.

Given the nature of the study, the sample sizes were unequal. Several times more women who received assistance at a women's shelter were available to participate in this study than women who were incarcerated for killing their abusive boyfriends or husbands. Many of the findings of this study support those of numerous studies: spouses were the majority of abusers, most incidences of violence occurred in the victims' homes, and the majority of battered women left their own homes in their attempts to stop the abuse (which in some cases resulted in an escalation of abuse). All participants in each group reported multiple forms of abuse. There were no significant differences by group for type of abuse, threats of harm, or abuse of children. It should be noted that the data collection instrument used in this study did not measure escalation in intensity or severity of the abuse over time. Subsequent studies that include measures of change in intensity and severity of the abuse could determine whether battered women convicted of homicide experienced intensification of the violence just prior to or at the time of the homicide.

Several findings were unexpected. Although the two samples of battered women did not differ in help-seeking behavior that involved calling 911 for emergency assistance, police response differed by group. The majority of women in the prison sample reported that they had repeatedly attempted to secure assistance from the police and rated the responses by the police as Not At All Helpful, while women in the shelter sample reported that the police provided Very Helpful or Somewhat Helpful service by arresting the abuser. None of the women in the prison sample was transported to a shelter. None of the abusers was arrested. It is important to note that in each of these instances, the woman who had contacted the police was later arrested and tried for homicide of the abuser. Clearly, the visits by the police did not end the abuse.

Additionally, no woman in the prison group gave a rating of Very Helpful to community-funded resources such as the police or mental health professionals. Nor did they rate private resources (minister, medical professional) or even friends as Very Helpful. The implication of these findings is clear. The consistency of the ratings of Not At All Helpful by women in the prison sample reflect their belief that the community resources they had contacted would not or could not help, effectively reinforcing their isolation in the midst of violence. The single category of persons who were rated as Very Helpful by the prison sample was family, specifically, mother, grandmother, and sister. Yet, family (parents, grandparents) homes were the places that the abusers knew and could easily track and confront the women who had fled the violence. Perhaps this was the reason that more of the women did not leave their homes to move into their families' homes for refuge: they knew that the abuser would follow and this would place others in their families in harm's way.

Questions raised but not answered by this study include possible differences in availability of shelters in the communities of those who participated in this study. Also, were there differences in the training of the shelter staff that accounted for the perception of the prison sample that they would find no help from the shelter? Or were the shelters so full that they could not house any more women? Why were police responses so different across these groups of battered women? Were the women in the prison sample intimidated by their abusers and asked the police not to arrest their abuser? Is non-arrest of the batterer a causal factor in domestic homicide? Researchers are currently conducting a second phase of this study to address a number of these unanswered questions.

The following conclusions may be drawn from the results of this study.

The experiences of this sample of battered women incarcerated for homicide differed in crucial ways from the experiences of the sample of battered women who received services from a shelter. Perhaps the most obvious difference is in the histories of treatment by the police. Clearly, the police play a major role in stopping domestic violence. Effective police response to domestic violence calls is crucial. Simon (1995, p. 65) explains, "By taking the offender into custody, the police are communicating to him and the victim that he has committed a criminal act and that he is responsible for his violent behavior." Arresting the offender provides clear evidence of support for the family as well as enforcing the law against assault and battery. Effective police response provides tangible help in the form of providing safe alternatives for the victim so she is no longer isolated in the violence.

A second obvious difference in the histories reflects the isolation of the women in the prison sample from resources that provide information, support, and alternatives. As demonstrated by the findings of this study, a number of factors function to reinforce the belief of many battered women that there is no escape from the violence. In addition to abuser-imposed isolation, the discovery that community resources cannot provide a safe, realistic plan for ending the violence further isolates the victims of domestic violence. Mandating that police be trained in, and implement, strategies that have been found effective in situations of domestic violence would be a first line of defense for all persons in domestic violence situations. Medical and mental health professionals must be trained to recognize and intervene in abusive situations. Without these basic changes, the battered woman is left with no solutions except to stop the batterer herself with the means she has at hand. Failure of the community to respond to domestic violence can and does result in homicides, of victim and of abuser.

REFERENCES

Bowker, L. H. (1983). *Beating wife beating.* Lexington, MA: Lexington Books.

Browne, A. (1987). *When battered women kill.* New York: Free Press.

Browne, A., & Williams, K. (1989). Exploring the effect of resource availability on the likelihood of female-perpetrated homicides. *Law and Society Review, 23,* 75-94.

Campbell, J. C. (1986). Nursing assessment for risk of homicide with battered women. *Advances in Nursing Science, 8,* 36-51.

Ewing, C. P. (1987). *Battered women who kill: Psychological self-defense as legal justification.* Lexington, MA: D. C. Heath.

Foster, L. A., Veale, C. M., & Fogel, C. I. (1989). Factors present when battered women kill. *Issues in Mental Health Nursing, 10,* 273-284.

Frank, P. D., & Houghton, B. D. (1981). *Dealing with the batterer* (Report of the Domestic Violence Project of the Volunteer Counseling Service of Rockland Co., Inc.). New York: Volunteer Counseling Service.

Gelles, R. J., & Strauss, M. A. (1988). *Intimate violence: The definitive study of the causes and consequences of abuse in the American family.* New York: Simon and Schuster.

Jurik, N. C., & Winn, R. (1990). Gender and homicide: A comparison of men and women who kill. *Violence and Victims, 5(4),* 227-241.

Simon, L. M. (1995). A therapeutic jurisprudence approach to the legal processing of domestic violence cases. *Psychology, Public Policy, and Law, 1,* 43-79.

Walker, L. E. (1979). *The battered woman.* New York: Harper & Row.

Walker, L. E. (1984). *Battered women syndrome.* New York: Springer.

Walker, L. E. (1989). *Terrifying love.* New York: Springer.

Managing Motherhood in Prison: The Impact of Race and Ethnicity on Child Placements

Sandra Enos

SUMMARY. The vast majority of the women who are imprisoned in our nation's correctional facilities are mothers. These women face considerable challenges in managing motherhood tasks while incarcerated. The options available for women in placing their children, maintaining contact, and maintaining place in families vary widely and are related to race, ethnicity and other variables. This article examines how motherhood is enacted under the circumstances of incarceration through the use of qualitative research undertaken in a women's prison. *[Article copies available for a fee from The Haworth Document Delivery Service: 1-800-342-9678. E-mail address: getinfo@haworth.com]*

INTRODUCTION

Since 1985, the inmate population has more than doubled from 744,000 to 1,585,000, giving the United States the highest incarceration rate of the

Sandra Enos, MA, is Assistant Professor of Sociology at Rhode Island College and a doctoral candidate at the University of Connecticut.

Special appreciation is extended to the women at the Adult Correctional Institution in Rhode Island along with the warden and staff associated with the parenting program for their time, interest and support of this project.

Address correspondence to: Sandra Enos, Rhode Island College, Department of Sociology and Justice Studies, Providence, RI 02908.

[Haworth co-indexing entry note]: "Managing Motherhood in Prison: The Impact of Race and Ethnicity on Child Placements." Enos, Sandra. Co-published simultaneously in *Women & Therapy* (The Haworth Press, Inc.) Vol. 20, No. 4, 1997, pp. 57-73; and: *Breaking the Rules: Women in Prison and Feminist Therapy* (ed: Judy Harden, and Marcia Hill) The Haworth Press, Inc., 1998, pp. 57-73; and: *Breaking the Rules: Women in Prison and Feminist Therapy* (ed: Judy Harden, and Marcia Hill) The Harrington Park Press, an imprint of The Haworth Press, Inc., 1998, pp. 57-73. Single or multiple copies of this article are available for a fee from The Haworth Document Delivery Service [1-800-342-9678, 9:00 a.m. - 5:00 p.m. (EST). E-mail address: getinfo@haworth.com].

industrialized world (Gilliard & Beck, 1996). Reflecting to some degree a steady and significant increase in the incarcerated population in the U.S. since 1979, the rate of increase for women (340%) has outpaced that of men (207%) (Beck & Gilliard, 1995). Despite their growing numbers, women still represent less than 7% of the imprisoned population. In some demographic characteristics, the female population mirrors the male population (Owen & Bloom, 1995). Both populations are made up of large numbers of ethnic and racial minorities (46% of the females and 45.5% of the males are black; 14% of the females and 16.8% of the males are Hispanic). The median age for female inmates and male inmates is 31 and 30 years respectively; 62% of the women and 66% of the men have less than a high school education (Snell, 1994). However, women inmates differ from male inmates along several dimensions. A higher percentage of women have had members of their family in prison (47% of the women vs. 37% of the men); they are less likely to be serving time for violent offenses (32% of females vs. 47% of males); they are serving shorter sentences (mean of 105 months vs. 153 months for men); and are more likely to be parents (78% vs. 64%) than are their male counterparts (Snell, 1994). It is estimated that 80% of these women are mothers with children, 66% with children under the age of 18 (Bloom & Steinhart, 1993). Seventy percent of these women were living with their children before incarceration (Snell, 1994). Of the males, only 64% are parents and about half of the inmates (53%) were living with their children at the time of arrest. This fact of parenthood has some significant effects for the population and reflects gendered aspects of the criminal justice and correctional systems that are usually ignored.

Arranging and managing the care of children of female inmates presents incarcerated women and their families with a variety of tasks and burdens. Unlike male inmates who may be somewhat peripheral to work associated with family caretaking and kinwork (Swan, 1981), female inmates are embedded, in some cases, in complex arrangements of shared child care, shared resources and so on. Their absence from their families often places the family itself in jeopardy.

That women offenders are in fact active members of families and mothers is not widely known. The image of the female offender is a woman who is estranged and isolated from family members relying on and dependent upon a pimp. While this may be the case for a minority of offenders, many female criminals remain closely aligned with families during their criminal careers. The family as a social institution plays a paradoxical role as it relates to crime. The family is used to explain the relatively low participation by women in crime. As a unit of social control, the family works to minimize deviancy by constraining the behavior of women. This theory holds that women are dependent on the family unit for economic support and this maintains social control over behavior (Kruttschnitt, 1991). Women with family responsibilities are less available to commit crimes because of the over-arching and powerful responsibilities of child-rearing and family maintenance.

While some families may exert the sort of social control theorists suggest, Miller (1986) demonstrates how embedded female offenders are in networks of relationships involving family members. The family, rather than being a protection against a criminal lifestyle as suggested by Kruttschnitt (1981), in fact, enables and nurtures a life of crime. Access to criminal opportunities, like drug trafficking and hustling, may be as available for some females as it is for males via family networks. The embeddedness of criminal opportunities and family networks may make crime-free lifestyles even harder to maintain for women than they are for men (Arnold, 1994). With the exception of a few studies like Miller's, little is known about how women balance criminal lifestyles and motherhood. How women manage motherhood while they are incarcerated, the sanctioned outcome of these lifestyles, is the focus of this research.

CHILDREN AND INCARCERATION

As a result of incarceration, inmates confront several challenges and suffer what Sykes refers to as the "pains of imprisonment" (Sykes, 1958). For men, this pain revolves around loss of freedom, autonomy, personal security, heterosexual relationships, and goods and services that can be found in the larger society. For women, the pains of imprisonment revolve around family relations, specifically separation from children (Henriques, 1981; Kiser, 1991; Neto & Bainer, 1983; Stanton, 1980) and the loss of the maternal role. The loss of maternal duties and roles are especially difficult for women who are concerned about the whereabouts and well-being of their children.

Options and Patterns of Placements

Where children live during the incarceration of their parents depends upon the resources available to their parent(s) and this availability appears to be related to the sex and race and ethnicity of their parents. National data on state prisoners reveals that 90% of the children of male inmates are likely to be placed or remain with their mothers (Snell, 1994) as a result of the imprisonment of the father. For children of female inmates, incarceration of the mother is much more disruptive. Upon imprisonment, 25% of the children of females were living with their fathers, 51% with grandparents, 20% with other relatives, 9% in foster care and the balance in other placements (Beck & Gilliard, 1995; Snell, 1994).

According to data reported from the most comprehensive survey of women in state prison and jails, there are also differences in placements attributable to race and ethnicity (Snell, 1994). White children are more likely to live with fathers (35%) than are black (19%) or Hispanic (24%) children. Grandparents are more likely to be the caretakers of black children (57%) and Hispanic children (55%) than of white children (41%), and white children are twice (12.6%) as likely to be in foster care as other children (6% for black and Hispanic children).

There have been relatively few research studies completed on the living arrangements of children when their mothers are incarcerated (Bloom and Steinhart, 1993; Fessler, 1991; Henriques, 1981; Johnston, 1995a; Johnston, 1995b; Stanton, 1980) and fewer still that examine the relationship of ethnicity and race and living arrangements for children.

One work that did include a race/ethnic breakdown of placement examined living arrangements of 285 children of 190 mothers incarcerated in two states (Baunach, 1985). Half of the mothers in the study were African-American and the other half white. Children of white women were more likely than children of African-American women to be placed in foster care (25% vs. 10%); black children were more likely to be placed in the care of grandparents (51% vs. 34%) and in the care of other relatives (29% vs. 23%) and white children were more likely to be placed with their father (25% vs. 10%). Although these differences are reported as statistically significant, Baunach does not examine factors that may contribute to some of these differences.

These questions are somewhat addressed in a study by Bresler and Lewis (1986). The authors compared white and black female inmates and found sharp differences in the incarcerated populations with respect to a variety of family-related demographics. Although the authors were interested in family-related issues, no data is presented on the placement of children. Black women were more likely to have been raised in single parent female-headed homes (62%) while white women's families of origin were more likely to be two parent families (95%). In this sample, only 20% of the white women were living with their children prior to incarceration compared to 54% of the black mothers. Twenty percent of the white women expected help from their family after their release while a majority (54%) of black women reported help would be forthcoming. Additionally, white women identified family help by naming one sibling or a parent while black women listed a wider network of help, with potential assistance from aunts, cousins, grandparents, and in-laws in addition to parents and siblings.

Bresler and Lewis (1986) suggest that for black women, families provide an extensive source of support and that imprisonment does not bring with it factors of isolation that seem to accompany the incarceration of white women. White women's isolation from their families and their children pushed them to rely to a greater extent on boyfriends, casual contacts and other sources of support. While Bresler and Lewis do not provide detailed data on the placement of children in their research, they do point to important differences in the family resources available to white and black women. To date, there has been no research examining differences in placement by race and ethnicity and attempting to uncover some reasons for these differences and the impact these differences have on how women think about and do "motherhood." As shown below, the incarceration event itself brings into sharp focus the possibilities, limitations and expectations associated with making child care arrangements for children. The response of families of women to the incarceration event and her ability to enlist, accept or reject care from kin reveals important and significant differences among women and their families. Burton and Stack (1992) refer to these phenomena as kinscripts which involve kin-work, kin-time and kinscription. Some of these differences reflect race/ethnic and class differences in family forms.

Another concept which may be useful here is the concept of family elasticity, the ability of family units to accommodate additional members and responsibilities during times of crisis. Stack's (1974) study of kinship groups and child-taking clearly illustrates the permeability of family groups in poor communities. Finch (1989) argues that family obligations are a result of normative principles that come from larger cultural and social norms about what family members should do for each other and negotiated commitments that govern what happens in individual families. White families and families of color may differ in their cultural understanding of family obligations (Angel & Tienda, 1982). White families steeped in a commitment to conjugal units may feel little obligation to a family member who was gotten into trouble, especially a female. Families of color, on the other hand, may rely to a greater extent on obligations that extend beyond the conjugal unit, providing a safety net in the case that conjugal relations do not provide economic or social support required to survive and raise children. There may also be differences in the bases of exchange and obligations. While balanced exchanges may be dominant in some cultural groups, that is to say, exchanges of like goods and services between two individuals, other cultural groups may rely more on generalized exchanges that encompass more members of the family to a wider system of support and need. Several researchers have suggested that these generalized exchanges characterize economically marginal communities and communities of color. The question of how women come to rely on families and on the state in arranging for care of their children will be examined below.

The imprisonment of women puts into sharp focus how family obligations are acted out in times of crises. The structural and cultural differences among families are revealed in the acting out of family obligations. How imprisoned women in families resist and enlist caretaking for their children from family, from the state and from others provides important insights into how race, class and gender interact in families.

SPECIFIC AIMS

The major focus of this research is to understand how motherhood and mothering are put together and unpacked as a concept and how women in these circumstances work to create meaning for themselves as mothers while others are taking care of children. Here, as well, we need to examine how this work may differ across race, ethnicity, class and experiences with the criminal justice system and other agencies of social control. If we can believe the statistics and limited observations that African-American, Hispanic and white women exhibit different strategies in placing and arranging care for their children, what impact does this have on managing motherhood and one's interpretation and enactment of it while incarcerated, pre- and post-release?

BACKGROUND AND PRELIMINARY FINDINGS

In 1993, I began fieldwork at a parenting program in a northeastern women's correctional facility. Initially focused on the operation of an extended visiting program in the prison, the research evolved into a more focused examination of how motherhood was enacted by women in prison. (An extended discussion of the history of this investigation and the methodology appears in Adler & Clark, in press.) At an early stage of the fieldwork at the parenting program, it became apparent that there were definite patterns that distinguished placements of children by mothers. White mothers more often relied on foster care and husbands while African-American mothers relied on their mother, sisters and other extended kin. Through informal conversations, the complex nature of being and doing motherhood while incarcerated revealed itself. While some mothers saw themselves as the central figure in the lives of their children, others related a much more casual intermittent involvement. While some were critical of the care provided by other caretakers, others considered that care superior to the care they themselves could provide. Finally, while some claimed sole ownership of their children, others suggested a shared ownership with others interested in the child's welfare.

To investigate these patterns more closely, thirteen women were recruited for intensive interviews during the summer of 1993. See the Appendix for a list of women interviewed, their race/ethnicity and the living arrangements of their children during incarceration. While most of the interviews were with women who fit the dominant pattern of race and placement of children (African-American children with kin; whites in foster care and with husbands), interviews were conducted with women who were exceptions to the pattern, as well. These interviews ranged in time from 45 minutes to several hours and were held in the medium and minimum security units of the correctional facility. Some of these interviews were tape-recorded. In other instances, notes were taken during the interview.

For women inmates, children represent both a "normal" part of an offender's life and yet define her as not only a law violator but as breaking gendered expectations that her children will be her primary focus. The charge of "unfit mother" is easily attached to women inmates from a variety of sources, including official agents, such as child welfare workers, correctional staff, as well as kin and others. For some women, this duality presents challenges where parental fitness must be proved during incarceration to formal agents of social control and to informal sources, such as family members. As we will see subsequently, contests over children place mothers in the dubious position of proving fitness while incarcerated and in some cases, understanding that their "right" to their children is a matter of their conforming to normative mothering behavior while away from their children (Genders & Players, 1987; Kersten, 1989). The gendered nature of conformity to their role and place as mothers becomes an important part of rehabilitation.

While significant attention has been paid to the formal system of child welfare and its formalistic means of determining "ownership" of children, little attention has been paid to the role of immediate and extended family and kin in managing these relations. Here, in addition to contests for claims to children engaged between mothers and the state, we also see battles over children mounted between mothers and other relatives.

As other research indicates, placements in non-kin arrangements were more likely for children from white families than they were for African-American and Hispanic women. White women reported that they were estranged from their families, so that placing children with relatives was not a viable option. These women identified themselves as the only "deviant" in their family and that most members were unwilling to lend a hand in a crisis that they considered the doing of the mother. Women also reported that their own mothers were done with raising children and not interested in resuming responsibility for rearing grandchildren, even on a temporary basis.

Arranging for the child to live with relatives was equated with "losing place" with the child; that is, relatives assuming sole "ownership of mothering." Paying back the child-caring obligation to relatives was a matter these women argued was impossible to do, suggesting an unpayable non-economic debt (Curtis, 1986). In these situations, mothers opted for placements in foster care as a way to care for children that might be both superior to the care provided by family and as a means to retain some control over the child. Even in these situations, there is the challenge to maintain place in relationship to the child. For example, Louise:

Enos: So, you had a baby just before you came to jail. Where is he now?

Louise: He's with foster parents who really love him a lot. They are just great with him.

Enos: Does he visit you here?

Louise: Sure he does, a little, the foster parents bring him to me.

Enos: And does he know you?

Louise: Well, he knows who I am. But, he doesn't *know* me know me.

Enos: Can you explain that?

Louise: Well, he knows I'm his mother, but he doesn't know me that way.

Other white women also expressed satisfaction with the foster care provided for their child, characterizing it as a "life-saver." Louise here makes a distinction as many do about being a child's mother while others do the caretaking of the child. This separates the identity and practice of mother as a biological producer from women in social and psychological places as caregivers. These distinctions bring special challenges when women resume caretaking of the child or when they reflect upon tasks associated with caretaking and how they themselves may enact those activities.

For one white woman who was serving time for a white collar crime and facing her first sentence for a crime, the challenge in parenting was to understand and accept her husband's taking over responsibility for their developmentally delayed young boy. They had recently gone shopping for school shoes.

> Pam: I looked at what they picked out and thought to myself, "My God, I would have never bought such a thing for him." No mother would have. There is a difference in what a mother would have done.

Pam carefully admits that there are tasks that others can do but reserves for mothers a special dimension. Unlike other women, Pam had no difficulty maintaining her position in her family. As major caretaker, her husband visited often and maintained their close "working relationship" that parenting a special child required.

White mothers suggested that retrieving a child from foster care was a simpler matter than getting a child back from relatives. After the child welfare agency was "satisfied" and the burden of proving fitness was fulfilled, the case was closed and the mother could reestablish herself as the mother independent of past failures. This is not to say that this is a simple matter (Beckerman, 1994). In contrast, reestablishing motherhood in the context of family caretaking presented the mother with continued involvement of others who had taken care of children in crisis. For white women, this brought the prospect that family members would constantly and forever remind the mother of previous failure and lapses as a mother. For other women, grandparents were unavailable because of other contingencies and the prospect of suggesting that they had an obligation to their grandchildren was not a consideration. Holly's analysis of this follows:

> My folks have troubles of their own. They don't know nothing about this baby. They are done with raising babies. They worked hard all their lives. They want to travel. When I had my kids and thought I was covering my drugs (use of drugs), I thought they would welcome them with open arms. But they didn't and I haven't been back since.

For some women, the available options for children are few and far from ideal. Stacey, a white woman in her twenties, is the mother of a four-year-old boy who is living with his father. She has heard from friends that the father is resuming a drug habit and is selling narcotics to maintain his own addiction. She is left with a difficult choice. Contacting the child welfare authorities will prompt an investigation of the father but will also bring the family to the attention of an agency that can remove the child from the home. The contradictory nature of public policy on families is reflected by Stacey who is both trying to protect her child but also to keep state attention and intrusion away from her family. On the other hand, her distance from the family weakens her ability to monitor and manage caretaking of her child and to exert any power in the unit. Maintaining presence and "force" as a mother of a child is difficult when a woman is absent from the home and all the more problematic when the mother has few resources to effect control of the other caretaker.

White women were also more likely to attribute their paths to prison to deficiencies in their families of origin, identifying alcoholism among parents, childhood sexual and physical abuse and other problems. It should also be noted here that white mothers identified kin caretakers as potentially harmful or as much more powerful or resource heavy than they were. Some relatives, particularly siblings, were characterized as "middle class," with plenty of money, suggesting here a significant power imbalance and social distance within family units. The reluctance to extend family resources might in fact be tied to factors related to perceived threat to the family unit by responding to this crisis (Hill, 1948).

On the other hand, as noted in other works, African-American mothers were more likely to rely on kin resources for child care before and during incarceration. In many instances, these arrangements avoided involvement with child welfare authorities and allowed women to maintain contact with children without the intervention of social workers and without the need to demonstrate parental fitness to authorities. African-American women proposed that foster care was the least desirable placement for a black child and that most mothers can find a caretaker for their children. Bernice, a pregnant African-American mother of a five-year-old son who had been in many foster homes, echoed Stacey's concern.

> Bernice: I feel like I'm having babies for the state. Once they (the child welfare agency) get in your life, they're always there. They stick with you forever.

This mother remarked that foster care was the worst place for an African-American child to be but that her family and friends didn't (or couldn't) respond to her need for a place to put her child while she was incarcerated. Unlike most African-American women in this sample, Bernice was somewhat estranged from her family, having been the subject of sexual and physical abuse when she was a girl and not eager to rely on her family for help.

Here, denial of services from the state, as suggested by Solinger (1992) and others (Billingsley & Giovannoni, 1972), does not seem to be the case. Rather, there appears to be a distrust that these arrangements with strangers are suitable for black children. Mothers feared that their children would face racism and poor treatment in white placements. As noted by Hill (1993), a very small percentage of black children who are without parents are in foster care, demonstrating avoidance of the child welfare system by families in need.

Additionally, in the state where this research was conducted, most social workers and foster homes are white, suggesting that managing relations with workers and foster homes may be more difficult for these mothers than for white mothers. While getting a child back from foster care is seen as a simple matter for white women, it may in fact be more difficult for African-American mothers to prove fitness. In fact, African-American women noted the importance of getting the "right" social worker, suggesting that maintaining good personal relations was essential to assure return of children or closing of the case. Randie speaks about managing social workers and the balance between relying on the state for help and fighting off the charge that she is a "bad mother."

Randie: My kids were being abused by the man I was with and I was starting drugs again because of him. I wanted some safe place for my kids to be but with DCF (child welfare) they had to prove you were bad first before you got help.

While arrangements with kin were seen by the black mothers as much superior to those with strangers (foster care with the state), these placements were not problem-free. These women also struggle, in some instances, to maintain their place in the family and to distinguish their own relationship with the child from that of other caretakers. In some cases, mothers had already informally relinquished child care to others.

In other instances where other caretakers who are family members assume care immediately after birth, women characterize these situations a bit differently. In some instances, babies are appropriated by older women and in other cases, women are sporadically involved in the lives of their children.

Vanessa: . . . ever since he was born, he was her (referring to her mother) baby. I never had a chance. No matter what, though, I am still his mother.

Here, Vanessa suggests a marginal role in the child's life as his mother, because others have asserted ownership in the mother's absence. There remains, however, the biological link and the grounds for claiming motherhood that this entails. In other instances, women speak about the threat on the part of their mothers that they will cease caring for children but consider this an empty threat. For some women, the availability of caretakers that are trusted and constant enables them to pursue and maintain lifestyles that brought them to prison in the first place.

In the case of a Hispanic woman, imprisonment resulted from a conviction of manslaughter related to domestic abuse. Here, the family was conventional and the woman's imprisonment was considered not of her doing. Her acts were seen by her family as defending herself and protecting her children from abuse. Her three children visited weekly and her mother was supportive. She sees her situation in terms of "maintaining place" with her children very differently from that faced by other mothers.

> Helena: For some of the girls in here, it's real sad. Their kids call foster mothers and aunts and all sorts of people "Mom" and they have to deal with it. One four-year-old came in to visit last week and called his mother by her first name. She got real upset and doesn't want to see the kid anymore. My mother makes it real clear who I am and they know I am their mother.

In other situations, mothers were contesting "motherhood" with caretakers. The children of another Hispanic woman were living with her husband in Puerto Rico where the husband's family was moving to assume custody of the children. For this woman, facing a twenty-year sentence, the relationship with her family had deteriorated since she had moved to the United States. While the woman was somewhat satisfied with her children's living arrangements, she was deeply concerned that her relationship with her children would end with a court decision giving her husband custody.

In still other cases, prison mothers were preparing to assume child care of children born to their own teenage children. Unlike white women in similar situations, black women remained in contact with families even when ownership of children was in dispute and others were "winning the battle." Here, relationships with particular biological children seem less important and specific than the relationship with the kin network as a caretaker of children generally.

African-American women were more likely to attribute imprisonment to lifestyle choices, exposure to criminal opportunities and less apt to identify families of origin as the source and reason for their criminal involvement. These attributions are very similar to those found by Miller (1986) in her research. Entry to criminal lifestyles was eased by relatives or family friends, but not one's parents.

For some black and white women, return to the households they had occupied prior to incarceration meant continued contact with opportunities for crime. Many women noted that going back home confronted them with challenges to refuse criminal opportunities on a daily basis. Once again, connections to families and households present contradictory meanings where both threats to survival and improved chances of survival coexist in the same household.

Exceptions to these patterns do exist, of course. In some instances, white women relied on their immediate families and placed their children with their mothers. In some instances, these mothers were previously involved in deviant lifestyles themselves and did not reject the criminal lifestyle of children.

Kate: I don't know what was wrong with me then. I just never had any feeling for my first (child). I just had it and then my Mom took over. She dressed up the baby in the hospital and left without a word. We used to do drugs together and party all the time and then she went straight and was preaching to me all the time. Then, the baby came and she took over.

In other instances, grandmothers provided child care when the mother was serving a long sentence and in prison on a first conviction for a serious crime.

There also were children of African-American women who were in foster care. For the most part, these women were without family resources that were "acceptable" to child welfare authorities and to the woman herself. These women came from families they described as very unsatisfactory with living situations that put them in danger at an early age. Upon release, these women planned to live apart and independent from their families of origin, contrary to what is the prevalent belief about the embrace of the extended family living patterns of black single mothers. Here, we see estrangement from the family of origin.

In suggesting explanations for the overall patterns of placements, the incarcerated women suggested explanations tied to the elasticity of families and "expectations of trouble." Cast as a hypothesis, these explanations tie family location in the economic and social structure to responses to the potential of interaction with external agencies.

Families and households located at economic and social margins may anticipate conflicts with the law, educational institutions, landlords and other agents of social control. While individuals who confront these agencies may be typed as offenders by the agencies, family members may characterize this as expected. In other words, certain families, perhaps those who are lower income and minority, are elastic enough to maintain the deviant in the family unit without risking harm to the status of the family as a unit. Conflicts with the law may be expected as young people are exposed to opportunities for crime or simply reside in areas where law enforcement is active. It might be argued that there are gender differences here and class differences as well. This expectation of trouble may not obtain for white middle-class families, who do not anticipate conflicts with the law or have the capability of handling such conflicts privately. Trouble brought upon the family by young women may be especially difficult for the family to manage. Young women may be more likely to be expelled from the family unit than are boys because of chances for disruption to family reputation or status.

These interviews begin to reveal the complexity of women's relationships to their families. While theorists have pushed analysts to take race and ethnicity into account, care needs to be exercised not to use these categories to over-explain differences in outcomes. As this small sample reveals, what appeared to be racial differences, in fact, faded as paths to deviance and access to criminal lifestyles and family resources were explored. This is not to suggest that family structures and organization do not differ across racial and ethnic groups. It is simply to suggest that care be exercised as we examine the dynamics underlying the practice of motherhood in this and in other settings.

Indeed, with respect to motherhood as a status and doing mothering as an activity and a relationship, we may discover a set of different activities as well as meanings that constitute accomplishing this role or position across race, class and gender. So that not only might it be expected that different meanings are attached to activities, but that the constellation of tasks are different as well.

CONCLUSION

The lack of research on women offenders has been noted by many in the field of deviance and criminal justice (Schur, 1984; Daly & Chesney-Lind, 1988; Smart, 1976). Feminist scholars have also pointed to the need for research that accounts for families as they are situated across class and ethnic/racial classifications. Finally, there is a need to reexamine and unpack what we mean by mothering and motherhood in circumstances and situations that are stressful. Examination of mothers in these situations can reveal important dynamics of family responses that would not obtain in more routine interactions (Osmond, 1987). It is hoped that this research will provide the basis for the generation of additional research questions and make an important contribution to forging links among the fields of criminal justice, family and feminist theory.

Finally, the development of a more comprehensive picture of the challenges women face in arranging care for their children while incarcerated may provide policy makers with increased ability to recognize the variation in family forms that comprise the prison population. While some women come to prison with intact families and supportive relationships, many do not. While some are able to rely on family and kin for the care of their children, these relationships are by no means trouble-free. While some women feel free to rely on the state for care of their children, it is clear that for some mothers, this option remains untenable. The resources that women have available to them to support and care for children while they are incarcerated vary widely. Recognition of these differences and sensitivity to a variety of family forms should help prison officials to tailor programs to meet the needs of mothers and their children.

REFERENCES

Adler, E. S., & Clark, R. (in press). *How's it's done: An invitation to social research.* Belmont: West/Wadsworth.

Angel, R., & Tienda, M. (1982). Determinants of extended household structure: Cultural pattern or economic need? *American Journal of Sociology, 87,* 1360-83.

Arnold, R. (1994). Black women in prison: The price of resistance. In M. B. Zinn & B. T. Dill (Eds.), *Women of color in U.S. society.* Philadelphia: Temple University Press.

Baunach, P. J. (1985). *Mothers in prison.* New Brunswick: Transaction Books.

Beck, A. J. & Gilliard, D. K. (1995). *Prisoners in 1994.* Bureau of Justice Statistics: U.S. Department of Justice.

Beckerman, A. (1994). Mothers in prison: Meeting the prerequisite conditions for permanency planning. *Social Work, 39,* 9-13.

Billingsley, A., & Giovannoni, J. H. (1972). *Children of the storm: Black children and the American child welfare system.* New York: Harcourt, Brace, Janovich.

Bloom, B., & Steinhart, D. (1993). *Why punish the children? A reappraisal of the children of incarcerated mothers in America.* Washington: National Council on Crime and Delinquency.

Bresler, L., & Lewis, D. K. (1986). Black and white women prisoners: Differences in family ties and their programmatic implications. *The Prison Journal, 63,* 116-22.

Burton, L. M., & Stack, C. B. (1992). Conscripting kin: Reflections on family, generation and culture. In P. A. Cowan et al. (Eds.), *Family, self and society: Toward a new agenda for family research* (pp. 103-113). Hillsdale: Lawrence Erlbaum Associates.

Curtis, R. (1986). Household and family in theory on inequality. *American Sociological Review, 51,* 168-83.

Daly, K., & Chesney-Lind, M. (1988). Feminism and criminology. *Justice Quarterly, 5,* 497-535.

Fessler, S. R. (1991). *Mothers in the correctional system: Separation from children and reunification after incarceration.* PhD dissertation. State University at Albany.

Finch, J. (1989). *Family obligations and social change.* Cambridge: Polity Press.

Genders, E., & Players, E. (1987). Women in prison: The treatment, the control and the experience. In P. Carlen & A. Worrall (Eds.), *Gender, crime and justice.* London: Open University Press.

Gilliard, D. K., & Beck, A. J. (1996). *Prison and jail inmates, 1995.* Bureau of Justice Statistics: U.S. Department of Justice.

Henriques, Z. W. (1981). *Imprisoned mothers and their children: A descriptive and analytical study.* Washington: University Press of America.

Hill, R. (1948). *Families under stress.* New York: Harper.

Hill, R. B. (1993). *Research on the African-American family: A holistic perspective.* Westport: Auburn House.

Johnston, D. (1995a). Child custody issues of women prisoners: A preliminary report from the CHICAS Project. *The Prison Journal, 75,* 22-239.

Johnston, D. (1995b). The care and placement of prisoners' children. In. K. Gabel & D. Johnston (Eds.), *Children of incarcerated parents* (pp. 103-123). New York: Lexington Books.

Kersten, J. (1989). The institutional control of girls and boys. In M. Cain (Ed.), *Growing up good: Policing the behavior of girls.* London: Sage Publications.

Kiser, G. (1991). Female inmates and their families. *Federal Probation,* September, 56-63.

Kruttschnitt, C. (1981). Social status and the sentencing of female offenders. *Law and Society Review, 15,* 247-265.

Miller, E. M. (1986). *Street woman.* Philadelphia: Temple University Press.

Miller, E. M. (1988). "Some peoples calls it crime": Hustling, the illegal work of underclass women. In A. Strathan, E. Miller & H. Mausch (Eds.), *The worth of women's work* (pp. 109-32). Albany, NY: State University Press.

Neto, V., & Bainer, L. M. (1983). Mother and wife locked up: A day with the family. *The Prison Journal, 63,* 124-141.

Osmond, M. W. (1987). Radical-critical theories. In M. B. Sussman & S. K. Steinmetz (Eds.), *Handbook of marriage and the family.* New York: Plenum Press.

Owen, B., & Bloom, B. (1995). Profiling women prisoners. *The Prison Journal, 75,* 165-185.

Schur, E. M. (1983). *Labeling women deviant: Gender, stigma and social control.* Philadelphia: Temple University Press.

Smart, C. (1976). *Women, crime and criminology: A feminist critique.* London: Routledge.

Snell, T. L. (1994). *Women in prison: Survey of state prison inmates, 1991.* Bureau of Justice Statistics: U.S. Department of Justice.

Solinger, R. (1992). *Wake up little Susie: Single pregnancy and race before Roe v. Wade.* London: Routledge.

Stack, C. (1974). *All our kin: Strategies for survival in the black community.* New York: Harper and Row.

Stanton, A. M. (1980). *When mothers go to jail.* Lexington: D. C. Heath and Company.

Swan, A. L. (1981). *Families of black prisoners: Survival and progress.* Boston: G. K. Hall & Co.

Sykes, G. (1958). *The society of captives.* Princeton: Princeton University Press.

APPENDIX

Women interviewed*	Race/ethnicity	Placement of children
Cases Fitting Dominant Placement Pattern		
Pam	White	Husband
Linda	White	Foster care
Stacey	White	Husband
Holly	White	Foster care
Sandy	White	Husband
MaryAnn	White	Foster care
Marylou	African-American	Mother
Tee	African-American	Mother/sister
Randie	African-American	Mother
Rachel	Hispanic	Husband
Helena	Hispanic	Mother
Cases that are Exceptions to Dominant Placement Patterns		
Kate	White	Mother
Bernice	African-American	Foster care
Others Interviewed Informally		
Louise	White	Foster care
Lonnie	White	Foster care
Vanessa	African-American	Mother/sister
Sara	African-American	Mother/sister
Erin	African-American	Foster care
Cathy	African-American	Mother/sister

*All names are pseudonyms.

Restricted Love

Dominik Morgan

SUMMARY. The increase in prison populations in America has given rise to a completely new set of societal expectations and impressions of the penal system. Modern women especially suffer from abject stereotyping and media portrayal of the tough, remorseless, manipulative lesbian femme fatale. In reality, many of the women being forced to wear this label are mothers, non-violent offenders and victims of abuse. Once incarcerated, these women turn to each other for support and companionship, often through lesbian relationships. This creates not the angry, violent lesbian relationships of prime time television, but more complex and intricate relationships based on learned behavior and social attitudes developed long before the women were ever arrested. This essay explores the myriad lesbian relationships in prison, the differences between inside and outside gay love, and implications for counseling gay inmates or ex-inmates dealing with issues relating to their sexuality. *[Article copies available for a fee from The Haworth Document Delivery Service: 1-800-342-9678. E-mail address: getinfo@haworth.com]*

Prison homosexuality as seen from the inside is of a completely different genre than its free-world counterpart. As an inmate for the past four

Dominik Morgan was born on the west coast and grew up in a metropolitan area. She is well traveled and attended a private prep school. She is currently incarcerated and in the fifth year of a 19-year sentence.

Address correspondence to: Dominik Morgan, c/o 1815 NE 82nd Street, Seattle, WA 98115.

[Haworth co-indexing entry note]: "Restricted Love." Morgan, Dominik. Co-published simultaneously in *Women & Therapy* (The Haworth Press, Inc.) Vol. 20, No. 4, 1997, pp. 75-84; and: *Breaking the Rules: Women in Prison and Feminist Therapy* (ed: Judy Harden, and Marcia Hill) The Haworth Press, Inc., 1998, pp. 75-84; and: *Breaking the Rules: Women in Prison and Feminist Therapy* (ed: Judy Harden, and Marcia Hill) The Harrington Park Press, an imprint of The Haworth Press, Inc., 1998, pp. 75-84. Single or multiple copies of this article are available for a fee from The Haworth Document Delivery Service [1-800-342-9678, 9:00 a.m. - 5:00 p.m. (EST). E-mail address: getinfo@haworth.com].

years, I have had a chance to observe prison culture firsthand. My reactions to my environment and my observations of it are not simple or detached: this is my home, and the women around me my only companions. My childhood curiosity about human behavior has not lessened in prison. Through friendships, conversation and the close social contact a prison environment provides, I have observed that the reasons women engage in same-sex relationships as well as the nature of the relationships themselves bear little resemblance to similar relationships developed in a non-restrictive setting, and as such, a woman dealing with the ramifications of a prison relationship may not relate well to conventional attitudes and therapies when seeking counseling. She may not trust or relate to a therapist who she feels cannot understand her particular circumstances. Counter to what many may believe, in a prison for women homosexuality isn't always the release of sexual energy or the manipulation of the weak. It can be true love, or a substitute for the love a woman may be seeking but unable to find. It can be a social activity, an excuse simply to touch, or a venue for social acceptance within prison cliques. Since the majority of women prisoners are engaged in homosexual relations, prison may be one of the few places in America today where lesbianism is commonplace.

REASONS FOR LESBIAN RELATIONSHIPS IN PRISON

Many inmates have past patterns of criminal behavior and have often received a great deal of counseling and therapy through prior incarcerations, drug treatment centers or mental health services exposure. The general awareness level of psychological behaviors and motivations is surprisingly high in prisons, but the ability to relate those patterns to daily behavior and to effect change of any sort is sorely lacking. Women who are in unhealthy relationships in prison may not recognize that they are repeating a pattern of abusive male-dominated relationships previously established because they do not recognize that behavior when it is perpetrated by another woman, even if it is the same type of treatment as experienced at the hands of a man.

Most female inmates have been victims of physical abuse, sexual abuse, neglect and a plethora of other detrimental psychological attacks. This brings with it a horde of adult social and psychological problems, most of which are common in "acceptable" society. These women don't know how to have a healthy relationship with themselves. Their self-esteem is so battered and intrusive on their day-to-day perceptions that any relationship with another warm body will suffice to fulfill their companionship needs. Often prison lesbians are only looking for physical contact:

someone to hold them, to touch them and to be their friend. These women have been taught to base their entire self-value system on their sexuality. They often have no friends in the traditional sense. Non-sexual relationships are almost always superficial. Most of their time, attention and money is focused on one individual who makes them feel good. In return, the woman usually offers sex to her partner, thinking that love and desire are indivisible. The strength of the emotions she may feel for her friend can easily be confused this way, especially if she hasn't had the life experience to teach her to differentiate among her emotions. Again, this same pattern is observable in these women in their relationships outside of the prison. It may not be the homosexuality they are seeking, it is simply repeating behaviors established with others before incarceration. Sadly, there are too many women who are completely aware of their motivations and behaviors but simply don't want to change.

Being "with" someone in prison carries a desirable social standing in a prison environment. For women who respect each other and themselves only as far as their sexual attractiveness can be gauged, homosexual relationships are the only discernible measure of worth in the prison. Inmates often lie about their relationships outside the prison, and can only prove their sexual (therefore total) worth by displaying their "woman" or their "bitch." The tragedy of all dysfunctional relationships is that a partner can never feel whole without the attentions of another person. This, coupled with the common issue of sexual activity being the only recognized measure of worth, creates an environment ripe for promiscuity and unemotional attachments.

In the free world, or "on the outs," a woman who decides at some point in her life that she is a lesbian or desires same-sex experiences has "come out" of the proverbial closet. The word "come" reflects the personally voluntary nature of the action. In prison, however, homosexuals do not "come out," but are "turned out." Notice the difference in phrasing: the prison terminology infers that the action was facilitated by an outside party. There are numerous theories about why this particular phrasing is used prevalently.

Historically, homosexuals in prisons were not always acting voluntarily. Although very few women are gang raped by other women inmates, it has been known to happen in isolated instances. However, these instances are not prevalent enough for this phrase to reflect an inherently violent experience for women, though many prisoners in male institutions have related histories of gang rape and forced sodomy. Women who are incarcerated constitute very few of the nation's total prison population; as a minority group, women often pick up male prison phrasing and terminology.

Another possible source of this terminology could lie in pre-incarcerated values. Most women who become homosexual in prison were straight before their incarceration for reasons such as moral or religious dictates, aversion to homosexuality, socialization, or of course, personal preference for heterosexuality. Using a non-voluntary phrase like "turned," which places responsibility for the action on the outside party, may make it easier for a woman to accept herself for an act which she may not feel is redeemable either socially or personally.

Conversely, women who are dominant personalities or who may be dominant members of abusive pattern relationships may subconsciously prefer a phrase which makes them the powerful facilitators of another person's behavior. To "turn" another woman out is to enjoy a special relationship with her not unlike that of a first sexual encounter as a teenager. Women have recounted their first gay experience in prison as being like losing their virginity all over again. On a more base level, some women find it stimulating to control other women, especially if the woman being turned out is not comfortable with the relationship. Aggressive prisoners often see relationships as a route to gain control over unwilling partners in an almost sadistic way.

Women sometimes also first discover their own sexuality through their lesbian relationships while in prison. Coming from strictly heterosexual backgrounds, there can be an element of surprise when she finds her ideal lover in another inmate in prison. For these women, lesbianism exposes them to an entirely new realm of caring and sexual gratification. Many women have their first orgasm ever in prison, where the lesbian atmosphere is stronger than in the environments they had come from, and engaging in same-sex relationships is more permissible.

No matter what attitude a woman herself has about lesbianism in prison, the environment created by the prison itself is not usually conducive to engaging in caring relationships or sexual encounters of any sort. The element of sneaking around attracts some women to prison relationships. More often a woman is frustrated by the amount of effort required simply to touch her lover on the cheek or hand. Prisons often have over-restrictive rules born of homophobic administrators which forbid touching of any sort: on the hand, back, even innocuous hugs. However, other prisons allow gay couples to live together in special housing wings reserved especially for couples. These more progressive penitentiaries have less of a problem managing gay inmates and much lower infraction rates. The prisons which forbid any sort of physical contact can develop problems in inmates in the form of overcompensating for the lack of touching, or under-compensating through self-isolating behavior.

THE EXPERIENCE OF BEING LESBIAN IN PRISON

In some instances, a prison lesbian may not engage in sexual activity with her woman at all. She may find one person to be her friend and that person becomes her companion for emotional support and simple touching. As stated above, the environment in prisons is not conducive to any physical contact between inmates and a lesbian relationship can be a convenient excuse just to touch one's friend. In other instances, women do actually engage in sex with their partners, but only out of desire to be touched, not from deriving any real sexual pleasure or desire from other women. Of course, there are women for whom lesbian sex is more gratifying and desirable than heterosexual encounters as well.

There are a number of different kinds of "prison dykes." These can be generally divided into two groups: those who consider themselves "truly" gay and those who are considered by others to be playing with their sexuality, or involved with women for reasons other than a serious relationship. There is a rift between these two groups which is not unlike the differences between upper and lower classmen in any high school. Those who consider themselves to be gay in the true sense often disdain and dislike women who are, in their eyes, only being lesbian for a fling or out of ennui while incarcerated.

Couples who consider themselves really and truly gay are usually comprised of women who were strictly gay before entering prison. There are exceptions when some women discover their sexuality while in prison and remain gay for the rest of their lives, but these women are the exception, not the rule. Interestingly, most of these "serious" relationships are the most stable and bear the greatest resemblance to gay relationships on the outside, where homosexuality isn't socially influenced in the same way as it is in prison. This predominantly gay atmosphere inside a prison can be often linked to the high number of women who comprise the other group mentioned–the "players."

Most women come to prison the first time without a homosexual background. Most new inmates vehemently deny any possible interest in homosexual activities. However, casual observation suggests that about 7 out of 10 new admissions have a homosexual encounter within their first six months of incarceration.

It is not uncommon for a newly turned out lesbian to jump from partner to partner every week or two. Sometimes she is not truly gay at all, but simply playing a part she feels necessary and withdraws from relationships as soon as they become too intimate. Other women will be "with" someone only for popularity or security–emotional or physical. When her partner is no longer useful to her, she is dumped and the woman moves on. As on the outside, there are also women who feel the need to show off their sexual prowess and desirability by attempting to seduce everyone they know. As soon as the woman is successful, she becomes disinterested. Similarly, there are some women who cannot seem to decide between women and men. Instead of accepting a lifestyle which allows for the attraction to both sexes, some feel that they must choose back and forth between their love interests, alternately accepting and denouncing contrary sexualities. These women are generally disliked by the longer-term, more serious couples because they seem to trivialize the lifestyle which other women take extremely seriously. The difference may be an ethical one, but is recognized within the penitentiary only by its social aspect.

For those women who are turned out in the penitentiary, there is a prevalent belief on the part of the other inmates that they are "tricks" or unimportant sources of money and easy targets for manipulation. Some of the dangers that a woman who has recently been turned out faces are from those inmates who are exploitive and recognize in her a person who can be easily convinced to do things she might not normally do. This can lead to her exploitation for canteen (personal items and food bought through the institution store), money, or even prostitution within the prison. These victims make perfect targets for predatory personalities.

Some inmates who are turned out and used as tricks are ignorant of the use to which they are being put by their partner. They are usually reliving the same relationship patterns which they established with men before ever coming to prison, but are unable to recognize it under the guise of a lesbian relationship. Still other women engage in these same relationships precisely because they derive comfort from the familiarity of an abusive or exploitive relationship. The predatory women seek out other women to dominate. They turn the woman out and then use her to buy them canteen, food, clothing, etc. For many of the women who allow themselves to be used like this, they feel that the exchange is fair or don't believe they are being exploited at all.

There are groups of prisoners who exclude non-homosexuals. These groups can be very isolated and devoted to a strict social structure within themselves. This sort of almost a gang mentality can be very appealing to a lonely woman. She can use her sexual availability as a ticket to popularity or acceptance in these groups. Her level of attraction to other women is irrelevant, as improving her social standing is the focus of her actions.

TRANSITION OUT OF PRISON

Lesbianism in prisons is more prevalent than heterosexuality. Heterosexuals in prisons often find themselves in a small minority for the first time in their lives. Younger inmates and more impressionable inmates sometimes come to prison and turn out in an attempt to conform with what they see as a behavior norm. Once these women are released, their liberal perceptions of homosexual relationships can be so far removed from the oppressive norms of American society that their transition back into society can be difficult. Ex-inmates may go to their families and friends expecting the kind of support and encouragement for their homosexuality that they got in prison and find instead derision and shame. Especially for the women who first discover their libido inside prison, this can be an extremely destructive transition if handled badly. Occasionally, the woman leaves an environment where codependency is the psyche du jour and enters into a world of self-motivated lesbians who are looking for real relationships, creating a confusion and anger which she may not know how to deal with or recognize. Generally, women who have been lesbians in prisons are able to readjust eventually to their former norms of male-female relationships. Some women are not. Other women immediately enter into heterosexual relations upon their release but discover that their gay relations in prison were more fulfilling or discover that their attraction to men has been diminished.

Sometimes, inmates will engage in lesbian relationships inside a prison but deny their involvement once they get out. This sort of shame-related behavior can make it difficult for a woman to readjust to life on the outside if she is unable to cope with the feelings of guilt and shame she is experiencing from actions which were permissible in one societal group but not another.

Of course, incarcerated women can enter into lesbian relationships as a sexual outlet. While enjoying sexual relations with other women, they may be fantasizing about the men who they remember or desire. Upon release, these women have sometimes built up the vision of heterosexual sex to such an extent that it is not fulfilling when they experience it. These women can experience a kind of limbo for a while as they try to sort out their sexual frustrations of having strong sexual desires but being unattracted to either sex.

Any woman recently released from a prison setting will be affected by the differences in social setting and mores. Even those who never participated in a gay experience are affected by the juxtaposition of structure and lack of structure which they may find turned opposite in free society from what they had become accustomed to on the inside. This can be especially true for lesbian inmates or women who have had gay experiences while incarcerated. Relationships of any sort have such an important impact on our daily lives and perceptions that an ex-inmate reevaluating her place in a social structure upon release may find relationships the hardest part of her reintegration into society. A very small number of prison relationships effectively parallel lesbian relationships on the outside, and an ex-inmate looking for a relationship similar to what she had in prison may be hard pressed to find what she feels is correct for her.

Women recently released from prison may be afraid to pursue heterosexual relations because of their own low self-esteem. Whether prison instilled it or not, many women exit the penitentiary thinking that sex with women is somehow inferior and that they are only good for sex with women since no man will want them. This attitude is reinforced by the popular ostracism of ex-inmates and the hatred that goes along with it. Thus, women who have experienced relationships with women throughout their incarceration may find it difficult to reestablish relations with existing male partners upon their release. Self-esteem building is important for any woman within and without the prison.

IMPLICATIONS FOR COUNSELING

Some women's prisons have comprehensive mental health counseling services either provided by the state or through volunteer efforts. Even though some prison therapy programs are effective and professional, an equal number are not. Inmates who have had negative, abusive or exploitive experiences with prison psychologists may be reluctant in the extreme when confronted by a therapist in the free world. State-hired therapists are sometimes required by prison administrators to follow certain agendas when dealing with inmates and/or to report much of their counseling sessions to individual inmates' case managers or probation officers. The lack of privacy and sincerity that inmates can experience with prison therapists often creates a defensive, protective shell which must be broken through with trust before a new therapist can begin counseling in earnest. A sad but true fact is that in prison, women learn that lying is a necessary survival tactic—even lying to counselors to protect their right to having feelings without being judged or punished for them as is often the case inside many prison therapy sessions. An ex-inmate may enter her first free-world counseling session ready to take on her therapist head-to-head, refusing to reveal any of her true emotions or problems and instead telling her counselor what she thinks she is supposed to say or what she thinks is shocking.

The best way to establish trust with any ex-inmate is through sincerity. Of all human qualities, prisoners rank honesty, fairness and sincerity the highest of all personal attributes. False sympathy, wandering attention, or bravado on the part of a therapist will be seen through immediately in a counseling session. Inmates are experts in human behavior and nonverbal messages; the best way to approach a potentially defensive woman is through sincere friendship. Therapists who are not afraid to admit that they "don't know" will have the most luck finding out and gaining the counselee's trust. Most prisoners are more trusting and attentive to a person who has had similar experiences to their own, and are very sensitive to others who presumptively relate to them without credibility.

It is deceptively easy for a counselor to assume that the prison experience with lesbianism is akin to that experienced outside of a penitentiary. It is important for every therapist to recognize the potential for deeper and more complex motivations than first appear in any woman confronting a homosexuality issue upon her release from a prison. It is highly likely that there may be issues of relationship patterns, the transference of drug or alcohol addiction to addiction to relationship crises, or simple confusion, which is likely to have been exacerbated by her shift from one social environment into another. Coming from an environment which is sometimes dangerous and often hostile, she may not be prepared with the emotional tools necessary to tackle these issues on her own.

In dealing with a woman who is experiencing sexuality issues either in prison or upon her release, it is imperative first to find out *why* she was/is lesbian, whether or not the feelings for women are sincere and will continue, and how best to communicate with the individual. For example, a woman who is experiencing severe childhood psychosexual trauma and has turned to homosexuality as a coping mechanism will probably not relate well to therapy directed toward coping with relationship addiction, even though the initial prognosis may indicate such a course of treatment as appropriate. Taking time to get to know the client is the only way to peel back the facade and layers of deception which any ex-inmate will have necessarily placed around her.

Women choosing lesbian relationships outside of a prison usually have healthier motivations than women who make that choice inside prison. It is important to be sensitive to the possibility that ex-inmates who are lesbian are not aware of their own motivations and will not recognize the types of lesbian relationships they may encounter on the outside.

The most important point for any therapist to recognize, when counseling inmates either inside and outside of a prison, is that prison lesbianism does not automatically equate to the lesbian experience outside of the prison. Prison culture is a social island unlike any experience imaginable outside of the walls, and the women within it are a breed unto themselves. Recognizing each woman's individual experiences, past and current, will help to formulate the answers or even the questions she is seeking. The lesbian experience in prison can be a nightmare or fantasy, apathy or epiphany, but will never be the culture that exists outside of the walls that define it. This is the infinite enigma of prison sexuality: it can never be wholly understood without firsthand experience but will rarely be experienced when understood.

Children Without Childhoods:
A Feminist Intervention Strategy Utilizing Systems Theory and Restorative Justice in Treating Female Adolescent Offenders

Carol Lee O'Hara Pepi

SUMMARY. The numbers of female adolescents entering the Juvenile Justice systems of this country are increasing at a rapid rate. Are these girls subjected to a gender bias that detains girls in greater numbers and for lesser offenses than their male counterparts? Drawing upon the work of juvenile justice experts, developmental psychologists and current research documents, this paper will put forth a theoretical framework for viewing the causal issues of female adolescent offending, the gender inequities in arrest, sentencing and program options and gender-specific treatment implications for mental health professionals. Giving recognition to Carol Gilligan's research on the developmental phenomenon of adolescent girls "losing their voice," issues of self-identity and self-advocacy will be discussed

Carol O'Hara Pepi, MEd, LMFT, is a graduate of the Marriage and Family Therapy Program of Cambridge College and is currently pursuing a doctorate in Social Psychology at The Union Institute. She is a juvenile justice consultant, a licensed Marriage and Family Therapist and an instructor at Cambridge College and North Shore Community College.

Address correspondence to: Carol Lee O'Hara Pepi, Cambridge College, 1000 Massachusetts Avenue, Cambridge, MA 02138.

[Haworth co-indexing entry note]: "Children Without Childhoods: A Feminist Intervention Strategy Utilizing Systems Theory and Restorative Justice in Treating Female Adolescent Offenders." Pepi, Carol Lee O'Hara. Co-published simultaneously in *Women & Therapy* (The Haworth Press, Inc.) Vol. 20, No. 4, 1997, pp. 85-101; and: *Breaking the Rules: Women in Prison and Feminist Therapy* (ed: Judy Harden, and Marcia Hill) The Haworth Press, Inc., 1998, pp. 85-101; and: *Breaking the Rules: Women in Prison and Feminist Therapy* (ed: Judy Harden, and Marcia Hill) The Harrington Park Press, an imprint of The Haworth Press, Inc., 1998, pp. 85-101. Single or multiple copies of this article are available for a fee from The Haworth Document Delivery Service [1-800-342-9678, 9:00 a.m. - 5:00 p.m. (EST). E-mail address: getinfo@haworth.com].

discussed from a feminist perspective. Mental health treatment methods in detention facilities will be examined with a critical look at the limited access female adolescents have to comprehensive counseling that addresses their victimization. Strength-based treatment planning based on a systems theory model will be explored as an effective method of facilitating the female adolescent's ability to self-advocate within a support network. This paper will call for a paradigm shift away from society's current retributive justice response to female adolescent offending and toward the healing model of restorative justice. *[Article copies available for a fee from The Haworth Document Delivery Service: 1-800-342-9678. E-mail address: getinfo@haworth.com]*

Marissa Dawson was arrested for "shoplifting by asportation," a violation of the Massachusetts General Laws, C266 S30A, on 2/12/93. At the time of her arrest, Marissa was 15 years of age and four months pregnant. Throughout the next 12 months Marissa would receive services from no less than ten social service agencies or programs. The state juvenile correctional system would eventually place her in a staff secure shelter program for 18 weeks and, after the birth of her son, move her to a foster home where she could live with her baby.

Small in stature, Marissa was a young black woman born into a dysfunctional family and disorganized community. Her closest relationship was with her sister, Cheryl, one year older. During her time at the state shelter care program Marissa maintained almost daily contact with her mother, but it was Cheryl who appeared to hold the strongest influence in Marissa's life.

Marissa was cooperative and only occasionally "acted out" her anger. The shelter care program, considered progressive in its philosophy of respecting the dignity of the client, assisted Marissa through limit-setting and behavioral methods to control her anger. Staff often allowed Marissa to claim "space" from the other residents as a way of avoiding conflict situations. Marissa left shelter care for a pregnant teen program where she remained until she delivered her son a few weeks hence.

A foster placement appeared to be successful for a while but Marissa began to get restless with the suburban setting and often traveled into the city. In time Marissa left the placement and stayed with family members. Within a few weeks she reestablished contact with the staff of the shelter care program and told them she was then living in a homeless shelter with her baby and needed money for diapers.

Sixteen months after the birth of her son and at the age of 18 years, Marissa was shot dead on the front steps of her sister's home. She was pregnant with her second child.

While Marissa's story cannot be rewritten, this year thousands of young women will be brought into the juvenile justice systems of this country. The mental health community has a rich opportunity to advocate for the provision of just and equitable resources for each girl and the mental health clinician can become a significant change-agent in the creation of a systemic approach toward the accomplishment of long-range goals. Additionally, the mental health clinician can be actively involved: (1) in assessing the causal factors influencing offending behavior, (2) in developing a biopsychosocial treatment model based on systems theory and (3) in assisting the female offender, the victim of her offending behavior and the community to apply a restorative justice model of intervention.

During the many months in which Marissa was in residential custody, each of the social service providers involved with her worked in isolation. There was little networking of information and resources among health care resources, social service, educational and correctional staff. Lack of available services was not a problem; lack of coordination of services was.

If the primary clinician or case worker had incorporated a systems theory model of intervention, all involved services as well as family members, school, court, social welfare and health care systems, etc., would have been in conversation with and about Marissa. By operating from a strength-based approach, Marissa's competencies could have been identified and utilized in the development of short-term goals and a long-range strategic plan for her and her child. Marissa's support system could have been identified and united around these positive life goals.

Since Marissa had a strong bond with her sister, and a caring, if casual, relationship with her mother, both family members could have been encouraged in the strengthening of their roles in her life. Marissa received positive, supportive services; they simply did not prepare her for life beyond the structure of residential care.

The creation of a system of competency-based support offers the female adolescent offender more than dignity and hope in seeking to confront the many issues that led to the offending behavior. It offers a safety net of people and communities working with her to achieve life goals.

Marissa's story is based upon actual events. While her name and some non-substantive information have been changed to ensure confidentiality, the issues remain tragic. Her story is unfortunately not unique in the annals of juvenile systems throughout the country. Whether adolescents languish in "kiddie jails" without appropriate and basic services or receive carefully planned and regimented care in state-of-the-art modern facilities, the fact remains that the time has come for a serious look at the rationale for detaining female adolescent offenders and to review the scope of mental health treatment options offered to these youth. Responsibility rests heavily on the mental health community to understand how and why females enter the system in order to create new, more effective interventions for these adolescents at risk. Thus, the mental health community needs a framework for viewing the unique situation females in the juvenile justice system face.

FRAMEWORK FOR VIEWING FEMALES IN THE JUVENILE JUSTICE SYSTEM

Many issues affect the lives of young women in the nation's juvenile correctional systems both before and after their entrance into the system. Among them are:

- current social and political attitudes in the nation;
- the gender biases inherent in juvenile justice systems working with female adolescent offenders;
- the gender-specific and developmental needs of young women;
- the lack of appropriate treatment resources.

Social/Political Attitudes

The social and political climates of the nation not only contribute negatively to criminal behavior or status offenses, they negatively affect the models of response.

Social service funding initiatives must focus less on reactive intervention than on proactive diversion strategies which could not only affect the likelihood of future criminality but also assist in the identification of at-risk behaviors. From the economic impact of the Reaganomics of the 80s which eliminated or cut funding for thousands of social welfare programs affecting children, to the Welfare Reform Bill of 1996 (P.L. 104-193, The Personal Responsibility and Work Opportunity Reconciliation Act), which, upon enactment, created an estimated 1.2 million more children living in poverty in the United States, we, in effect, witness a lack of value placed upon the lives of our children.

Young people like Marissa, who have lived through economic deprivation, violence, substance abuse and hopelessness in their families and communities, are now subject to the new public youth system of the 1990s, the juvenile justice system. Marissa's charge of shoplifting was a misdemeanor offense, and yet, like many other girls with non-violent or status offenses, it resulted in her commitment to the state youth services department and her placement in detention.

> Status offenders are described (Weiss, Nicholson, & Cretella, 1996) in the following statement: The vast majority of girls who enter the juvenile justice system are status offenders. A status offense is a behavior that is a law violation only when committed by a juvenile. These offenses include running away, being ungovernable, underage drinking, truancy and curfew violations. Thus, offenses with which girls are charged are typically nonviolent. In addition, the conduct that triggers a girl's arrest may be neither extreme nor exceptional, especially within the context of adolescence. (p. 3)

Once identified with the system, the female adolescent is negatively affected by the nation's current view of criminal behavior. Crime remains a serious concern of the majority of citizens in the United States. Recent political initiatives have addressed this concern in the adult system by implementing tougher laws such as the Violent Crime and Law Enforcement Act of 1994 which instituted mandatory sentencing and ("Three strikes you're out") life imprisonment for repeat felony offenses. The Supreme Court has decreased the appeal processes available to death row inmates, steadily increasing the number of states with Death Penalty statutes and allowing for the execution of women, developmentally delayed persons and in 1989 (Stanford v. Kentucky) persons whose offenses were committed as juveniles. As of June 30, 1995, forty-two individuals were on death row for crimes committed when they were juveniles (Bartollas, 1997).

In response to public outrage against crime, there has been an equally reactive response from the juvenile system which increasingly places a greater focus on punishment rather than treatment.

> . . . the 1991 survey of detention centers found that 62 percent of these facilities offered no treatment programs. One of the serious concerns about this failure to provide treatment programs is that detention is often a turbulent time for a youth. (Bartollas, 1997)

Paralleling the "get tough stance" in the adult system, many states have lowered the juvenile age of waiver to the adult court/prison systems. Bartollas (1997) states:

Since 1978, legislation aimed at transfer to the adult courts of serious juvenile delinquents has been enacted in nearly half the states. These statutory charges fall into three categories: (1) making it easier to prosecute delinquents in adult courts, (2) lowering the age of judicial waiver, and (3) excluding certain offenses from juvenile court jurisdiction (Krisberg, Schwartz, Litsky, & Austin, 1986). The impact of this legislation has been unmistakable in some states. Juveniles in these states have been propelled into adult prison in record numbers. (p. 379)

Juveniles now incur greater sanctions and more secure placements, including Boot Camps, and programs whose principles are based on a justice that punishes. The mental health community must advocate for a justice that restores.

Gender Bias

Gender bias affects the disposition of girls' juvenile cases in two significant ways: (1) given the patriarchal attitudes of parents and courts alike and the urgency to "protect" girls from the consequences of their sexuality, girls are disproportionately detained for both criminal and status offenses; (2) treatment options are generally modeled after programs designed for male adolescents and, therefore, often do not address the gender-specific needs of the detained females.

Rev. George M. Anderson in an article in the January 20, 1994, edition of *America* (*Juvenile Justice and the Double-Standard*) draws upon the research of Chesney-Lind and Shelden (1992) when he states that female offenders suffer higher arrest rates and more punitive sentences than males. Anderson cites a 1991 study by Virginia's Department of Youth and Family Services entitled, "Young Women in the Juvenile System," which concluded that girls serve more time in training schools than their male counterparts, and for less serious offenses. The Office of Juvenile Justice and Delinquency Prevention's 1993 Children in Custody census conducted on February 15, 1993 found that 6,408 girls and 53,846 boys were being held in public juvenile facilities (Weiss et al., 1996). The census also determined the following:

- Twelve percent of the girls in custody (versus 27% of the boys) had committed violent crimes.
- Twelve percent of the girls (versus 1% of the boys) were in custody for status offenses (p. 6).

The disproportionate number of girls held in custody as status offenders is relevant as a paternalistic response of a biased system. Anderson further states that especially troubling are arrests of young women who have run away from home to evade abuse. The facts above give credence to the assertion of Chesney-Lind and Shelden (1992) that

> . . . statutes written to protect young people have, in the case of girls' delinquency, criminalized their survival strategies. If girls persist in their refusal to stay in abusive homes, they become embedded in the juvenile justice system, which has few alternatives other than incarceration. (p. 91)

The offense which brought Marissa into the juvenile justice system was shoplifting; for others, their offenses are simply fleeing bad relationships, abusive relationships. Chesney-Lind and Shelden (1992) state that very high rates of physical and sexual abuse have been reported by those working with delinquent girls, from a low of 40 percent to a high of 73 percent. They have addressed this abuse as an important element for consideration in the formation of current delinquency theory.

> . . . a feminist perspective might add to traditional delinquency theories an explicit concern about the role of sexual abuse in girls' delinquency. Like young men, young women are frequently the objects of violence and abuse, but, unlike young men's victimization, young women's victimization and their response to it is shaped by their status as young women. Hence, young women are much more likely than their opposites to be the victim of sexual abuse . . . In addition, their vulnerability is heightened by norms that require that they stay at home, where their victimizers have greater access to them. (p. 91)

Given the high number of girls coming into the system not simply as perpetrator but also as victim, it would seem imperative that specific gender-based strategies be universally incorporated into juvenile justice program goals for females in custody. At the present time, however, one of the great operational problems of juvenile justice is that female adolescent offenders are brought into a system that has been designed around the needs and behaviors of adolescent males. Programs and services are replicated for female adolescents based on the male model of juvenile corrections and, therefore, fail to address the gender-specific needs of females.

Tim Keough, psychologist for Juvenile Justice, New South Wales, Australia, completed a study of the effectiveness of U.S. programs for female adolescent offenders and subsequently reported in a paper presented to the Australian Institute of Criminology (1994): " . . . discrimination which affects young women who end up in custody is seen to be part of a broad systemic abuse based on gender. Through such systemic influences the system is seen to repeatedly fail to meet the needs of young women from abusive backgrounds" (p. 3).

Similarly, *Prevention and Parity* (Weiss et al., 1996) states:

> Given the fact that juvenile delinquency has been and continues to be perceived as primarily a male problem, the correctional industry and profession revolves around establishing programs that meet the needs of boys. This approach has resulted in few prevention, intervention and treatment programs and facilities that are designed specifically for girls . . . Where programs are single-sex, far more options exist for boys than for girls. For example, a recent list of "potentially promising programs" identified by OJJDP (Howell, 1995) cites 24 programs specifically for boys in contrast to two programs specifically for girls. (p. 24)

While there are various girls' programs throughout the nation that are outstanding in their commitment to gender-specific program design and services, they are few in number and, often, are dependent on the funding priorities of governmental agencies and private foundations. Chesney-Lind and Shelden (1992) state: "Many innovative programs have relied on funds or private foundational grants, and very few have survived for any length of time" (p. 214).

Gender-Specific and Developmental Needs

The majority of juvenile correctional programs offer scant attention to the gender-specific psychosocial factors which have influenced the developmental, psychological and moral growth of young women presented to the court system. The OJJDP funded study *Prevention and Parity* (Weiss et al., 1996) states:

> The Juvenile Justice system reflects society's assumptions about gender. Boys are perceived to threaten the community with violent behavior, girls by flouting moral standards. Society is presumed to need protection from boys; girls are presumed to need protection from themselves. The dearth of research about girls adds to confusion both about the nature and extent of girls' involvement in delinquency and their treatment in the juvenile justice system . . . Race

and socioeconomic status also affect the treatment of girls . . . The limited placement options available specifically for girls interact with gender, race and socioeconomic status to directly affect the disposition of girls in the juvenile justice system. (p. v)

In addition to viewing the offending behavior within the context of the developmental tasks of adolescence, all systems which affect the lives of the adolescent female must be examined and treatment strategies developed from a biopsychosocial model. It becomes important, then, to employ strength-based systemic methods to assist the adolescent in recognizing resilience they have developed in previous stress and coping events and to identify alternative support systems. Gender-based determinants of delinquent behavior such as family history, self-identity and gender role-definition, social and personal victimization, power-control variants and social bonding issues deeply affect the female adolescent.

For the adolescent who has had inadequate, absent or negative role-modeling in her quest to understand "what it means to be a woman in my family, my community, my culture," her ability to claim membership in these social groups is impaired and issues of self-identity and gender role-definition are developed from a deficit perspective. The resultant posture of vulnerability further exacerbates already existing gender biases and the young woman often finds herself aligned with subordinate cultural groups while experiencing the social and personal victimization of dominant groups and individuals. It becomes quite difficult, then, to view the self from a strength-based perspective. These issues affect the adolescent offender's ability to confront delinquent behaviors, to develop a sense of accountability for wrong-doing, to recognize her strengths and abilities, and to acquire the resolve required to self-actualize.

Colin Wastell (1996) discusses the importance of utilizing a counseling approach which is operational from a life-span developmental model. Wastell contrasts the traditional male posited model of Erikson (1963) with the feminist developmental model of S. Conarton and L. Kreger-Silverman (1988) in viewing the gender-specific developmental stages of women. The feminist developmental model provides therapists working with female adolescent offenders an alternative theoretical posture that counseling can assume in order to work from a feminist framework of connection and relationship.

As noted in the case of Marissa presented above, Marissa was rewarded for not acting on her feelings and, in fact, was allowed to isolate or "claim some space from the other residents as a way of avoiding conflict situations." While this may have facilitated her success in the program, it did not teach her the value of vocalization of her feelings. In essence, Marissa was affirmed and supported in her cultural adaptation to the program environment, thus figuratively reinforcing the theory that cultural adaptation as a feminist developmental stage corresponds with the time when, according to Gilligan, most girls "lose their voice" (Gilligan, 1991).

Treatment Resources

In 1994, an estimated 678,500 girls were arrested, accounting for one-quarter of all juvenile arrests (Snyder, Sickmund and Poe-Yamagata, 1996). The FBI reports that the large majority of these girls (91 percent) were adolescents–young women ages 13 to 17 (Weiss et al., 1996). Limited information exists regarding the number of these who had access to mental health counseling. As the number of young women in custody escalates, there is an abiding need for strategies which will assist young women in the discovery of a positive self-identity and equip them with self-advocacy skills.

Once it is understood that girls are often detained for being poor, female, and victims of abuse and neglect, it becomes apparent that the response of mental health professionals must be focused within a systemic biopsychosocial framework. To move beyond traditional models of counseling, treatment must include a more systemic view of the child's ecosystem and its potential avenues of support.

To date, counseling efforts for detained girls have focused on "maintenance therapy," that is, a behavioral approach to counseling that concentrates solely on the issues the young woman is experiencing around her immediate life circumstance, i.e., being in custody. Practical considerations such as the short length of stay of young women in any one facility, the system's inability to implement aftercare plans and limited access to mental health staff have led to the use of behavioral methods for youth in custody. Siegel and Senna (1991) state that behavior modification is used in almost three-quarters of all institutions. They further state that behavior modification is effective in controlled settings, where a counselor can manipulate the situation, but once the youth is back in the real world, it becomes difficult to use.

The reality remains, then, that very troubled young women who come into the system with a history of physical, sexual and emotional victimization are not offered the opportunity to deal with some of the causal issues which have affected their previous delinquent behavior and will, likely, lead them to recidivist activity.

Sheila was remanded to a shelter care detention program at the age of 14. Her offense was assault and battery on a classmate. After three months in the program, Sheila was very compliant with program rules and was described by one staff person as very sweet and child-like. In fact Sheila began to develop signs of regression and infantile behavior such as thumb-sucking.

The local youth authority began to make plans for Sheila's return home based on her compliance. After developing a level of trust with Sheila the program counselor began to work with her from a frame-work of relationship, encouraging self-esteem and self-advocacy strategies. Sheila slowly began to disclose information about her family. Eventually it was learned that from the age of three, Sheila had been ritually beaten every Saturday evening by her father. Her mother was aware of the beatings and remained calm and unin-volved as the set time approached and throughout the beating.

Sheila had learned within the family and through her mother's role-modeling that she had neither power nor voice and compliance was her only possible response.

Oftentimes in juvenile justice programs the suppression of feelings is viewed as appropriate when it allows the adolescent to better adapt to her program. Thus, her history is neglected and her voice stifled when the need for her to speak and be heard is crucial especially because she is female. She is counseled in ways that will best adapt her to the juvenile justice program, even if that includes avoidance of real issues. In Sheila's circumstance, without any of the causal issues being addressed, her com-pliance almost facilitated her return to the same abusive environment where her self-worth and her voice were originally "lost." In this case, the counselor's role in working with Sheila from a framework of relationship allowed for Sheila to move into risk-taking activity, i.e., disclosing the "family secret."

Colin Wastell (1996) speaks of the role of counseling from the feminist perspective of relationship and "knowing."

> Counseling provides an opportunity for women to reclaim their "voice." Gilligan (1991) discussed the phenomenon in which ado-lescent girls lose their ability to speak of that which they know from their own experience of interrelatedness. The denigration of this intuitive voice occurs to women during adolescence and early adult-hood. Gilligan (1991) asserted that a "revision washes away the grounds of girls' feelings and thoughts and undermines the transfor-matory potential which lies in women's development" (p. 7). The cost to both themselves and society at large, according to Gilligan, is enormous. However, Gilligan exhorted counselors to "strengthen

healthy resistance and courage, to help women recover lost voices and tell lost stories and to provide safe houses for the underground" (p. 27). Women come to counseling often as a result of their struggle to take on a role they feel is expected of them. During their counseling, women can be assisted to rediscover their voice by a counselor who values connectedness. (p. 579)

Utilizing a strong systems-based treatment focus which incorporates a feminist model of therapy assists the female adolescent in the development of self-advocacy strategies. By learning how to access the network of services within her support system, the adolescent becomes empowered to proactively identify and utilize intervention strategies. This treatment goal is, ultimately, far more effective than the goal of controlling perceived maladaptive behavior.

Recognition of the ways in which the adolescent, charged with victimizing another, has first been victimized herself is basic to the facilitation of healing and the counselor's role in assisting the adolescent's development of esteem for self and empathy toward others. Effective and appropriate treatment planning rests upon the identification and acknowledgment of the role that personal and social isolation has upon the adolescent's ability to view themselves as competent members of the community.

Competency-based counseling assists the female adolescent in the reclaiming of her voice and recognition of the privileges and responsibilities of self-identity and membership in the greater society. Just as society needs to be accountable for the conditions which denigrate young women, female offenders need to be accountable for their victimization of others.

MOVEMENT TOWARD RESTORATION OF THAT WHICH HAS BEEN BROKEN

For female adolescents whose offending behavior has precipitated their involvement in the juvenile justice system, there remains yet another dimension which facilitates self-growth and healing: restorative justice.

Drawing upon the previously-stated theories of female adolescent identity being based within a framework of relationship and connection, application of the principles of balanced and restorative justice becomes a natural adjunct to the therapeutic process of self-identity and growth.

Criminal offenses have three levels of victimization: the actual victim of the crime, the perpetrator of the offense and the community broken and scarred by violence and mistrust. True justice must facilitate a restoration to wholeness on all three levels. While current societal attitudes place great emphasis on the punishment of the offender, retributive justice provides no healing nor relief for victim, offender and community. The answer, then, must rest with the restoration of that which has been broken. Gordon Bazemore, PhD (1994, p. 21), School of Public Administration, Florida Atlantic University, states:

> . . . restorative justice provides a coherent alternative to the increasingly retributive focus of current sanctioning and supervision processes, while also moving beyond the limits of individual treatment based on "the medical model." Restorative justice is based on a unique value orientation and on the primary assumptions that crime results in injuries to victims, communities and offenders; all parties should be included in the response to crime–victim, offender and community; government and community play complementary roles in that response; and accountability is based on offenders' accepting responsibility and repairing the harm done. (McLagan, 1992)

Restorative justice offers to the female adolescent offender the opportunity to confront her delinquent behavior in the context of relationship. The victim and offender meet and confront the offending behavior and its consequences to the victim and the community. Victim and offender are active participants in developing a plan that would offer the victim some restitution of material goods; provide the offender opportunity to view the human consequences of her criminal behavior and actively work toward providing restitution for material and emotional loss; provide benefit to the community through the community service work assigned to the offender as restitution for community costs. The empowerment of the victim to become an active participant in the decision-making process and the acknowledgment of the offender's ability to offer some healing to the victim gives dignity to both parties. It moves the offense out of the exclusive domain of the courts and into the mediating realm of relationship.

The three-prong approach of restorative justice, community protection, accountability, and competency development, eliminates a view of the victim as a nameless, faceless object and calls the offender beyond the role of detached participant in the legal process. While working within the boundaries of community safety, the offender is accountable in a social context for wrong-doing and given the opportunity, often for the first time, to develop the necessary competencies to participate as a responsible member of the community toward restitution. Restorative justice calls for a paradigm shift away from punitive and retributive concepts of justice to a justice that restores that which has been broken in the lives of both victim and offender.

In the case of Marissa, application of restorative justice would have involved a meeting with the store manager from whom she shoplifted merchandise. In that meeting the store manager would have been able to tell Marissa what her actions cost him, personally, and the public who pay higher retail prices because of the high rate of stolen goods. Marissa would have had the opportunity to apologize to the manager and, together, they would have been able to work out a contract for the restitution of the cost of the stolen goods. In addition, the store manager could have proposed that Marissa do community service by working in the store or providing service to a charity of his choice.

In this scenario, Marissa would have had an opportunity to learn, in the context of relationship to the actual victim, that there are no victimless crimes. She might have experienced the manager's frustration around his loss. She, too, would have had the opportunity to face the harmed person and explain and/or apologize for her behavior. Together they would plan the healing process.

In this manner, the three-prong approach of restorative justice would have been a reasonable and effective alternative to Marissa's placement in detention. By being accountable for her actions, Marissa would have learned valuable life lessons that would, in the future, ensure community safety. Marissa's restitution and community service work would, ideally, have provided opportunity for her to feel that she was acting as a competent member of society.

> Meanwhile, across the country, many young offenders sit in detention centers, where in the interests of "community protection" and "rehabilitation," they shuffle from their cell to the TV room in slippers and orange overalls.
>
> . . . Society must ask: Which approach advances genuine public safety? Which approach gives priority to the offender's responsibility for restoration? Which approach imparts values and behavior patterns necessary for long-term change? Which approach begins the process of reintegration of offenders into communities by helping to build a sense of belonging and changing public perception of these youths? (Maloney & Bazemore, 1994, 76-77)

While today's concept of restorative justice is, most often, applied to property crimes, the basic elements of healing through participation for victim and community and offender accountability for wrongdoing are central to the process.

Our society's common understanding of the need for juvenile offenders to be held "accountable" is closely linked to the concepts of
punishment and retribution ... "when you violate the law, you incur
a debt to society." In this viewpoint, offenders are held accountable
when they have received or taken a certain amount of punishment.

In the restorative justice paradigm the meaning of accountability
shifts the focus from incurring a debt to society to that of incurring a
responsibility for making amends to the victimized person; from
passively taking punishment to actively making things right. Rather
than emphasizing punishment of past criminal behavior, accountability in the restorative justice paradigm taps into the offender's
strengths and competencies to take direct and active responsibility to
compensate the victim for material and emotional losses. (Umbreit,
1995, p. 31)

By applying the restorative justice model to adolescent offending, the
adolescent female is able to confront her wrongdoing and the human face
of its consequences within the experience of connection and relationship.
She develops competency in accepting responsibility for her actions and in
believing that she does have something to contribute to the society from
which she has previously felt excluded.

By eliciting accountability for the harm caused to the victim and community and offering an active plan for restitution or making right the
wrong, the female adolescent is encouraged in reclaiming an identity as a
participant of community, not a peripheral outsider. Through this healing
process the female adolescent offender develops relational competency
and both victim and offender are empowered in restoring the balance of a
community wronged.

CONCLUSION

Treatment based on a feminist model of intervention that, in essence,
assists the young woman in "finding her voice," can lead to a systemic
homeostatic response in her family, and, consequently, the greater society.
This response supports the re-parenting of the child and the self-identifica-
tion of her strengths and competencies. Participation in a process of accountability for offending behavior based on restorative justice principles
can help create a sense of belonging rather than alienation from community. Systemic work with the family or alternate support network and the
young woman's efforts to move into responsible living can significantly
reduce the incidence of recidivistic crime.

Mental health professionals are in a unique position to speak for the needs of children who have never been parented, children whose gender often prevents them from receiving just and adequate services, children who are asking the adult community to work with them toward a restoration of that which has been broken in their lives.

It is in the domain of relationship that young offenders can completely and competently choose to work through a restorative justice model of accountability for wrongdoing and become active participants in the victim-offender healing process. By proactively addressing the causes of female juvenile offending and the importance of developing systems-based counseling strategies that effectively give voice to the gender-specific needs of young women, the mental health clinician can not only facilitate the restoration to wholeness of the individual female offender, but can also present to the young woman a modeling of a society that, once again, values and cares for its young.

REFERENCES

Anderson, George M. (1994, January 20). Juvenile justice and the double standard. *America,* 13-15.
Bartollas, C. (1997). *Juvenile delinquency (4th Ed.).* Needham Heights, MA: Allyn and Bacon.
Bazemore, Gordon. (1994). Developing a victim orientation for community corrections: A restorative justice paradigm and a balanced mission. *Perspectives.* American Probation and Parole Association, 19-24.
Chesney-Lind, Meda, & Shelden, Randall G. (1992). *Girls, delinquency and juvenile justice.* Pacific Grove, CA: Brooks/Cole Publishing Co.
Conarton, S., & Kreger-Silverman, L. (1988). Feminist development through the life cycle. In Dutton-Douglas, M.A., & Walker, L.E. (Eds.). *Feminist psychotherapies: Integration of therapeutic and feminist systems.* Norwood, NJ: Ablex 37-67.
Erikson, Erik H. (1963). *Childhood and society.* New York: Norton.
Gilligan, C. (1991). Women's psychological development: Implications for psychocounseling. In Gilligan, C., Rogers, A.C. & Tolman, D.L. (Eds.). *Women, girls and psychocounseling: Reframing resistance.* New York: The Haworth Press, Inc., 5-32.
Howell, J. C. (Ed.). (1995). Guide for implementing the comprehensive strategy for serious, violent and chronic offenders. Washington, DC: Office of Juvenile Justice and Delinquency Prevention.
Keough, Tim. (1994). *The psychology of adolescent female offenders: Programs and their response to the challenge.* Paper presented to the Australian Institute of Criminology Conference, Terrigal, New South Wales, Australia.
Krisberg, B., Schwartz, I. M., Litsky, P., & Austin, J. (1986). The watershed of juvenile justice reform. *Crime and Delinquency, 32.*

Maloney, Dennis, & Bazemore, Gordon. (1994, December). Juveniles–A generation at risk; Community service helps heal troubled youths. *Corrections Today,* 76-77.

McLagan, J. (1992). Committee recommendations on restorative justice. Working paper presented to the Minnesota Planning Group.

Siegel, L. J., & Senna, J. J. (1991). *Juvenile delinquency, theory, practice and law,* 4th Ed. St. Paul: West.

Snyder, H. N., Sickmund, M., & Poe-Yamagata, E. (1996). *Juvenile offenders and victims: 1996 update on violence.* Washington, DC: U.S. Department of Justice, Office of Justice Programs, Office of Juvenile Justice and Delinquency Prevention.

Umbreit, Mark S. (1995, Spring). Holding juvenile offenders accountable: A restorative justice perspective. *Juvenile and Family Court Journal,* 31-41.

Wastell, Colin. (1996). Feminist developmental theory: Implications for counseling. *Journal of Counseling and Development, 74,* 575-581.

Weiss, F. L., Nicholson, H. J., & Cretella, M. M. (1996). *Prevention and parity: Girls in juvenile justice.* New York: Girls, Inc. National Resource Center.

Lessons from a Mother's Program in Prison: A Psychosocial Approach Supports Women and Their Children

Kathy Boudin

SUMMARY. This article examines a psychosocial group model among women in prison focusing on their roles and identities as mothers. The group is co-facilitated by the author and another woman who are prisoners and mothers themselves. The goals of the group are two: to provide women with the opportunity to grow through examining their roles as mothers in the past and present and to strengthen the mother-child relationship during incarceration. The article illustrates that when a mother works on her own emotional issues, this process can also improve her ability to parent her children, if her children's needs are kept in the forefront. The article will

Kathy Boudin has been incarcerated for more than fifteen years. During her incarceration she has worked in the areas of mother/child relationships including parenting from prison and foster care/child custody issues, AIDS/women's health, and literacy. She has worked on both an emotional and educational level and in program development. She has published in each of the above three areas in journals including *The Harvard Educational Review, Social Justice,* and *Journal of Correctional Association.* She received her Master's degree in Adult Education and Adult Literacy from Norwich University in 1989.

Address correspondence to: Kathy Boudin, #84G0171, P.O. Box 1000, Bedford Hills, NY 10507.

[Haworth co-indexing entry note]: "Lessons from a Mother's Program in Prison: A Psychosocial Approach Supports Women and Their Children." Boudin, Kathy. Co-published simultaneously in *Women & Therapy* (The Haworth Press, Inc.) Vol. 21, No. 1, 1998, pp. 103-125; and: *Breaking the Rules: Women in Prison and Feminist Therapy* (ed: Judy Harden, and Marcia Hill) The Haworth Press, Inc., 1998, pp. 103-125; and: *Breaking the Rules: Women in Prison and Feminist Therapy* (ed: Judy Harden, and Marcia Hill) The Harrington Park Press, an imprint of The Haworth Press, Inc., 1998, pp. 103-125. Single or multiple copies of this article are available for a fee from The Haworth Document Delivery Service [1-800-342-9678, 9:00 a.m. - 5:00 p.m. (EST). E-mail address: getinfo@haworth.com].

103

discuss the strengths of a peer support model within the prison context while defining issues raised by utilizing peers rather than a professional therapist to facilitate the group. *[Article copies available for a
fee from The Haworth Document Delivery Service: 1-800-342-9678. E-mail
address: getinfo@haworth.com]*

I listened to other mothers. Listening to them, knowing that I was
amongst them, and to be a person, to feel human again, to talk about
the skeletons in our closets. To feel that I'm not hiding as much. I hid
all these feelings of shame and guilt, I didn't allow people to see me
for how I was. But once I became more open, it broke the barrier. I
could relate to my children better.

* * *

Other people in the group would talk, saying the same things
about themselves, negative things, things in their past that they
needed to get out but they didn't have anywhere to tell it, and it
made me feel like I wasn't alone. I'm walking around here, and
people see me one way but inside I'm keeping hidden the real
person that I was, and I never had a chance to get it out of me–you
know, using drugs while my kid was in the house, having to give
him away to his father–it helps me to talk about all the things I did
wrong, come face to face with them. Now that I've shared, I will be
able to deal with them better, because as long as they were inside I
could pretend that it didn't happen, it wasn't real. By talking about
it, I had to face it.

* * * *

I'm glad that I was able to help other mothers with dealing with
their situations. It made me feel important and wanted, a feeling we
all know is lacking behind these prison walls.

* * * *

When a woman goes to prison, her relationship to her children is a
central emotional focus: she is torn by guilt, anxiety and a sense of failure,
yet, at the same time, her child continues to be a source of hope, a connection to a part of herself, a motivation for her to change. This crisis is
potentially an opportunity for enormous growth if it is faced, growth in a
woman's ability to develop emotionally and growth in her ability to parent

her child. I am one of these women. I am an inmate at Bedford Hills Correctional Facility and also a mother. I have been in prison for more than 15 years; my son was 14 months old when I was arrested. I have utilized the remarkable Children's Center Programs at the prison to build my relationship with my son and I also work in these programs as an inmate staff member. The Children's Center, a national model for maintaining the bond of incarcerated mothers and their children, includes visitation programs, parenting programs and activities to allow a mother to support and communicate with her children, and a Nursery.

Many years into my time in prison, I wanted to attempt to answer the question that hovered over me, "How is it that I loved my son so much, yet I made choices that resulted in my arrest, and in my leaving him? What was going on in my life? Inside of me?" Trying to face this question is one of the factors that took me on an internal journey, a journey that included creating a program called Parenting From a Distance with Rozann Greco, another inmate and mother. Our goals were two: to provide a context for women to explore their experience as mothers through a review of their lives, and simultaneously, to work on parenting from prison.

We were motivated to create such a program out of our personal experiences but also out of our work as inmate staff in the Children's Center. Between us we had worked in a number of the programs, as teachers of foster care laws and child custody issues, topics of parenting using films, and bilingual parenting; as a caregiver for the visiting children; and as an advocate and peer counselor. We felt the need for a program that would give women the opportunity to reflect on who they had been as mothers before coming to prison, what the forces were in their lives that affected how they were as mothers, and what had led them to the point of becoming a parent from a distance. We believed that this kind of process would create a stronger foundation to parent from a distance from prison and also to prepare for the future when women could resume the role of mother outside of prison. We also felt the potential that a *social* process could bring to working on being a parent from prison.

I hope to illustrate that when a mother works on her own emotional needs, this process can also improve her ability to parent her children, if her children's needs are kept in the forefront. I will review how the group worked to find the balance between reflecting upon and learning from the past and actively working on the present, between focusing on the mother's own experience and working on the child's needs. I will define three central emotional issues that repeatedly came up for the mothers and show how each affects the relationship with their children: the mothers' own traumatic experiences as children or young adults; shame and guilt about the choices they made before coming to prison; and grief at being separated from their children while in prison.

I will examine the process which we developed to encourage the mother's growth and support for the children. I will emphasize two processes: one, we relied on a *social* or *group* process for individuals to examine their own history; two, we linked the therapeutic process to *acting* on the issues being explored, making an impact on existing situations, in this case the relationship with the children or the children's caretakers. We emphasized these techniques because they helped to counter the overwhelming powerlessness that is experienced by women in the prison context.

BACKGROUND

Bedford Hills Correctional Facility is New York State's maximum security prison for women. Located about 50 miles from New York City, it houses about 800 women, 75% of whom are mothers. The women in Bedford Hills C.F. face the same problems of powerlessness that characterize most women in prison: women of color are 80% of the prisoners at Bedford–50% are black and 30% are Hispanic, a far greater proportion than in society at large. A New York State Department of Correctional Services publication (1992) states:

> Victimization in the lives of incarcerated women is pervasive. In an ACA survey, a third of the adult women and more than half of the juvenile offenders surveyed had a history of sexual abuse. Most of the abuse had occurred before the age of 14 and had been generally perpetrated by a male member of the family. Two thirds of incarcerated women were runaways, 74% had histories of alcohol abuse, with drug abuse ranging from 22% to 49% depending on the drug of choice. Our experience indicates that conservatively 65% of the female inmate population has a history of extreme physical and/or sexual abuse, primarily as children. (p. 180)

Over half of the women do not have a high school degree yet the majority had dependent children. The problems created by economic dependency were exacerbated by the frequent history of abuse and drug and alcohol dependency (New York State Department of Correctional Services, 1995).

Hence, women come to the group experiencing three levels of powerlessness: (1) being in prison; (2) being separated from their children yet trying to be a mother for them; and (3) coping with the legacies of powerlessness in their own lives.

This points to the importance of women developing their efficacy, self-reliance, a sense of autonomy, and skills to become self-supporting. Yet prison, by its nature, is authoritarian and controlling. Women cannot even make the most basic decisions of life such as when to go to sleep or get up, what to eat and wear, who or when to visit, not to mention building normal relationships (Hannah-Moffat, 1995). The concept of rehabilitation and treatment still places women in a passive role, either as "victims" who need to be helped or people who need to be "rehabilitated."

Even in the context of Bedford Hills Correctional Facility where there are model programs which encourage and provide means for women to take responsibility and to be self-reliant, the overall prison environment overwhelmingly pushes towards passivity and dependency. According to the present Superintendent of Bedford Hills C.F.:

> The rigidity and authoritarianism of prisons by their very nature can be yet another experience of power and control as belonging to other, not the women. Prison does not allow women to experiment with their own decision making but rather reduces them to an immature state in which most decisions of consequence are made for them. (Lord, 1995, p. 262)

With this in mind we wanted to create a process that would set loose the capacity of women to be active participants in their own process of growth and to facilitate making a difference in their own lives and in the lives of others. We designed the program to encourage the active role of women in several ways:

1. women would individually and together reconstruct a definition of their own history by telling the stories about their lives which were important to them;
2. women would help one another with their process of self-investigation;
3. time in the group would be spent actively trying to change and have an effect on their relationship with their children and on their children's needs–i.e., they would work at being parents, even from a distance;
4. finally, we had as a goal that the group experience would lead to a final product–out of their own experience they would write something to help others, either for their children, for other mothers, or caretakers of their children. In addition, the fact that the group

would be facilitated by inmates and function totally as an inmate group we felt would play some role in creating the sense of self-reliance and autonomy.

For three months, five days a week, two-and-a-half hours a day, the group of ten women meet and have the opportunity both to review their own lives and work on issues about their children. New groups have met successively over the past two-and-a-half years. Although some cognitive material is presented at certain points, for example, information about child development, and about the social history of women as healers, the primary material for the group is the life stories of the women themselves.

Voices and stories in this article are largely drawn from the book which the women in the first group wrote. They very much wanted their experiences to be shared and to be of use to others. Some of the material is taken from interviews with other women from subsequent classes who also felt strongly that they wanted to share their experience.

THEORETICAL FRAMEWORK

The approach we developed draws from three other models of group work; however, the theoretical bases have been defined more in hindsight and reflection. The process evolved out of the day-to-day experience in the group commensurate with our goals.

We draw from feminist consciousness-raising groups: women tell the stories of their lives, looking at certain topics related to mothers and children, and in doing so in a group situation, there is a process of seeing patterns, learning that certain experiences are not personal but come from the social context. The biggest difference from the feminist consciousness-raising is that the focus is not about changing society–although we do discuss the impact of social realities on the experience of being mothers–but rather on the growth of the individual woman and improving the interaction with the children and the support for them (Hole & Levine, 1971).

Second, we rely on aspects of group psychotherapy. We noticed in our own experience many of the strengths of group therapy, named as the "curative factors" by an expert on group psychotherapy (Yalom, 1975). They included hope, universality, altruism, group cohesiveness, catharsis, and existential factors. Our work differs from group therapy in that the focus is not on interpersonal difficulties in the present, or conflicts and differences among group members. Our focus is on past relationships and experiences that a woman had relevant to her experience as a mother and on her current relationships with her children and their caretakers.

Finally, the process draws on trauma recovery process (Herman, 1992). Many of the women told stories of traumatic events they had endured. The group was a safe place to work on recovery from those traumatic events, a place to build trust and connections. However, usually women were in–or we suggested that they become part of–more specialized groups in the facility such as the Family Violence Program or AIDS Counseling and Education or Mental Health where they would have a more in-depth opportunity to focus on these traumas.

THREE AREAS OF CONCERN/FOCUS OF THE MOTHERS

Relooking at Our Own Childhood and Young Adult Experience: The Need of Mothers to Be Mothered, or Who Is the Mother and Who Is the Child

A central theme in our group was the traumatic experiences that women themselves had as children or as young adults and the impact these had on their ability to be a mother. The most common ones were the sexual, physical and emotional abuse that women had experienced either as children or with boyfriends or their spouses. We worked as a group to piece together how these experiences affected our role as mothers, our ability to mother, and our children.

One pattern was that some women who had been abused as children and did not get protection, support and love from their parents, often found it difficult to mother and protect their own children. Many said they had sworn to themselves that they would be a different kind of mother than their own had been. Yet tragically the pattern often repeated itself. Often drug or alcohol addiction and/or abuse from a boyfriend or spouse followed their childhood experiences. This often meant that they were unable to be the emotionally stable mother that they had hoped to be.

Role reversal–a mother depending on her child–was common. For some women, the absence of mothering in their own childhood seemed to mean they were looking for that from their child. One woman says,

> I think I had children because I needed someone to love me. I am 34 years old, with two children that I have never been a mother to. I had my kids, mostly because I didn't want to feel alone. I thought I would have someone to love me, no matter what.

Another woman says,

> I think my main reason for wanting a child was for him or her to love
> me. I have always doubted love from husbands, boyfriends, parents.
> But this was going to be *my* child–it had to love me . . . or so I
> thought. I could make it love me, it was supposed to, I was its Mom.

Either because of the violence or the drug or alcohol abuse, women
described situations that illustrated how their children actually took care of
them, or even helped to protect them. Women would frequently begin a
description of their children as "very mature": "My little girl was able to
handle a lot, she even helped me." As the women and the group reflected
upon the stories, it became clear that their children were being exposed to
and having to handle experiences and responsibilities way beyond what
was reasonable for children. When the mothers spoke about their own
childhoods, often we saw a cycle of premature loss of parental support. I
drew on related literature for insights about the impact of a woman's own
childhood losses of parental support on her role as a mother (Baunach,
1988; Edelman, 1994; Jackson, 1994; Miller, 1981).

Through the group process, we tried to create a safe space for women to
retell their own traumatic experiences as girls or women. And for many,
when they worked at expressing their feelings and when they felt that they
were understood, this increased their ability to focus on their children's
needs. When they could begin to see their children's needs, they could
then begin to take on a different role in practice with their children. The
group, in giving women support and understanding about their own experiences, then freed them to focus on their children and to begin to be a
more stable figure.

Below is a summary about one woman who was eager to have her story
told:

Jerri did not participate very much during the first weeks of the group.
Then she learned that her children, in foster care, were acting out so badly
that they had to be split up and put in two therapeutic homes. When she got
off the phone with her social worker she was panicked and in tears. The
worker had told her that her children had a problem which she had trouble
pronouncing, let alone understanding: "intermittent explosive disorder."
She kept trembling and saying, "It's not my drinking that did this, is it?
It's not my drinking that did this, is it?" After calming down, she shared
her phone call with the class. We asked what her greatest fear was. She
said "that my kids will end up like me." She expressed concern that they
would be medicated and then begin the same problems as she had with
drinking since they would have no place for their feelings. In this period

she insisted that the only problem her children had was that they were not being allowed to visit her in the prison, otherwise, everything had always been fine in their lives. And she was very angry at the social workers for not bringing them for visits.

About three weeks later, she began to describe her life with her children before the arrest. She detailed her drinking and violent life including one incident when her boyfriend bit off part of her nose and lip; how she left him and then went back; how he beat her and how once, to get away, her ten-year-old daughter who had watched all of this, helped distract him while she dialed the police. She slid down the stairs, bloody and drunk, which her daughter also watched.

Previously she had said that her own childhood had been perfect. Soon in the class she began to describe her own childhood which had included abuse from a mother, living with her father who at nine decided to put her in a foster home and then she went into a group home. She began drinking at age nine, dropped out of high school and became pregnant.

The group gave her the space to talk about herself, to feel how horrible her own childhood had been and what she must have been going through to become an alcoholic at age nine.

A change took place after she had described stories of drinking and violence that her children witnessed and after she received attention about her own childhood experience. One day she said she was beginning to learn that she had some responsibility for where her kids were today, in terms of their behavior, something that the social worker had been trying to get her to see. Soon she began to work with the children's therapist by letter and phone, trying to detail as much background as she could as to what the children had lived through. Now she was actually taking responsibility for the problems her children were having and actively working to help them through working on a weekly basis with their therapists.

Some months after the class finished, Jerri said,

> With my 11 year old, I'm not as hard on her now. I expected her to be an adult. I'm now telling her, "be the little girl. You don't have to worry about big people things." I don't tell her things her little mind can't handle.

Her process was not a linear one. Jerri chose to be in a program where she would focus on herself and her children. The crisis that her children went through while she was in the group was the catalyst for her to begin talking about her own life and that of her children. Slowly, through the group's support, she could acknowledge her own pain at what she had survived as a child, young woman and mother. The group's acknowledgment of this seemed to help her in two ways: one, other women were empathetic and validated her experience and this began to free her to separate her own needs from her children's; two, by talking about what had happened and finding that she was accepted by others, she no longer had to deny how the troubles in her own life had negatively affected her children. This, in turn, began to allow her to take responsibility for them, to gain in self-confidence. She slowly defined a new role with her children, that of their mother, rather than depending on her children to help her.

Women brought situations to the group that they were facing with their children at that time. These concrete issues provided a way for women to test out and implement new ways of relating to their children and it allowed group members to help one another. For example, once the issue of role reversal became explicit in the class, group members would call each other on their behavior. One woman describes a situation with her 11-year-old daughter:

> The weekend when we first talked about it, people in the class told me "you better not cry, be the adult, and let her talk, don't you do all the talking." And when I was down there (in the visiting room) I saw two of you, and I felt that I had two angels, two angels from the class, looking at me, giving me the strength. And my daughter got her strength by talking to me, and I got my strength to just let her talk by feeling the eyes of people on me. You all told me not to cry so that she could see that I was handling it, letting her talk and she just opened up. And I remember that day was the best day of all, because you remember how I said she used to leave here crying, but that day she left here with a positive attitude. I think she was more open with me since she saw that I protected and that I didn't want to see anything happen to her, that I love her. She sees that I'm incarcerated and that even so I'm still able to take care of situations for her. Working out the situation in class helped. Talking with the group helped a lot, everybody gave me some support, nobody downed me or knocked me, they gave me advice, support, strength.

This dependency on children to meet our own needs is exacerbated by the prison context. We are not just struggling with the kind of roles that developed in the past but also with the impact of the present conditions. Women want their children to meet their needs for connecting to the outside world and to family, even when it may be more important for a child not to visit, not to communicate on the phone or even to be distant. You will hear women say things like, "It was Christmas, that day is hard

for me, my daughter should have stayed home so that I could call her."
Group members would ask one another empathetically, "Do you think that
your teenage daughter might have other needs, other things she wanted to
do?"

There were some for whom the violence in their own lives already had
irreversible tragic implications for their children. One woman wanted her
story to be known:

> I grew up in a violent household. I lived firsthand with the experi-
> ence of violence between my parents and was raped by my own
> father from the age of six years old to 13. I still bear the scars that my
> father inflicted upon me as well as reliving the nightmares. From
> there, as I grew older and started dating, it seems the only guys I
> attracted were those who were abusive, one after the other. I became
> fearful of those men, lost my self-esteem and was always thinking it
> was me. From having a violent childhood I became a very passive
> woman. The impact of the violence on my children is that one of
> them died because I tried to escape an abusive relationship and
> Carlos, my boyfriend, used my son, knowing he was my heart.
> Before that, both of my children suffered because I was constantly
> beaten upon and had a gun to my head, knife to my throat and beaten
> with extension cords while my oldest was forced to watch. At the
> time I was locked in closets like my father used to do to me. As for
> my ability to be a parent, it was hard because Carlos would ridicule
> me in front of my son but present himself as a devoted boyfriend to
> everyone else. Talking helped me to see I am not alone and there are
> places I can go and talk about being a battered woman. It helps me to
> see, that as a mother, whatever affects me will affect my son.

If the group became a place where women could work on recovering
from their own traumas, increase their understanding of events that already happened to their children, we considered this a success because we
believed this would create a stronger foundation for the children whom
they were parenting in the present.

When women shared their lives, the group had to absorb enormously
painful stories. People reiterated the importance of being with others who
could understand their ordeals. As pointed out by both Yalom (1975) and
Herman (1992), the cohesion and support of the group facilitated the
individual's ability to accept herself. Also, when individuals could help
others through their understanding or example they felt good about themselves, and this was often stated as one of the strengths of the process.

Collective empowerment also took place. Women in the group were all prisoners; in spite of diversity of backgrounds and experiences, this was a common equalizer. Although in the beginning there may have been a sense of "how can we help each other, it is like the blind leading the blind," something different emerged. By the end most women felt as though they had both contributed to and received from others. In our experience, there is truth to the observation of Herman (1992) who writes, ". . . the group as a whole has the capacity to bear and integrate traumatic experience that is greater than that of any individual member and each member can draw upon the resources of the group" (p. 216).

Guilt and Shame over What We Have Done and the Impact of This on Our Ability to Respond to Our Children's Needs

One of the most crippling emotions is that of the profound guilt and shame that many mothers have about what they have done before they were arrested. Many were parenting from a distance before they came to prison, either because of drug use or actual separations due to other arrests or foster care. We found that it was important for mothers to share their stories about the very things that they had hidden and were ashamed of. By sharing the stories with others, it allowed them to feel less alone, less wretched, more like human beings. When the group accepted them in spite of the things they had done, that acceptance became a basis for their beginning to accept themselves. The piecing together of their lives meant they could place the "horrible" things they had done within the context of their life story. This contributed to an understanding about why things had happened; it also helped them take responsibility for their choices. All of this was a foundation for better relating to their children.

Sharing their stories helped them to be more open with their children in general, less defensive or anxious to hide things that their children already knew about. It aided them in answering their children's questions about why they lost their mother to prison, and it played a critical role in helping them to cope positively with the anger of teenagers. Finally, in coming more to terms with herself, a mother is more likely to be able to help her child understand him/herself.

Here is one woman's story about the development of that process and her interaction with her teenage son during and after the group. It begins with her pregnancy, then her years before her arrest, the three months in the group and finally a year and a half since the group ended. Her story illustrates her own emotional process and how this process within herself helped her son.

When I became pregnant with my second son, I was so happy that joy showed in my life, as everyone kept telling me how great I looked. I was exceptionally happy the first three months of pregnancy, but then something happened. Today, 16 years later, I cannot account for the dread that I experienced. I began to dip and dab with cocaine and then it became an everyday thing. As my pregnancy progressed, so did my habit. Pre-natal care was now twice a week as I was diagnosed with "prolonged pregnancy." With a lot of help, I delivered my son, but to my surprise, I never heard him cry as all babies do. When I looked, I saw staff running with my baby and the doctor said "knocked out."

Then I saw my husband come in, his face was ashened and I knew something terrible was happening. My husband couldn't speak, but his eyes were red. He had been crying. I said, "Where's my baby? What's wrong? Tell me." He stood up and held me in his arms and I began to cry uncontrollably. I kept yelling "What's happened? I want my baby, where is he?" Then the doctor came in and said, "Take it easy, I'll try to answer your questions as best I can." Then I said again, "I want my baby." The doctor proceeded to explain that my son was born asphyxiated and he was presently on a respirator and that because of prolonged delivery and his size that the next 72 hours were critical. Then they wheeled me to Neonatal Intensive Care Unit. There, with what seemed hundreds of machines attached, my son lay motionless. All I could do was stare and say "Oh my God, please save my baby." I finally touched his fingers and hands, then his face and hair and then his tummy where very carefully in his naval a large needle protruded. The nurse came over and said "Don't worry, he doesn't feel any pain."

Later the doctor told me that after the baby was resuscitated, he had 3 seizures, back to back, and that he was on phenobarbital to prevent any more. Later that night I went back to NICU to see my baby. They said, "No change." His condition was still critical.

I sat in my room and cried and asked God to forgive me, because only He knew that I was to blame for my son's suffering and condition. Today, my son is well and thriving as any young man his age; however, he is in special ed classes due to his condition at birth. I never told him what I did when we were one. I will someday.

After telling her story, weeping, she said that her son had a significant learning disability, that she felt responsible for it due to her drug use during the pregnancy. She said she had never talked about the drug use during pregnancy nor the relationship to the learning disability to anyone.

As the group continued and we moved into the topic of "Who we were as mothers before coming to prison," this same woman shared the story of her drug addiction with the group, summarizing it by writing:

> Where was I when my children needed me? When the kids called out and said "mommy." I felt nothing because my yearning within was for drugs. I cheated with whatever had any meaning in my life and this was the cause of my destruction. Drugs were calling for me 24 hours plus and it was more than I realize I could handle.

When we sat down as a group to write a booklet for other mothers, she wrote about how talking in the group had helped her become more honest with her children:

> I had a lot of shame and guilt, leaving the children with their father, remarrying, and not focussing on my boys' life too much. I was afraid to tell them that I was on drugs and the importance of drugs at that time in my life. It seemed that it was more important to get my drugs then, and I took it for granted that they were being taken care of. They were not my priority, I can see my priorities were not in order. But now, after airing this in the group, I was able to speak to them. I became more confident with them about where I stood in their lives. They told me that they could see, that they had known I was on drugs. It drew us closer, confirming just their own feelings, when I could talk about what I was doing.

Nothing is static, and not long after that process, her son went for five months without talking to her.

> I went for five months with my 16 year old refusing to see me. Every time I called I could speak with my other two sons but he always told them to say he wasn't home, or he was busy, he had nothing to speak to me about. When we finally spoke I was able to take his anger. He was right. I told him I was very sorry for being out of his life and for placing all the responsibility for the younger boys on him. And he said he was going to visit me. That he was going to blow me out of the water. This, he isn't saying this to hurt me but that he just wants me understand what he feels, he just wants me to look at him as the young man that he is, with his own mind and own feelings.
>
> Dealing with his anger was hard. It helped talking to other mothers who have been in prison longer than myself. To know that in one way or another we all go through something similar. If I hadn't

accepted his anger would mean to lose him totally so to accept was to be able to talk to him and not hide anymore.

The more the mother has accepted herself, the more she is able to accept the anger of the children in a manner that supports them. These issues are particularly relevant for dealing with children's desires to understand where the mother is and why she is there. Mothers feel terribly ashamed of both being in prison and of why they are there. Yet children have their own needs to understand why their mother is not with them. As one psychologist who has worked with the children of incarcerated parents said,

> We are all shaped by our parents. What they have done in their life helps to determine what we ourselves will do. . . . If a child is allowed to interact with the parent, the child will learn that the parent is capable of both good and bad actions, and, therefore part of the child is good as well. Knowing the parent, coming to terms with his or her criminal activity, seeing it as one part of a complex multifaceted personality is a start. (Gamer & Gamer, 1983)

This mother reached a point of feeling confident enough in herself to be more real with her son about herself. This was also encouraged by her son's own maturing process, his age, and his own questions and directness to her:

> He expected me to be a role model. I let him know that I had many faults, that I wasn't perfect, and that I made mistakes some more severe than others. He now knows that drugs played a big part in what brought me here. That if I had dealt with his brother's death before, and then hadn't waited until his father died, maybe I would have been able to face things, not run to drugs. There comes a time when you want to make things right regardless of how wrong they are, especially with your children. And to face it was to have hope that whether he accepted my wrongs or not, the truth was the priority now. It was no more lying, hiding behind this prison wall, to know that I would have to face it sooner or later and what better time to do it but now. Being able to tell him the truth was a way of helping him be more independent. It was part of my letting go, letting go a myth about me, but by telling him the truth I was letting him know that I trusted him. Now he is 17, he can be trusted.

This relationship between an incarcerated mother and her son is constantly unfolding and developing as any relationship. Recent news about her son and her feelings about her relationship with him has been very positive:

> The good things now–he's getting very involved in positive things. He is in his last year of high school and he is in a construction program. And he has signed up for an environmental program after he graduates, he will be working away from home for 5 days a week. He's very confident. He's using all of his math. Feeling proud about using it in his training and that's encouraging to me who is working at basic math myself. We're able to talk more–our time that we do spend together, whether on the phone or in the visiting room, we're friends and that's important to me.

Loss: "We Have Lost Being Able to Be Mothers."

There is enormous grief in the class about missing the years of their children's childhood and of being able to be mothers. Even though many women were taking only partial responsibility for their children before coming to prison, due to drugs or living an illegal life, the total separation that prison brings creates a qualitative difference. The grief of a mother, the sense of loss, if not faced directly, had different ramifications which affected children negatively.

Sometimes the grief manifested itself in anger at the people who were now in charge of the children. The mother in prison, attempting to hold on to a certain kind of decision-making would be in constant conflict with the caretakers of the child and in an ongoing state of anger at them. Accepting that many basic decisions are no longer in our hands but in the hands of another family is very difficult. It is a process. However, if a mother comes to terms about her own loss, can grieve it, and define a more limited yet different and usually important role in the child's life, she can have a positive impact. This can help the child because the mother is able to work more constructively and cooperatively with the child's day-to-day family.

One woman expressed this process in a letter she wrote to us one year after her group finished. She was in another prison:

> My self-esteem has risen, I am now able to accept life for what it really is, not for what I perceive it to be. My children have been coming along just fine, even though my mother is planning to move down South. When I first found out I went through all of the normal feelings and I thought to myself, "Why is she leaving me and taking my children with her?" But as I thought it out and used some of the tools of the group, I realized that it was the best for my children. And

for me not to accept it would be very selfish. I now take my children's feelings into consideration and not just my own. Without the group I may not have been so open with the relationship with my children.

This grief at times manifested itself in making demands on the children which were not helpful to the child and didn't take into account the child's needs and reality. One major issue that comes up over and over again is the complaint that their child calls someone else "mommy." We focused on how important it was to us as mothers to have our child call us "mommy," something which becomes even more important because we are not acting as "mommy" and we want that as an identity and human connection. And then we ask for women to put themselves in their children's reality, living for many years with someone who is meeting their emotional needs on a day-to-day level. It is a difficult process for the woman to identify her own needs as separate from that of her child's and to learn that sometimes the most important gift she can give to her child is to allow her/him to build that kind of secure bond with someone else. One woman speaks about this:

> Before when I heard my daughter call my mother "mommy" I used to go in a room and cry. But in all reality she had a right to call her "mommy," because my mother was there for everything. When she got her first cold, she was there; when she was withdrawing from drugs, she was there. I never was a mother. I never had the responsibilities of a mother. It is painful to realize but I realize I have to accept it.

For women whose children are teenagers there is a particular experience of loss. At this time women feel that their role of mothers to their children is over forever and because of being in prison the loss of being a mother feels particularly intense. Sometimes this can manifest itself with the mother trying to make demands on the child about decisions that teenagers are normally taking on themselves, whether it is hair style, gradual lengthening of curfew, or clothes style. Cognitive information about adolescence has helped women to understand that our own losses are part of a universal process that parents of teenagers have to go through as their children grow up, and that we have a responsibility to help our children be more independent, which is our job in helping them grow up.

Yet prison separation brings a particular sense of loss. Often the teenage years reconfirm that a mother has missed being home with her child. In addition, the separation frequently has affected the relationship in negative ways which cannot be reversed; the mother is faced with the indelible loss.

Perhaps there is anger which leads the child not to want to visit, or an ambivalence towards the mother which means the child keeps promising to visit and then doesn't, or an emotional distance. Crises develop such as children dropping out of school, getting arrested, using or selling drugs. The mother is going to assume these would not have happened had she been home. She combines her own feelings of loss with the heightened guilt and anxiety about her children. One woman struggles within herself around the inevitable process of growth and her separation from it:

> When I got here I thought "my babies, my boys" but life doesn't stop. My boys were growing up without me. Eddie's interests are basketball, school, friends, girls and of course I feel a little jealous. And I have to struggle with my feelings. Why are all these things more important than mommy? How did this group help? When we started envisioning our children, it was mainly in my head and I saw them as babies. And mommy had to be there. Then we spoke about Shauna, how her baby was born there and then she had to let him go. That helped me to look at my boys and realize that I also must let go and let them become men, that they already are doing this. At one time I just wanted to hold them as babies forever, yet when they came on the next visit I could see Eddie had a moustache, Josh was older and bolder and the baby was no more in Pampers. And a mother always loves her children, but I like these guys, I like them, too.

Finally, there are the losses which bring with them no relief: women whose children have died and it is that which brought the mother to prison, women whose children died while they were in prison, women whose parental rights have been terminated and who have no contact with their children, women whose caretakers have been so determined not to allow the children to visit that the relationship with their mother is very limited. The group was the bearer of each of these griefs.

Listening to others talk and withstand the pains provided a kind of existential process of growth. Pain and loss are basic parts of life–whatever form they may take–and in facing these issues in the group, hearing of others' struggle with their losses, many of which were even worse than one's own, there was a process of acceptance of the reality, of facing one's own responsibility for one's situation and the beginning of defining things differently.

In the context of accepting losses, the group also provided hope as each person's relationship with her children was constantly unfolding and going through ups and downs. The participants in the group always include women who have been in prison for widely varying amounts of time: one year, six years or even fifteen or more years. Hearing the stories of those who have been here for a long time and who had to accept the losses, had to redefine their roles, and yet who had found a way to build a meaningful relationship with their children, gave a sense of hope.

One woman wrote, after her first two weeks in the class, a piece that ties together the role of grief, anger at the caretakers and learning from others in the group:

> When I first came into the group I was furious with my sister. I made a decision not to put my baby in the Nursery here at Bedford because I felt she would be better off with my sister. It would be a more normal situation. My sister agreed to take her. Now, I don't even get to see my daughter. I thought I would have regular contact with her. True, my daughter lives upstate and it's a long drive, but I thought I would get to see her. I know she's bonded with me and now she can't come but every couple of months. After I let my anger out, I began to listen. People in the group helped me see that I made a choice about where it would be best for my baby to be. And I don't regret it. My sister just can't drive down here much. I have to accept that and I am grateful that she took my baby days after she was born and is taking care of her. Then I listened to the other mother who had just sent her baby home. She made me realize that my baby wasn't bonded with me, she's bonded with my sister; she can't know me because she's only 5 months old and I've only seen her a few times. I need her but she really doesn't need me right now. It's hard to accept all this, but it's what's real. When I called my sister on the phone, instead of attacking her with my anger and frustration, I just broke down and cried and she cried and we shared our feelings about how hard it is. It's hard but this group helped me to let go and to accept being a parent from a distance. I feel more at peace.

ASSESSMENT

How does one assess the impact of such an intense three-month process? While the group was meeting, it helped most of the participants–including me and my co-facilitator–in their own emotional growth and in their relationships with their children. However, when the group was over, women said there was an abrupt loss. The group provided enormous emotional support and suddenly it was missing. Fortunately, usually a network of support grew during the group. If women lived on the same unit, they were especially able to continue connecting about their children. Even if they lived on separate units, frequently the three months provided enough of a basis that they continued to support one another whenever they met. However, the support and hope that was reinforced during the group was difficult to sustain without it.

A group experience such as Parenting From a Distance is most effective in a prison when there are other ways for women to grow within themselves and to interact with their children. In this prison they have other programs which help women cope with emotional issues—such as family violence or AIDS, the ability to improve their capacity to become self-supporting or to grow intellectually which the vocational or academic programs can encourage, different programs in the Children's Center such as the program in which mothers work at learning how to negotiate the system of foster care and family court laws or in working with the teachers or therapists through the Children's Advocacy Program.

Unfortunately, in this period of budget cuts and cries to "stop coddling prisoners," options for women's growth within the prison are being eroded. For example, the GED program, once available five days a week is now only two evenings each week; and college was entirely eliminated throughout the state prison system in June of 1995 when all public funding for higher education in prisons was eliminated. Women in the prison have been trying to make up for the losses through creating new approaches. For example, they have been working with the prison administration and individuals and colleges from the community to create a full college program based on private funding and it was prepared to open in the spring of 1997.

We are not in a position to evaluate the long-term impact of such a group on a woman's ability to parent her children when she goes home. Clearly, when issues of economic self-sufficiency, relationships with men, access to drugs and alcohol, lack of day care, housing, and poverty all become pressing, a group that solely focuses on emotional interaction will need to be in a context of concrete support in order to be most effective.

IN THE ROLE OF FACILITATORS: PEER OR PROFESSIONAL THERAPIST

The group is facilitated by peers, not a professional therapist. What issues does this raise? The participants frequently comment that they liked having peers as facilitators, rather than "outsiders." When everyone in the group is a prisoner, including the facilitators, this increases the feeling of autonomy and self-reliance which the prison environment of control and infantilization erodes. Additionally, a facilitator who shares similar personal experiences and problems as the participants is a role model. Participants have often commented on this and have said that it increases their own self-esteem and hope for themselves.

If a professional therapist were to lead such a group, it would be important for the person to have the goal of unleashing the potential of each participant and the group itself to take on the work. The group process works best when peers are helping each other through sharing experience, asking one another questions, and problem-solving. Through the process, they learn how to help one another in new ways.

A full review of the issues raised by having peers as facilitators is beyond the scope of this article. The peer process brings with it the strengths of identification, empathy, moral stance and empowerment. However, it raises issues of boundaries, over-identification, and neutrality. In the prison, we live with one another and know many details about each others' lives. This is true not just for facilitators but for the participants in the group as well. What is the impact of this on building trust and a safe context? What is the impact of having friends or people with whom we have a negative history in the group? When one of us who facilitates the group shares her own experience, how does this undercut the necessary distance that promotes the likelihood for a participant to define her own understandings and course?

There are elements within the model which we developed that draw on traditional therapy, yet it is clearly not the same. Throughout the prison, peer counselors in other programs such as the AIDS Counseling and Education and Family Violence programs struggle with these and related issues in their practice.

We draw on the weekly supervision of a licensed social worker who is also a professor of social work to give us perspective as we chart a new course. We draw on our own educational backgrounds–the two of us who created the program have Master's degrees–and our many years of experience in working with women in different prison programs.

REFLECTIONS

Often when I think about the program, I reflect on how far I have moved from approaching problems from the point of view of structural analysis. The statistics appearing in the beginning of this article suggest that many of the factors underlying the women's difficulties in fulfilling their dreams as mothers as well as underlying their incarceration were rooted in the social, economic and political realities of our society. I have wondered whether our process focuses too much on individual patterns and solutions rather than responding to what are at root social problems with social solutions. How do we not "privatize psychic damage" (Lykes, Brabeck, Ferns and Radan, 1993)? How do we focus on an individual's history and yet not place full responsibility for the mistakes and failures on that person, thereby increasing her own guilt? Yet if we define problems as overwhelmingly rooted in the social structure, how can we avoid leaving people feeling passive and unable to change their lives? How can we combine a process of both introspection and social analysis and the relationship between them? These are questions which I continue to struggle with within myself, among friends in prison and in carrying out the program, and they will undoubtedly affect the evolution of Parenting From a Distance as a program over time.

In the meantime, I continue to find the process of looking inward in a collective process useful and rewarding. It helps overcome the powerlessness of prison, allows women to grow stronger and more effectively to meet their children's needs. From my experience, prison can be a time when women have an opportunity to try to redirect their lives. In fact, most women who are here for any length of time very much want to figure out what happened to them and how they can do things differently. The most important resource we have is ourselves, as individuals and collectively. The Parenting From a Distance Program tries to maximize the capacity of each woman and the cooperative effort among us to grow ourselves and to parent as best as we can from the distance of prison.

AUTHOR NOTE

The author wishes to acknowledge Rozann Greco with whom she developed the Parenting From a Distance Program and had the pleasure of co-facilitating for a year and a half. And she wants to thank Rozlyn Smith with whom she now co-facilitates and shares the day-to-day work and journey of the group. Thank you to Cay Caicedo for her professional weekly supervision, to Thea Jackson for her dialogue about the content of the program and her ongoing support for its work, and to Lucia Scott for providing a model for us through her program Choices and Changes. Thank you to Suzanne Kessler, Michelle Fine and Judy Clark for their input about the content of the article itself; to Precious Bedell for many years of dialogue; and to Sister Elaine Roulet, the Director of the Children's Center, both for her belief in the importance and possibility of our role as mothers from prison and for her support of us as inmates to create and facilitate such a program as Parenting From a Distance. Finally, the author's great appreciation to all of the women who were in Parenting From a Distance over the past three years and whose experiences and voices made possible the wisdom that we have all gained as well as this article.

REFERENCES

Baunach, P. (1988). *Mothers in prison.* New Brunswick, NJ: Transaction.

Edelman, H. (1994). *Motherless daughters: The legacy of loss.* New York: Addison-Wesley.

Gamer, E., & Gamer, C. (1983). *There is no solitary confinement—A look at the impact of incarceration upon the family.* Paper presented at Pine Hill College, MA.

Hannah-Moffat, K. (1995). Women-centered prisons. *The Prison Journal, 75,* 135-163.

Herman, J. L. (1992). *Trauma and recovery.* New York: Basic Books.

Hole, J., & Levine, E. (1971). *Rebirth of feminism.* New York: Quadrangle Books.

Jackson, R. (1994). *Mothers who leave: Behind the myth of women without their children.* London, England: Harper Collins.

Lord, E. (1995). Prison superintendent's perspective. *The Prison Journal, 75,* 257-269.

Lykes, M. B., Brabeck, M. M., Ferns, T., & Radan, A. (1993). Human rights and mental health among Latin American women in situations of state sponsored violence. *Psychology of Women Quarterly, 17,* 525-544.

Miller, A. (1981). *The drama of the gifted child.* New York: Basic Books.

New York State Department of Correctional Services. (1992). *Female cluster program services action plan.*

New York State Department of Correctional Services. (1995). *Women under custody.*

Yalom, I. (1975). *The theory and practice of group psychotherapy.* New York: Basic Books.

Girls in Jail

Verna J. Tuesday

SUMMARY. This article will explore the process of introducing a weekly all-girls group inside a juvenile detention facility. It presents the facilitators' experiences of utilizing feminist topics and discussion, primarily focusing on and challenging the young women on internalized sexism and in the process, confronting their own. Successes and failures will be described and some of the effects of running the group on the facilitators will be shared. The girls' own voices are included. *[Article copies available for a fee from The Haworth Document Delivery Service: 1-800-342-9678. E-mail address: getinfo@haworth.com]*

A literature review suggests that sexism and internalized sexism may affect young women involved in delinquency behaviors. One study that examines the effect of changing gender roles on female delinquency argues that the concept of "role strain" offers a promising explanation of current patterns of adolescent female crime (Berger, 1989). The nature of girls' crime has changed from status offenses and "sexual misconduct" to more serious and violent offenses (Calhoun, Jurgens, & Chen, 1993). The relationship between girls' victimization and girls' crime has been systematically ignored (Chesney, 1989).

Verna J. Tuesday, MC, NCC, is a counselor in private practice in Eugene, OR. Her business, Women's Counseling Services, provides individual, couple and group counseling and consultation and training to professionals and groups.

The author would like to thank J. Elaine Walters, Mary Ann Klausner, and Karen Howell for their feedback and editorial suggestions.

Address correspondence to: Verna J. Tuesday, Women's Counseling Services, 132 East Broadway, Suite 801, Eugene, OR 97401 or (Wmscounser@aol.com).

[Haworth co-indexing entry note]: "Girls in Jail." Tuesday, Verna J. Co-published simultaneously in *Women & Therapy* (The Haworth Press, Inc.) Vol. 21, No. 1, 1998, pp. 127-139; and: *Breaking the Rules: Women in Prison and Feminist Therapy* (ed: Judy Harden, and Marcia Hill) The Haworth Press, Inc., 1998, pp. 127-139; and: *Breaking the Rules: Women in Prison and Feminist Therapy* (ed: Judy Harden, and Marcia Hill) The Harrington Park Press, an imprint of The Haworth Press, Inc., 1998, pp. 127-139. Single or multiple copies of this article are available for a fee from The Haworth Document Delivery Service [1-800-342-9678, 9:00 a.m. - 5:00 p.m. (EST). E-mail address: getinfo@haworth.com].

Recently, the subject of girls in juvenile justice has received national attention in a collaborative effort between Girls Incorporated (1996) and the Office of Juvenile Justice and Delinquency Prevention (OJJDP). They conclude that: "Girls in juvenile justice need effective programs that do not perpetuate inequities based on gender, race, class, sexual orientation and other personal and cultural factors." The challenge for feminists and clinicians is to address the needs of this overlooked population.

HOW OUR GROUP STARTED

As a counselor working with adult battered women for 10 years, I heard women say many times that they wished they had received information about domestic violence when they were younger. I wanted to educate young women about domestic violence before they ended up in a shelter. Although the local battered women's shelter was doing outreach and education in high school classrooms, I wondered about the young women who were not in school, who were locked up in detention facilities or training schools. How were they going to get the information that may save their lives? Did they have access to services that addressed their abuse histories from a feminist perspective?

I learned that the girls in our county detention were not getting services specifically targeted for young women, and certainly no services that offer to help young women understand their life experiences in a feminist context. My colleague, J. Elaine Walters, had experience running support groups for "at risk" teens in the schools. I had experience facilitating groups for adult abuse survivors. Together we decided to approach the local detention facility with an idea to provide a group for young women utilizing a feminist model, and offer some training for staff on abuse and gender issues affecting young women.

We wrote a proposal for a weekly group for girls, covering topics such as domestic violence, sexual assault, sexual abuse and recovery, self-harm, self-esteem issues, and gender conditioning. We suggested in the proposal that the group be voluntary, and the decision to participate be left to each individual girl. We also insisted on complete confidentiality. In order to create the safest atmosphere we could, we did not want to share with detention staff what the girls were saying in group.

Our proposal was accepted. The supervisor arranged for us to have about an hour and a half with the girls during a shift change time that they normally would be in their rooms. Faced with a choice between staying in their rooms and checking out this new group, we got our first group of curious girls.

About Us

I am a professionally trained feminist counselor. Elaine is a feminist activist and a reevaluation counselor. It is a great combination. Elaine and I have very different styles and personalities and come from different class backgrounds. Recognizing these differences, we work on making them a strength in our relationship and our co-facilitation of the group.

Elaine and I have worked on our own relationship as friends and colleagues for many years, and have explored our own internalized sexism with each other. Elaine has more experience working with young people in a variety of settings. She also is a parent to two teenagers. I, on the other hand, was scared. I knew that teens are not bound by any adult notions of politeness or civility. Nor, as delinquents, would they have any compulsion toward compliance. I imagined a group of street-hardened thugs, who would refuse to speak with us, insult us, make fun of our topics, and see through our flimsy adult masks of supposed confidence and professionalism. Being briefed on security in the detention facility only increased my fears–what if we were attacked?

Almost none of my imagined fears were realized. The girls were curious, willing to give us a chance and were most forgiving of our mistakes and blunders. At first we thought they came to the group to get out of going to their rooms. It was some time before we realized that they enjoyed the group, and especially enjoyed the time together, away from the boys.

About the Girls

The ratio of girls to boys is about 1:5 in our detention facility. The girls share a common area, meals, groups and all daily activities with the boys. They sleep in a separate wing unless there is an overflow that necessitates a boy living in their wing.

The girls have an interesting mix of urban and rural backgrounds that present different challenges and different levels of sophistication in the group. The girls range in age from 12 to 17 years. Most report problems with drugs and/or alcohol. The girls do not talk openly about gang activity, although it is alluded to. Some of the local gangs are white supremacy groups. Our groups almost always include girls from different ethnic backgrounds. Racism and its subtle and not so subtle manifestations are a constant issue in the group. The girls seem accepting of each other on a personal level, but make generalized statements about ethnic groups other than their own.

We do not spend time in group discussing what crimes they have committed, but it appears that many are there for assaulting another girl. Several have discussed involvement in prostitution and pimping, stealing and drug offenses. All are sexually active and all report multiple partners. Some girls report engaging in intercourse before menstruation occurred (ages 8, 9, and 10). Most of the girls discuss being repeatedly sexually abused as children, and being raped as young women.

WHAT WE DO

We start the group by introducing ourselves to any new members and explaining the guidelines of the group. We have kept the guidelines as simple and concrete as possible. At the beginning, we described our own motivations for starting the group. Now we ask one of the other girls to explain the guidelines and what the group is about. Although they often start by saying they "don't know," they then describe the group in a poignant and simple fashion and reveal to the newcomer (and to us) what meaning the group has for them. We always emphasize our policy of confidentiality, that we are not part of detention staff and that we keep no files on them and do not report what they say to the staff. We also insist that the girls treat each other with complete respect at all times. This includes not "trashing" other women or talking about girls who are not present.

First Effects

The first effect we noticed after a few weeks is that the existence of the group challenged the invisibility of the girls in detention. In many ways the girls had been "going along" with the boys, trying to blend in and not be seen as different. The group changed that. Now they were separated, and getting special attention. This raised everyone's cognizance that the girls might have needs that were different from the boys, including the girls' own self-awareness. The girls got the expected complaint from the boys, "Where is the boys' group?" We resisted commenting that the whole world is a boys' group. The girls dismissed the boys' curiosity and questions about what happens in the group, and frankly expressed their desire to have something of their own, a place to talk about "girl stuff."

As time went on, they voiced their observations and personal experiences about being treated differently than boys. We quickly learned that utilizing the technical language of feminism and sexism resulted in instant glazed-over eyes, so we resisted offering our guidance and insight and decided to listen. The girls discussed an array of subjects from the guys making fun of their breasts when they ran, to the double standards about sex. They shared their experiences with each other of surviving abusive relationships, and sometimes choosing to remain in them.

About the detention facility itself, they shared their frustration in losing all the "majority rules" decisions to the boys in the milieu setting of detention. This resulted in a daily atmosphere saturated with male domination, not unlike their experiences on the street. The street and drug culture is predominately shaped by men and the girls describe adapting accordingly. They exchanged information with each other about ways to handle sexual harassment and unwanted physical contact in the facility from other boys and even problem-solved confronting a male staff member about his inappropriate comments.

If we agree that one of the consequences of sexism is to silence women and deny their experience, then listening to these young women's stories and experiences is in direct contradiction to that. Young people are frequently silenced in American culture. The healing and transformative power of listening respectfully to them cannot be underestimated.

Mothers

Almost all the girls talk about mothers who are addicted to drugs, have criminal histories, have gone from one abusive man to another, have not protected them, have chosen men over their children's safety, and have not believed them when they told about their own sexual abuse. One is struck by the overwhelming impact of women's betrayal to their girl children and the graphic examples of helplessness these mothers present to their daughters in the face of male terrorism in their lives. Yet these girls are fiercely attached to their mothers, believing in them, forgiving them, hoping for a reunion and brighter life together in the future. Several girls commented more than once that if their mother ever died, they would see no reason to go on living themselves. How do mothers sustain such a powerful lifeline to their girl children in the face of overwhelming betrayal and violence?

One girl who had fled her abusive household for the streets, took her younger siblings with her when her mother was not able to leave her abusive partner. She protected them because her mother could not. She is angry at her mother's failure to protect her, but more powerful by far is her longing for a reunion with her mom and her siblings. Years later, she is still waiting for her mom to choose them over her abusive partner.

Fathers

Noticeably little is mentioned about the girls' fathers. References to fathers or step-fathers are usually about the abuse they perpetrated on the girls and/or their mothers. Birth fathers are in jail, lost to drug addiction or dead. Sometimes the girls will have acceptable step-fathers or adoptive fathers, but this is rare. A few are bitter and angry about this absence but most seem unconcerned. When asked, few can identify an adult male who is a healthy role model to them. In contrast to the tenacity in which they fight to regain their connection to their mothers, the broken bonds with their fathers are met with shrugs and resignation.

Girls and Violence

Rarely do any of the girls come from stable homes to the detention facility. Most are picked up on the streets after an assault, a robbery or car theft, not usually sober or clean and not always in the company of creatures less dangerous than the home environment they were escaping. When homes are not safe, the safety of the street is the alternative. The street community has its own code of honor and its own rules by which the girls fight to stay embraced. The rules require the girls to be hard and unforgiving with each other, and violent to protect their status on the street and their street "family." Often their physical battles with each other are over men. An interesting question we ask in group when presented with this information is: "How many of you have lost a friendship with another girl over a guy?" All of them raise their hands. Then we ask how many of them are still with that same guy. The answer is always, none. We try to raise awareness of how hard it is to stay loyal to each other as women, with mixed results.

It is difficult to hear about the violence the girls perpetrate on each other. The level of betrayal and lack of feeling for other girls has been horrifying at times. Sometimes we are able to resolve disputes that arise among them in the group, always emphasizing that they have to rely on each other as women for support and it is worth the struggle to resolve things peacefully. At times they are able to apologize, recognize and acknowledge their mistakes or see how a particularly emotional topic could have led to a disruption. Other times they remain hardened to each other and we leave those groups with heavy hearts.

Girls and Sex

Being good at sex, liking sex and having a lot of sex are all sources of prestige with the boys, but in the company of just girls, the girls' confusion about sex is evident. Having too many (or too little) sexual experiences can result in judgment from other girls in the group, to the point that some remain silent for fear of censure from their peers. How many sexual partners are too many is quite variable, and dependent on the peer consensus of that particular group on that particular day. It is interesting that the older girls are quick to judge the younger girls for engaging in behaviors that are similar to their own.

The girls freely admit to cheating on their boyfriends and with each other's boyfriends. As expected, internalized sexism ensures that the anger about this is always directed at the female former-friend. Sex with older men is also prestigious and many do not date males their own age, although they will admit to attractions to other boys in detention. Girls with boyfriends "on the outside" engage in flirtations and romances with boys in detention to pass the time more pleasantly. One topic that always bonds the girls is discussing the boys in detention. We struggle to keep their attention when a particularly attractive male walks by the windowed area of the group. We continuously comment on the power that they give to these boys, to allow them to disrupt and distract them from their own focus and process.

The girls are open about their extremely varied sexual practices and experimentation. As the girls brag about their sexual prowess, we are often struck by the sexual objectification and victimization to which these girls are subjected. They derive a sense of power from being sexual and act as if they are in charge of these sexual encounters, but their stories reveal otherwise. Sex is always a topic they are excited to discuss and often leads into other issues.

Rarely do the girls feel the safety with one another to discuss any encounters that are not heterosexual. In one group that was very small, all the girls revealed experimentation with same sex attraction and identified themselves as bisexual. I believe it was the particular girls' self-confidence in identifying themselves as bisexual that allowed them to discuss sexual orientation in such detail. We are vigilant in interrupting homophobic remarks and sharing accurate information about homosexuality in order to make the group safe for every girl to discuss her sexual experiences.

WHAT WE ARE LEARNING

As we facilitate the group, Elaine and I are learning and changing. Every group presents a personal challenge or triggers our own memories of adolescence. The class differences between us, our individual experiences as teens, and our varying theoretical orientations always make for a lively discussion, and we learn from each other as well.

Our mistakes are teaching us to be more flexible. When we first presented information on stereotypical roles for men and women as a lead into a discussion about gender conditioning, we were startled that an exercise that worked so well with youth in high schools backfired with girls in detention. The girls actually thought we were advocating for traditional female role-playing. We have since revised it better to reflect their experiences.

We recognize that these are young women who do not fit into stereotypical images of femininity. They are aggressive, they are angry, they get in trouble, they run away, they have sex, use drugs, rob, cheat, and steal. They do not see themselves as conforming to any of society's expectations of female behavior. This is juxtaposed against their traditional and conservative views of marriage and family. It is an interesting contradiction that challenges and puzzles us.

These girls do not have the same choices or options as their non-delinquent counterparts. The choices they have for male companions due to their lifestyle on the streets and the stigma of delinquency, often lead them farther down the road of criminality and drug use. Yet the girls cling to the traditional housewife fantasy as a lifeline, exclaiming with pride that they will stay home and clean and cook for their husbands as their goal in life. These young women are already defying stereotypes in terms of their behavior. Perhaps the fierce attachment to a traditional female role is an attempt to still fit into society's ideal of femininity.

We struggle with how we can harness that rebellious energy into a productive (feminist) future in this sexist world. If ever there was a group that was ripe to embrace feminism, we believe this is it. We have yet to discover how to make that happen.

How Our Own Internalized Sexism Gets in Our Way

It is always difficult to admit one's mistakes. As a clinician and as a feminist, it is difficult to announce them to your colleagues in an article, but I do so with the hope that the reader can learn from them as I have. Fortunately, Elaine and I have a deep understanding of the subtle workings of internalized sexism, which helps us to put our mistakes in a context that assists our comprehension of our own dynamics and those of the group.

It is not uncommon for us to walk away from the group carrying the feelings of helplessness, wanting to give up, feeling ineffective. The task of combating sexism and internalized sexism is daunting. Is anything we are doing or saying making any difference? How are these young women going to overcome the enormous barriers to productive living? We inevitably recognize our own struggles against sexism and our cynicism and weariness. Are we transmitting these to the girls? Are we unconsciously reinforcing their own sense of helplessness?

Another way we saw the subtle workings of internalized sexism was noticing that we were liking girls who disliked the same girls we do (the ones that are difficult in group). Instead of combating the divisiveness, we were secretly siding against the girls who did not conform to our expectations of the group. In what ways are we subtly reinforcing notions of conformity in our unconscious signals of acceptance or rejection?

When a group would get disruptive, we would try various ways to regain their attention and to get back on track. Sometimes we would fail. After one such failure, Elaine and I recognized that by tolerating the level of disrespect to ourselves, we were modeling our own lack of self-esteem and our conditioning as women raised in a patriarchy to accept this level of disrespect as normal. With this revelation, we marched into next week's group with an ultimatum. They would behave respectfully to us, as respectfully as we treated them, or we would no longer do the group. By not demanding the respect we deserve, we were succumbing to our own internalized belief that we were not deserving.

The girls agreed that the level of disruption and disrespect was distressing to them as well. As we went around the group, each girl contributed her input into how to shape the structure of the group to meet everyone's needs. The final product allowed time for blowing off steam as well as structure to allow them to share without interruption. Once again, we were reminded that listening is valued more highly than any information we may have to offer.

Other Mistakes

Elaine and I preface our explanation of the respect guideline in group by the example that adults often do not treat young people with respect (adultism) which leads to young people internalizing this and disrespecting each other. Imagine our surprise when we found ourselves lapsing into adultist behaviors in the group: lecturing, trying to protect them, being uncomfortable with their silliness and their inability to stay as focused and quiet as adults, telling them in all sorts of ways that *we know better.* It was a humbling realization that we had so much more work to do in this area.

The girls utilize ageism against each other as a ferociously effective weapon. Any girl's feelings, ideas or beliefs can be instantly discounted by a remark from an older girl about her age, lack of experience, or level of maturity. It has created some of the most intense dialogue and defensiveness in the group. Younger girls, especially if there is only one, are ostracized by the other girls and their attention getting behaviors are resented and not understood by the older girls. It is one of the few avenues of power they have access to, and they wield it with a vengeance against each other.

WHAT THE GIRLS SAY

To contribute to this article, one group of six girls was asked a series of questions Elaine and I had prepared. Their condensed responses follow in their own voices.

What is good about being locked up?

I stopped drinking; you are taught respect; you get the help you need; you are learning structure; you have to look at reality–not on drugs; learning self-discipline; I think about things I have done; I feel safe.

What is hard?

No smoking; not able to see family, friends; no freedom; hate room, cell; have to ask to go to the bathroom, sometimes I wait for an hour; can't see out the window; claustrophobic; clothes are limited; staff uses their authority against us; sharing space with strangers; see the same people every day; can't get space when you need it.

What is good with sharing space with the boys?

Flirting; girls get on each other's nerves; some boys are easier to get along with than girls; boys become our "little friends."

What is hard?

Boys think they are hard, act like they are "all that"; they are mean, disrespectful to us; they embarrass and humiliate us sometimes; the girls change in front of the guys, act cold; the competition for the boys' attention with other girls; girls who switch their loyalty to the guys.

What do you never want to hear again?

That I'm never going to change–if you don't believe in me, why should I believe in myself?; adults who look down on us; being called a loser; don't hang out with her, she'll get you in trouble; you're out of control; there is something wrong with you.

What do you want others to know about you?

I'm not a ruthless person, just have problems in my life and I took the wrong way; I'm not out to hurt you, I have a lot of problems, I need to deal with them; I have a lot of problems, I dealt with them in the wrong way; I'm learning; I have a big heart, I'm intelligent, I'm going to make something of my life.

What kinds of women end up in prison?

Any kind of woman; my mother.

How are they different from you?

They aren't; maybe more problems, drugs; boyfriends use women to commit the crime and they get arrested; they do it for a hit of dope or to avoid abuse.

What else do you want people to know?

Groups for just girls will help other girls in detention.

It is tempting to summarize and analyze their remarks, but I will leave them to stand alone and speak for themselves.

Topics that Have Been Most Successful

One of the most successful group topics started with a question: what groups do you belong to? It continued by exploring times when they had been excluded from a group, what that felt like, and ways they have excluded others. Almost every girl's memory came from early childhood and led to some insight into her own judgment and rejection of other girls.

A discussion topic about lying revealed when girls lied because they needed to for their own survival, when it became a habit, and stories about when they were not believed when they told the truth. Levels of deception between themselves and adults, particularly parents, were disclosed. We encouraged them to imagine a time when it would be safe to always tell the truth, and what that would be like for them.

A very emotional topic occurred around Mother's Day. The girls were asked a series of questions about the relationship with their mothers, how they thought they were similar and different from them, and their grief about the loss of that connection. A tearful association was made between that loss and their current behaviors.

We are finding that moving away from specific structured topics to sharing personal experiences and listening more closely has improved the level of attentiveness of the girls, created a deeper level of sharing and increased our sense of effectiveness.

WHAT WE HOPE TO ACCOMPLISH

What happens when girls get to separate from boys and have their own time and space? Being together and being separate from the boys is in itself a healing and a revolutionary act (Frye, 1983). Focusing only on their ability to be supportive of each other contradicts the internalized sexism. Working through conflicts and getting them to see they are on the same side, constitutes the majority of what we accomplish. We have a theory that we work on constantly with the girls and with ourselves: If women could stand together, no one could oppress us.

Although we are sharing information about abuse issues, coping skills, healthy relationships and other relevant topics, I believe the biggest impact the group offers is the separation and the space to be supported as women and to learn to support each other. Having strong feminist women as models is perhaps just as important. How we behave and respond to these young women's problems, challenges and questions impacts them more than any lecture.

Factors that make the group successful are that it is voluntary, that confidentiality includes our not sharing disclosures with detention staff, and that the group is not scheduled at the same time as a fun activity.

The group's staying power may indicate its level of effectiveness. We started in April 1995 and are still going strong. We have seen some administrative changes since our group started. The female probation officers have started a group for young women on probation, and there has been a revision of the general intake form to include questions about abuse histories. I think general awareness of young women's issues has been raised throughout the juvenile department.

CONCLUSION

By facilitating this group, I have learned more about my own experience growing up female, the impact of sexism and internalized sexism, and the ways and techniques of utilizing education and therapy to transmit transformative information than in all of my experiences as a clinician and an activist combined.

Working with young women in detention is challenging and breathtaking. The times you do break through and connect with even one young woman motivates you to return. I can only exhort feminists and clinicians in the reading audience to challenge themselves to do this work. You will be presented with the opportunity to help transform the next generation of women, but the biggest risk and perhaps the greatest challenge will be in the transformation of yourself.

REFERENCES

Berger, R. (1989). Female delinquency in the emancipation era: A review of the literature. *Sex Roles, 21(5-6),* 375-399.

Calhoun, G., Jurgens, J., and Chen, F. (1993). The neophyte female delinquent: A review of the literature. *Adolescence, 28(110),* 461-471.

Chesney, L. (1989). Girls' crime and woman's place: Toward a feminist model of female delinquency. *Crime and Delinquency, 35(1),* 5-29.

Frye, M. (1983). *The politics of reality: Essays in feminist theory.* Freedom, CA: The Crossing Press.

Girls Incorporated. (1996, Summer). Prevention and parity: Creating solutions for girls in juvenile justice. *Girls Ink,* pp. 1-5.

Women in Prison:
Approaches in the Treatment
of Our Most Invisible Population

Stephanie S. Covington

SUMMARY. The issues and needs of addicted women are for the most part invisible in the criminal justice system. Historically, treatment, research and recovery have been based on men's lives, often neglecting women's experience. While statistics indicate that for women there is a high correlation between drug abuse and incarceration and parole/probation violations, a comprehensive continuum of care is missing. This article presents a relational model of treatment which incorporates the multiple issues in women's recovery and is based on the integration of three theoretical perspectives–addiction, trauma and women's psychological development. The strengths and limitations of Twelve Step programs for women are also discussed. *[Article copies available for a fee from The Haworth Document Delivery Service: 1-800-342-9678. E-mail address: getinfo@haworth.com]*

Stephanie S. Covington, PhD, LCSW, has an independent psychotherapy practice in La Jolla, CA, where she is Co-Director of the Institute for Relational Development. She has written and presented extensively on the issues of addiction, sexuality, and relationship in women's lives and her consulting work includes the Betty Ford Treatment Center, the National Women's Resource Center, and the National Institute of Corrections.

Address correspondence to: Dr. Stephanie S. Covington, 7946 Ivanhoe Avenue, Suite 201B, La Jolla, CA 92037.

[Haworth co-indexing entry note]: "Women in Prison: Approaches in the Treatment of Our Most Invisible Population." Covington, Stephanie S. Co-published simultaneously in *Women & Therapy* (The Haworth Press, Inc.) Vol. 21, No. 1, 1998, pp. 141-155; and: *Breaking the Rules: Women in Prison and Feminist Therapy* (ed: Judy Harden, and Marcia Hill) The Haworth Press, Inc., 1998, pp. 141-155; and: *Breaking the Rules: Women in Prison and Feminist Therapy* (ed: Judy Harden, and Marcia Hill) The Harrington Park Press, an imprint of The Haworth Press, Inc., 1998, pp. 141-155. Single or multiple copies of this article are available for a fee from The Haworth Document Delivery Service [1-800-342-9678, 9:00 a.m. - 5:00 p.m. (EST). E-mail address: getinfo@haworth.com].

141

OVERVIEW

Some of the most neglected, misunderstood and unseen women in our society are those in our jails, prisons and community correctional facilities. While women's rate of incarceration has increased dramatically, tripling in the last decade, prisons have not kept pace with the growth of the number of women in prison; nor has the criminal justice system been redesigned to meet women's needs, which are often quite different from the needs of men.

There are many reasons for the growing numbers of women in the criminal justice system, but the primary one is the increase in drug-related convictions and the advent of mandatory sentences for these offenses. According to the Federal Bureau of Prisons, over 60% of the women in their custody are serving sentences for drug offenses. For many states the rate is even higher for alcohol and drug-related crimes.

In spite of this, the issues of addicted women are, for the most part, invisible in the criminal justice system. Historically, treatment, research and recovery have been based on the male experience, often neglecting women's needs. While this neglect has a serious impact on women and treatment programs in the free world, the problem is magnified for women in the criminal justice population.

Statistics indicate that for women there is a high correlation between drug abuse and incarceration and parole/probation violations, and yet our society provides no comprehensive continuum of care for these women. This paper will discuss a relational model of treatment that incorporates the multiple issues involved in women's recovery. Three theoretical perspectives–addiction, trauma, and women's psychological development–are interwoven to provide the foundation for a model based on the concept of a woman's journey to recovery. This model can be adapted for both the prison population and community-based programs.

In summation, the objectives of this paper are:

1. To increase awareness of women's lives in the criminal justice system.
2. To discuss a comprehensive and integrated treatment model (theory of addiction, theory of trauma, theory of women's psychological development).
3. To examine the four areas that women report as being both most challenging, and their major triggers to relapse: self, relationships, sexuality, and spirituality.
4. To discuss Twelve Step programs for women.

Rising Numbers of Women in the Criminal Justice System

Since 1980, the number of women in United States prisons has tripled. During this time, the rate of incarceration for women has surpassed the male rate during every year but one; and in 1996, the number of women imprisoned nationally was 69,028 (LeBlanc, 1996).

The war on drugs has inadvertently become a war on women, clearly contributing to the explosive increase in the number of women who are incarcerated. The 1986 mandatory drug sentencing laws, with their "get tough on crime" philosophy specifying that anyone caught with possession of a drug should automatically be sentenced, were designed to rid society of drug dealers and major players in the illegal drug trade. Unfortunately, this law backfired in the case of women. The assumption that this law was only sending dangerous males to prison was a false one. Between 1986 and 1991, the number of women in state prisons for drug offenses increased by 433%, compared to a 283% increase for men (LeBlanc, 1996). Currently, 35.9% of women serving time for drug offenses were charged solely with "possession." "Instead of a policy of last resort, imprisonment has become the first-order response for a wide range of non-violent and petty offenses and women have been disproportionately swept up in this trend" (Bloom, Chesney-Lind, & Owen, 1994, p. 2).

To keep up with the high costs of incarceration—it takes $50,000 per cell to build a new prison and $20,000 per person per year to house offenders— many states have cut vitally needed social service, educational, and drug/ alcohol programs (Raspberry, 1991). Since there is a high rate of recidivism among women who are convicted for possession or use of drugs, curtailing drug and alcohol recovery programs has proven to be an expensive and illogical move.

One of the questions we must ask ourselves when faced with the issues surrounding the growing number of women in the criminal justice system is whether or not there is always a need for incarceration. In a private conversation, a warden at one of the largest women's prisons in the U.S. stated that 75% of the women in her custodial care would be better treated in the community (personal communication, May 1995). Clearly, this would be a more humane and economical solution to the overcrowding of our prisons by women who have committed nonviolent, petty offenses.

Profile of Women in the Criminal Justice System

Female prison populations differ from their male counterparts in several significant ways. First of all, they are less likely to have committed a violent offense and more likely to have been convicted of a crime involving alcohol, other drugs or property. It is important to point out that many property crimes are economically driven, often motivated by the abuse/addiction of alcohol and other drugs and/or poverty (Chesney-Lind & Bloom, 1997; Watterson, 1996). A 1994 study done in California showed that 71.9% of women had been convicted on a drug or property charge versus 49.7% of men. Men also commit nearly twice the violent crimes that women do (Bloom, Chesney-Lind, & Owen, 1994). These statistics are consistent with national trends (LeBlanc, 1996). Women are significantly less violent than their male counterparts, and show more responsiveness to prison programs, although they have less opportunity to participate in them than male prisoners do. While men often deal with their anxiety by working their bodies constantly, women tend to fear the central yard, working out their anxieties with too much sleep, food and prescription pills (LeBlanc, 1996).

Most female prisoners are poor, undereducated, unskilled, single mothers, and a disproportionate number of them are women of color. In a study of California prisons, over half of the women were African American (35%) and Hispanic (16.6%). One-third were Caucasian and the remaining 13% were made up of other racial groups. Of those who had been employed before incarceration, many were on the lower rungs of the economic ladder, with only 37% working at a legitimate job. Twenty-two percent were on some kind of public support, 16% made money from drug dealing and 15% were involved in prostitution, shoplifting or other illegal activities (Bloom, Chesney-Lind, & Owen, 1994). One of the things that these statistics clearly show is that there are issues of race and class involved in the criminal justice system. For example, there has been a law in the state of Minnesota (recently held unconstitutional) that says first-time users of crack cocaine will receive mandatory four-year sentences, but first-time users of cocaine in its powdered form will receive only probation. Since 92% of those arrested on charges for possession of crack in 1988 were African Americans and 85% of those arrested for possession of powdered cocaine were Caucasian, the law is clearly racist (Raspberry, 1991). When racial and economic factors drive the issue of who will be imprisoned, where is the "justice" in the criminal justice system (Belknap, 1996)?

One major health concern in prisons is AIDS. In a study done with 400 female volunteers in a Massachusetts prison, 35% of the women tested were HIV positive, compared with 13% of the men. In one California prison, women who tested positive were placed in a segregated AIDS unit, whether they showed signs of the disease or not (Salholz & Wright, 1990).

Two-thirds of incarcerated women have children under the age of 18

(Smith, 1991). Many feel enormous guilt about being absent from their children's lives and worry about whether they will still have custody of their children when they get out (Bloom & Steinhart, 1993). These and other concerns, including unresolved issues of physical and sexual abuse, lead female inmates to make requests for psychological counseling that far exceed those made by men. Penal experts agree that women would benefit from additional services (Salholz & Wright, 1990).

Many incarcerated women either abuse or are addicted to alcohol and/ or other drugs. In a study done in the Las Colinas Detention Facility in California, 37% of the women said that alcohol was their drug of choice, 21% said heroin, 24% crystal meth, and 18% cocaine (Covington, 1991c). Unfortunately, drugs are readily available in prisons, usually brought in and sold by prison guards (Salholz & Wright, 1990).

Along with their history of alcohol/drug use, many women in prison also have a history of physical and sexual abuse. In California prisons, nearly 80% have experienced some form of abuse. Twenty-nine percent report being physically abused as children, and 60% as adults, usually by their partners. Thirty-one percent experienced sexual abuse as a child and 23% as adults; and 40% reported emotional abuse as a child and 48% as an adult (Bloom, Chesney-Lind, & Owen, 1994). Women are also abused *within* the prison system. An ongoing investigation by the Human Rights Watch Women's Rights Project documented custodial misconduct in many forms including verbal degradation, rape, sexual assault, unwarranted visual supervision, denying goods and privileges, and use or threat of force. "Male correctional officers and staff contribute to a custodial environment in state prisons for women which is often highly sexualized and excessively hostile" (Human Rights Watch Women's Rights Project, 1996, p. 2).

WHAT KIND OF ADDICTION TREATMENT ARE WOMEN RECEIVING IN PRISONS?

With nearly 60% of women in prison for a drug-related crime, and with the number of addiction and abuse issues that women bring with them, it would not be unreasonable to expect prisons to invest some resources in alcohol/drug recovery programs, support groups, and psychological counseling. Unfortunately, although the current programs we have in men's prisons are few and inadequate, there are even fewer for women (Salholz & Wright, 1990). Health care, especially pre-natal care, education, job training and treatment for alcohol/other drug abuse are all missing from the women's prison system. Only 3% of California prisoners have any alcohol and/or drug treatment programs available to them, even if such voluntary programs as Alcoholics and Narcotics Anonymous are included (Bloom, Chesney-Lind, & Owen, 1994). In light of these facts, the term "correctional institutions" becomes a sad euphemism in a system that provides no programs to help redress the most basic needs and concerns that are shared by many women.

The lack of proper substance abuse treatment programs was recently confirmed by the National Criminal Justice Association. In a nationwide survey done under the U.S. Department of Justice, they found that "Virtually every survey respondent reported that there is too little funding for treatment services, that there are not enough drug treatment facilities or appropriate placements for drug dependent clients, and there is a lack of qualified personnel to staff treatment programs" (Zawistowski, 1991, p. 9).

There is also a wide gap between what our judicial system actually believes about the availability of health care and alcohol/drug recovery programs in prison, and the existence of such programs. In recent years, shrinking tax dollars for community based programs have led judges to believe that the best chance that pregnant, addicted women have for treatment is through sentencing and incarceration. Unfortunately, this belief is a myth, because the programs simply do not exist, often with tragic consequences for the high number of these women who enter the penal system. Although detoxification of pregnant, substance-dependent women can be accomplished safely, successfully and at low cost, many prisons force these women to go "cold turkey." Many times this results in the death of the fetus or serious damage to it. Nor do pregnant, addicted women in many prisons receive even the most basic of gynecological or maternity care. In addition, illegal drugs are often more readily available in prisons than they are on the street (Barry, 1991).

If we are to develop effective programs for women in prison and community corrections, we need to develop a theoretical approach to addiction treatment that is gender sensitive, addressing itself to the realities of women's lives.

DEVELOPING AN INTEGRATED MODEL OF ADDICTION

To develop an integrated model for the treatment of addiction, it is important first to develop a sound theoretical framework, asking ourselves to what theory of addiction we are subscribing. The next step is to utilize a theory of women's psychological development, which refers to what is known about how women learn, grow and heal. Lastly, it is important to incorporate a theory of trauma since the majority of women who are chemically dependent, especially those in the criminal justice system, have experienced emotional, physical and sexual abuse in their childhood and/ or adulthood. The definition of victimization and trauma also needs to be expanded to include racial prejudice, witnessing violence, and the stigma, stress, and abusiveness of incarceration.

Theory of Addiction

Traditionally, addiction treatment has been based on a medical model, which views addiction as a disease. The most commonly used analogy is that addiction is like diabetes, a physical disease that carries no moral or social stigma. This analogy is often useful because neither diabetes nor addiction can be managed by will power. They both require adherence to a lifestyle regimen for physical and emotional stability.

However, this analogy sees the disease/disorder rooted solely in the individual. As we move into the twenty-first century, health professionals in many disciplines are revising their concept of disease in general. Based on a holistic health model, we are now acknowledging not only the physical aspects of disease, but also the emotional, psychological, and spiritual aspects.

I believe we can best understand addiction as a disease/disorder if we understand it holistically and include cancer as an analogy. The diabetes model is useful, but too individualistic and simplistic to adequately explain addiction.

Like cancer, addiction has a physical component as well as emotional, psychological, and spiritual dimensions. I would argue that two other components of disease must also be added to a fully holistic model: the environmental and the sociopolitical dimensions. It's interesting that few people question that cancer is a disease even though some experts estimate that 80% of doctors link cancer to lifestyle choices (diet and exercise) and the environment (pesticides, emissions, nuclear waste, etc.) (Siegel, 1996). There are also sociopolitical aspects of cancer, especially when we realize the huge profits carcinogenic products make for powerful business interests. The same is true of addictive substances, both legal and illegal. For example, medical doctors prescribe 80% of the amphetamines, 60% of the psychoactive drugs and 71% of the antidepressants to women (Galbraith, 1991). Companies that produce and sell alcohol are indirectly responsible for over 23,000 deaths and three quarter of a million injuries each year— and these are only the figures reported to insurance companies (Zawistowski, 1991). Even though some women may have a strong genetic predisposition to addiction, an important treatment issue is acknowledging that many of them have grown up in an environment where drug dealing and addiction are a way of life.

Theory of Women's Development

The next important element for developing a treatment model is having a theory of women's psychological development. Traditional developmental psychology is based on a separation/individuation model. The Relational Model, developed by the Stone Center in Wellesley, Massachusetts, posits that the primary motivation for women throughout life is not separation, but establishing a strong sense of connection. When a woman is disconnected from others, or involved in abusive relationships, she experiences disempowerment, confusion, and diminished zest, vitality and self-worth—fertile ground for addiction. Healthy, growth-fostering relationships create increased zest and vitality, empowerment, self-knowledge, self-worth and a desire for more connection. In a growth-fostering relationship, a woman develops a sense of mutuality that is "creative, energy-releasing and empowering for all participants," and fundamental to her psychological well-being (Covington & Surrey, 1997).

If we are trying to create treatment for women to help them to change, grow and heal from addictions, it is critical that we place them in programs and environments where relationship and mutuality are core elements. The system needs to provide a setting where women can experience healthy relationships with their counselors and each other. Unfortunately, the criminal justice system is designed to discourage women from coming together, trusting, speaking about personal issues or forming bonds of relationship. Women who leave prison are often discouraged from associating with other women who have been incarcerated.

If women are to be successfully reintegrated back into the community after serving their sentences, there must be a *continuum of care* that can connect them in a community after they've been released. Ideally, these community programs should have a relational basis.

Theory of Trauma

The last element we need in order to create a model for treatment is a theory of trauma. A vast majority of chemically dependent women have been physically, sexually and emotionally abused for much of their lives, and these numbers are even greater within the criminal justice population. Traditional addiction treatment often does not deal with abuse issues in early recovery, even though they are a primary trigger for relapse among women (Covington & Surrey, 1997). Therefore, we need a theory of trauma that is appropriate for women in early recovery.

Psychiatrist Judith Herman (1992) writes that there are three stages in the process of healing from trauma: safety, remembrance and mourning, and reconnection. "Survivors feel unsafe in their bodies. Their emotions and their thinking feel out of control. They also feel unsafe in relation to other people" (Herman, 1992, p. 160). Stage One (safety) addresses the woman's safety concerns in all of these domains. In the second stage of recovery (remembrance and mourning) the survivor tells the story of the trauma and mourns the old self that the trauma destroyed. In Stage Three (reconnection) the survivor faces the task of creating a future; now she develops a new self. As we have seen above, the difficulty is that many women are *not* safe in our criminal justice system where they are vulnerable to abuse and harassment from correctional staff.

Stage One recovery from trauma, safety, is the appropriate level of intervention for women in early recovery from addiction. If we want women to heal from addiction, we must set up a safe environment in which the healing process can begin to take place. Dr. Herman uses Twelve Step groups as an example of the type of group appropriate for Stage One (safety) recovery because of their focus on present-tense issues of self-care, in a supportive, homogeneous environment.

ADDICTION RECOVERY FOR WOMEN

The Center for Substance Abuse Treatment (1994, p. 178) has developed the following list of issues that should be reflected in a comprehensive treatment model for women:

- The etiology of addiction, especially gender-specific issues related to addiction (including social, physiological, and psychological consequences of addiction and factors related to onset of addiction)
- Low self-esteem
- Race, ethnicity and cultural issues
- Gender discrimination and harassment
- Disability-related issues, where relevant
- Relationships with family and significant others
- Attachments to unhealthy interpersonal relationships
- Interpersonal violence, including incest, rape, battering, and other abuse
- Eating disorders
- Sexuality, including sexual functioning and sexual orientation

- Parenting
- Grief related to the loss of alcohol or other drugs, children, family members, or partners
- Work
- Appearance and overall health and hygiene
- Isolation related to a lack of support systems (which may or may not include family members and/or partners) and other resources
- Life plan development
- Child care and child custody

When I interviewed women around the country who had recovered in Twelve Step programs and asked them to describe both the things that had changed the most for them in their journey from using to recovery and the issues that contributed to relapse, they listed the self, relationships, sexuality and spirituality. It is interesting to note that these four issues incorporate the issues listed above. If we are going to create recovery programs for women in correctional settings, these four issues need to be understood and addressed. (For additional information, see *A Woman's Way Through the Twelve Steps*, Covington, 1994.)

The Self. The generic definition of addiction I use is "the chronic neglect of self in favor of something or someone else." Addiction can be conceptualized as a self-disorder. One of the first questions women in recovery need to begin to address is "Who am I?" Women in our culture are taught to identify themselves according to role: mother, professional, wife, daughter. One of the first tasks for women in recovery is to find words to describe who they are from a deep, interior place. In addiction, one loses the sense of oneself and, with it, the ability to have a real connection with others. Recovery is about expansion and growth of the self, both the inner and the outer self.

Many women enter the prison system with a poor self-image and a history of trauma and abuse. As we have seen, prisons actively discourage relationship. Creating the kinds of programs that help incarcerated women to develop a strong sense of self, an identification that goes beyond who they are in the criminal justice system, is vital to their recovery.

Relationship. Some women use addictive substances to maintain relationships with using partners, some use them to fill up the void of what is missing in relationship, and some use alcohol/other drugs to deal with the pain of being abused (Covington & Surrey, 1997). One of the tasks of any recovery program is to teach women self-soothing techniques in order to deal with the myriad of feelings that surface when abstinent.

Women in the prison system often have unhealthy, illusory or unequal relationships with spouses, partners, friends and family members. For that reason, it is important for recovery programs to model healthy relationships, among both staff and participants, providing a safe place and a container for healing (Covington & Beckett, 1988). Our greatest challenge is to overcome the alienation that is fostered within prison walls, and replace it with a greater sense of relationship in community.

Sexuality. Sexuality is one of the most neglected areas in the treatment of addiction, and one of the major causes for relapse. Healthy sexuality is integral to one's sense of self-worth. It represents the integration of the biological, emotional, social, and spiritual aspects of who one is and how one relates to others (Covington, 1991a; Covington, in press; Kaplan, 1981; Schnarch, 1991). Addiction is often defined as a physical, emotional, social, and spiritual disease. Since healthy sexuality is defined as the integration of all these aspects of the self, we can see that addiction can have an impact on every area of sexuality. Therefore, addressing and healing all aspects of the sexual self is critical to a woman's recovery process (Covington, 1991a; Covington, in press).

Creating healthy sexuality is a developmental process that occurs over time. This normal developmental process is often interrupted by addiction. In addition, many women entering the early stages of recovery report the following sexual concerns: sexual dysfunction, shame and guilt, sexual identity, prostitution, sexual abuse, and the fear of sex clean and sober. These issues need to be addressed if we expect women to maintain their recovery (Covington, 1991a; Covington, 1993).

Few women in prisons have a positive view of sex. Some have been prostitutes, many have been abused and most connect sex with shame and guilt. Even those who have been the most sexually active have little accurate information about sex. Developing programs that can work with this part of a woman's recovery can help to create a positive sense of self and a healthier image of relationship.

Spirituality. The root of the word psychology is "psyche," which means "the knowledge and the understanding of the soul." Although we live in a secular culture where traditional psychology does not focus on the spiritual, helping women to reconnect to their own definition of the spiritual is critical to their recovery process. Religion and spirituality are not the same–they may or may not be connected. Religion is about form, dogma and structure, and is institutionally based. Spirituality is about transformation, connection, wholeness, meaning and depth.

Women connect with their spirituality in many different ways. Some have rejected the religion of their childhood, and must find a new path for themselves. Some return to the religion of their youth. In recovery groups I have facilitated, I often find it useful to give women art history books to look at how, for thousands of years before the Patriarchy, the female was revered. Since the feminine has been so denigrated in our culture, it is often helpful to show women that they are a part of a long history of birthers, growers and caregivers, helping them to reconnect with the energy of the great goddess.

The design of the criminal justice system is antithetical to spiritual values, and it is essential that any recovery program designed for women in this system find a way to help each woman find her own definition of a "higher power."

TWELVE STEP PROGRAMS

In recent years, Twelve Step programs have been critiqued in various ways and, as some feminists have pointed out, the language used is simplistic, sexist and reductionist (Bepko, 1991; Berenson, 1991; Kasl, 1992; Rapping, 1996). Feminists are particularly concerned about the Twelve Steps' emphasis upon powerlessness as liberating. In contrasting the recovery movement with the women's movement, Marianne Walters (1990) points out that "one movement encourages individuals to surrender to a spiritual higher power, where the other encourages people to join together to challenge and restructure power arrangements in the larger society" (p. 55). What is often missed in feminist analysis is the masculine "power over" is what is being relinquished in order to experience the feminine "power with," "power to be able," i.e., a sense of empowerment (Miller, 1982). "The process of recovery from addiction is a process of recovering a different, more feminine, sense of power and will" (Berenson, 1991, p. 74). There is also a confusion between surrender and submission. "When we submit, we give in to a force that's trying to control us. When we surrender, we let go of our need to control" (Covington, 1994, p. 48). Recovery encourages surrender and giving up the illusion of control. Feminist writer Marilyn French (1985) describes " . . . life is the highest value for 'feminine' people; whereas control is the highest value for 'masculine' people" (p. 93).

If we look at the underpinnings of Alcoholics Anonymous we can see that it was actually very radical for the 1930s, the time it was founded, and that this continues to be true even today. Twelve Step programs are free, a radical concept in a capitalistic society; they are non-hierarchical, a radical idea in a patriarchal society; and they are spiritual, a radical stance in a non-spiritual society. As previously stated, women grow and develop in relationship, and Twelve Step programs can provide a growth-fostering relational context, and offer their members social support through the creation of a caring community (Covington, 1991b; Covington & Surrey,

1997). These programs can also create a safe environment, which is an essential element for recovery from trauma (Herman, 1992). Although some critics have focused on the sexist language in which the Twelve Steps are couched, I have found that women are able to interpret the steps in ways that are distinctly personal, meaningful and useful to themselves (Covington, 1994).

Since we know that women grow and develop in relationship and connection, and that these programs are free and available in our communities, it would make sense to enable women to have access to them both while they are incarcerated and while they are making the transition back into community. The Twelve Step programs also need to be incorporated into community correctional settings. These programs offer us an already existing "continuity of care" that we cannot afford to ignore.

CONCLUSION

With women being incarcerated for drug related offenses at an alarming rate, it is imperative that treatment services be designed to reflect the realities of their lives. This means comprehensive, integrated programs that understand and address the intersection of race, class, gender, and addiction. Even though most professionals believe addiction is a disease/disorder, societally we still respond to it chiefly as a crime. We can also no longer think only of individual addicts but must acknowledge that society fosters addiction.

On one level our task is to provide better services for the invisible women caught in our criminal justice system. These are women whose lives represent all women's issues–*magnified*. On a deeper level, we must question whether therapeutic, healing care can be provided in the ultimate system of oppression and domination.

Our criminal justice system is in desperate need of repair and revision. What changes would make a difference? The Human Kindness Foundation (1995) has suggested "Seven Ways to Fix the Criminal Justice System":

- Learn to recognize the influence of socially sanctioned hatred.
- Make drugs a public health problem instead of a criminal justice problem.
- Separate violent and nonviolent offenders right from the start.
- Regain compassion and respect for those who wrong us.
- Allow for transformation, not merely rehabilitation.
- Join and support the restorative justice movement.
- Take the issue of crime and punishment personally.

REFERENCES

Barry, E. (1991, Winter). Pregnant, addicted and sentenced. *Criminal Justice,* 23-27.

Belknap, Joanne. (1996). *The invisible woman: Gender, crime and justice.* Belmont, CA: Wadsworth.

Bepko, Claudia (Ed.) (1991). *Feminism and addiction.* New York: The Haworth Press, Inc.

Berenson, D. (1991). Powerlessness–liberation or enslaving? Responding to the feminist critique of the twelve steps. In C. Bepko (Ed.), *Feminism and addiction* (pp. 67-80). New York: The Haworth Press, Inc.

Bloom, B., Chesney-Lind, M., & Owen, B. (1994). *Women in California prisons: Hidden victims of the war on drugs.* San Francisco: Center on Juvenile and Criminal Justice.

Bloom, B., & Steinhart, D. (1993). *Why punish the children? A reappraisal of incarcerated mothers in America.* San Francisco: National Council on Crime and Delinquency.

Center for Substance Abuse Treatment. (1994). *Practical approaches in the treatment of women who abuse alcohol and other drugs.* Rockville, MD: Department of Health and Human Services, Public Health Service.

Chesney-Lind, M. & Bloom, B. (1997). Feminist criminology: Thinking about women and crime. In B. MacLean & D. Milovanovic (Eds.), *Thinking critically about crime* (pp. 54-65). Vancouver: Collective Press.

Covington, S. (in press). Women, addiction, and sexuality. In L. Straussner & E. Zelvin (Eds.), *Gender issues in addiction: Men and women in treatment.* Dunmore, PA: Jason Aronson.

Covington, S. (1991a). *Awakening your sexuality: A guide for recovering women and their partners.* San Francisco: Harper San Francisco.

Covington, S. (1991b). Sororities of helping and healing: Women and mutual help groups. In P. Roth (Ed.), *Alcohol and drugs are women's issues* (pp. 85-92). Metuchen, NJ: The Scarecrow Press, Inc.

Covington, S. (1991c). Unpublished research. From Las Colinas Detention Facility for Women in San Diego County, California.

Covington, S. (1993). Alcohol, addiction and sexual dysfunction. In E. Freeman (Ed.), *Substance abuse treatment* (pp. 189-216). Thousand Oaks, CA: Sage Publications.

Covington, S., (1994). *A woman's way through the twelve steps.* Center City, MN: Hazelden Educational Materials.

Covington, S., & Beckett, L. (1988). *Leaving the enchanted forest: The path from relationship to intimacy.* San Francisco: Harper San Francisco.

Covington, S. & Surrey, J. (1997). The relational model of women's psychological development: Implications for substance abuse. In S. Wilsnak & R. Wilsnak (Eds.), *Gender and alcohol: Individual and social perspectives* (pp. 335-351). Piscataway, NJ: Rutgers University.

French, M. (1985). *Beyond power: On women, men, and morals.* New York: Ballantine Books.

Galbraith, S. (1991). Women and legal drugs. In P. Roth (Ed.), *Alcohol and drugs are women's issues* (pp. 150-154). New York: The Scarecrow Press, Inc.

Herman, J. (1992). *Trauma and recovery.* New York: Basic Books.

Human Kindness Foundation. (1995). *Can we do better than our present prison system?* Durham, NC: Human Kindness Foundation.

Human Rights Watch Women's Rights Project. (1996). *All too familiar: Sexual abuse of women in U.S. state prisons.* New York: Human Rights Watch.

Kaplan, H. S. (1981). *The new sex therapy.* New York: Brunner/Mazel.

Kasl, C. (1992). *Many roads, one journey.* New York: Harper Collins.

LeBlanc, A. N. (1996, June). A woman behind bars is not a dangerous man. *The New York Times Magazine,* 35-40.

Miller, J. B. (1982). *Women and power.* Work in Progress, No. 82-01. Wellesley, MA: Stone Center Working Paper Series.

Northrup, C. (1994). *Women's bodies, women's wisdom.* New York: Bantam Books.

Rapping, E. (1996). *The culture of recovery.* Boston: Beacon Press.

Raspberry, W. (1991, June 2). Why are so many people in prison? *Washington Post,* p. 57.

Salholz, E., & Wright, L. (1990, June). Women in jail: Unequal justice. *Newsweek,* 37-38, 51.

Schnarch, D. (1991). *Constructing the sexual crucible.* New York: Norton.

Siegel, B. (1996). Personal communication.

Smith, S. (1991, March). Women in prison. *Bureau of Justice Statistics Special Report.*

Walters, M. (1990, July-August). The co-dependent Cinderella who loves too much . . . fights back. *The Family Therapy Networker,* 53-57.

Watterson, K. (1996). *Women in prison: Inside the concrete womb* (Rev. ed.). Boston: Northeastern University Press.

Zawistowski, T. A. (1991, March/April). Criminal addiction/illegal disease. *The Counselor,* 8-11.

To Find a Voice:
Art Therapy in a Women's Prison

Beth Merriam

SUMMARY. This article will present a compilation of case studies that will document the art therapy process utilized to assist incarcerated women with histories of severe trauma in expressing their feelings in an appropriate manner. These case studies will show how art images produced within this therapeutic milieu enabled the women described to reconnect with disowned thoughts, feelings and fantasies in a safe way. *[Article copies available for a fee from The Haworth Document Delivery Service: 1-800-342-9678. E-mail address: getinfo@haworth.com]*

The Kingston Prison for Women population is overwhelmingly comprised of women who have survived traumatic experiences. In one study (Task Force on Federally Incarcerated Women, 1990), 82% of the 102 women surveyed at the Prison for Women reported a history of physical or sexual abuse. A study on the general population (Haskell & Randall, 1993) showed significantly lower percentages of reported trauma experiences, with 17 percent of 420 women reporting at least one experience of incest before age 16, 40 percent reporting at least one experience of rape,

---

Beth Merriam, ATR, works in the Kingston Prison for Women as Art Therapist and in private practice. She has presented at both the Quebec and Canadian Art Therapy Conventions on art therapy with females in prison.

Address correspondence to: Beth Merriam, ATR, 473 Bagot Street, Kingston, Ontario, Canada, K7K 3C5.

[Haworth co-indexing entry note]: "To Find a Voice: Art Therapy in a Women's Prison." Merriam, Beth. Co-published simultaneously in *Women & Therapy* (The Haworth Press, Inc.) Vol. 21, No. 1, 1998, pp. 157-171; and: *Breaking the Rules: Women in Prison and Feminist Therapy* (ed: Judy Harden, and Marcia Hill) The Haworth Press, Inc., 1998, pp. 157-171; and: *Breaking the Rules: Women in Prison and Feminist Therapy* (ed: Judy Harden, and Marcia Hill) The Harrington Park Press, an imprint of The Haworth Press, Inc., 1998, pp. 157-171. Single or multiple copies of this article are available for a fee from The Haworth Document Delivery Service [1-800-342-9678, 9:00 a.m. - 5:00 p.m. (EST). E-mail address: getinfo@haworth.com].

and 27 percent reporting physical assault in an intimate relationship. This has shown a need for increased sensitivity to the significance of trauma within the female prison population.

The severe emotional effects from sexual abuse and from other major disruptions which include parental death at an early age, foster-care placement, residential placement, living on the streets, prostitution, suicide attempts, self-injury and substance abuse, present a bewildering range of treatment challenges. In this setting, the therapist is confronted daily with images of terror, rage and despair.

The prison presents a restrictive environment and a population diverse in personalities and needs. Therapy is a time and place where they can just be themselves, free to think about feelings. This poses a dilemma for many incarcerated women, however, who fear the strong emotions which therapy can release. They grope for diversions from fear, sadness, anger, terror, grief, anxiety, and rage through drugs, eating disorders, self-injurious behavior and suicide attempts. Severe dissociation is evident in a number of women.

Many studies (Howard, 1990; Peacock, 1991; Spring, 1985; Walker, 1992; Yates & Pawley, 1987) suggest that the benefits of art therapy with women who have been traumatized result from providing a protected environment for lowering defenses, releasing tension, and gaining insight. Sgroi (1988) argued that art therapy is helpful in gaining access to information that clients have repressed, denied or dissociated. Cox and Cohen (1995) discussed the graphic communications that are characteristic of Dissociative Identity Disorder, and how art therapy can facilitate communication among parts of self. Estep (1995) describes the capacity of art therapy to foster self-soothing in women who have been abused.

It is the focus on the image that makes art therapy distinct from verbal therapy and perhaps safer in that it seems less intrusive for some women. The art image is a personal statement that provides a focus for discussion and exploration, yet it also provides distance from the strong feelings evoked. This has proven to be especially helpful with the women whose cases I present in this paper who dissociated feelings and were withdrawn and resistant to verbal therapy. Art therapy allowed them to process and integrate information, to contain it in the artwork, thus gaining distance, as well as to nurture and self-soothe.

The potential of art therapy in prisons has barely been explored and the literature available is usually in regard to male offenders. *Art Therapy with Offenders,* published in England (Liebmann, 1994), outlines numerous advantages that art therapy offers to the prison population which include the alleviation of immediate crisis situations through catharsis, expression of pent-up emotions, and provision of a catalyst to promote discussions of suicidal ideation. Art therapy has also been found to be successful in engaging withdrawn and depressed individuals and alleviating inmates' feelings of isolation and desperation (Strait Day & Onorato, 1989).

Art therapy is based on a process of creating visual images through drawing, painting or clay modeling, in order to evoke self-awareness. It provides an alternative language for examining one's view of the world, both inner and outer, and can be a powerful medium for integrating different aspects of the self and human experience (Rubin, 1984).

Art therapy provides incarcerated women with a voice when they have otherwise lost their ability to verbalize their emotions because of trauma. This makes art therapy particularly beneficial to women with a history of trauma, because an inability to describe and discuss trauma creates tremendous obstacles for therapeutic intervention.

Restoring power and control is critical to the recovery of trauma survivors (Herman, 1992). How can one empower incarcerated women, however, when whatever autonomy they have left has been removed, and space and time are controlled by and defined by others? Add to this that the environment is usually associated with punishment. Art therapy offers the possibility of self-empowerment. This is because art making is such a highly personal and self-directed activity. I try to instill this in the women I work with by providing a client-directed approach where they are encouraged to attain control by choosing and manipulating the art materials. The structure is the art activity itself, and boundaries are marked by the paper edge. The end product or image is often experienced as something tangible and lends a feeling of containment for their fears and anxiety.

The therapeutic relationship is the key to effective therapy, and the establishment of trust is a priority and ongoing concern for many of the incarcerated women I see. I receive their art work with serious interest and a willingness to understand. The clarifications and responses I offer facilitate their increasing awareness of the meaning of their images and over time there is a growing sense of sharing in these images, even though no words may be exchanged about them.

CASE STUDIES

Marie

This was Marie's first incarceration as an adult and she was serving a seven-year sentence for attempted murder. She was nineteen. Marie was segregated from the general population because of her history of aggressive and hostile acting out and self-injurious behavior. The goal of art therapy was to provide a structured and positive outlet for the anger and frustration that Marie typically satisfied by self-injuring.

Marie was Native American and had a history of sexual abuse and trauma. She had been a heavy substance abuser from a very early age. Most of her adolescence was spent in psychiatric hospitals where she accumulated diagnoses that included schizophrenia, multiple personality disorder, and borderline personality disorder.

Picture 1 is the first painting that Marie did in art therapy. In this self-portrait Marie expressed her frustration and anger. Crying eyes, an open mouth that she said was "wailing," slashed arms and a body pressed against the bars indicated Marie's anguish and desperation. Much of Marie's art over the next few months graphically depicted images of trauma that she could not remember or feel connected to, and yet seemed compelled to continue producing. While this was cathartic for Marie it was not therapeutic in itself, because the painful intrusions from her past tormented her daily and she could not draw fast enough to contain all of them. It was important that she process these memories in order to assimilate them.

Marie did begin talking about her childhood trauma, and to consider

PICTURE 1

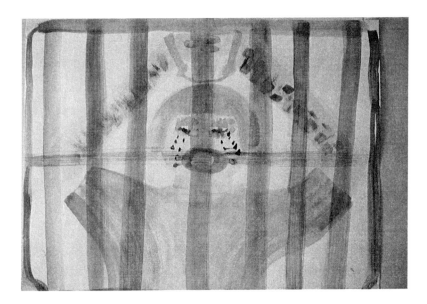

tentatively the concept of dissociation as being a response to the trauma in her childhood. Marie called Picture 2 the "hotel," with the bedroom windows representing the many parts of herself. This picture presented the structure and complexity of her internal personality system in relation to Dissociative Identity Disorder. No one is outside of the hotel and the playground is empty, indicating that Marie would not reveal who she was. The lightning suggested an impending storm to ensure that the parts of her personality system remained indoors, and unseen.

The first of many characters appeared soon after. Picture 3 was a villain and witch named "X-Marie." Red, pursed lips and glaring eyes suggested a warning that silence be maintained or the "hotel" would be destroyed. The hotel in this picture seems covered in a dark shroud, emphasizing secrecy. While Marie continued to present images representing aspects of herself which included a young girl, a teenaged male, and a dog, she did not verbally share information about their characteristics with me, thus heeding "X-Marie's" warning. Marie's artwork and process demonstrate how she was able, through art therapy, to reveal the trauma safely and to explore the concept of parts in relation to dissociation.

PICTURE 2

PICTURE 3

Grace

Grace is a 24-year-old woman described in prison reports as "severely personality disordered." Her violent and self-injurious behavior includes burning her body, attempts to hang herself, cutting, and head banging. An assault on a staff member and murder attempt on a fellow inmate made it necessary that she be placed in segregation. She experiences depression and despair, persecutory ideas, and anxiety about social contact. The goals of art therapy were to lessen her isolation through the stimulation of making art, and to explore issues that cause her anxiety.

When I first met Grace she claimed to remember nothing about her childhood, yet in her very first painting (Picture 4), and throughout most of her art work, there has been a childlike theme suggesting a need to return to that period in her life. Her adoptive mother claims that Grace became troubled beginning in grade four when there was some suspicion of her having been sexually abused by a teacher. Grace has no recollection of this. Grace has adamantly rejected any line of questioning suggesting her behavior is in response to childhood trauma and feels that she is just a "bad person."

Picture 5 is the same shape as the little girl in Picture 4, but has been

PICTURE 4

PICTURE 5

changed into a bomb about to go off. Grace has written "How will we diffuse it?" She related this painting to the internal pressures she often feels prior to self-injury. The little girl in the picture was about to fall apart and Grace felt her own self "going to pieces." Grace could not tell me who lit the fuse or how to stop it. She finds her own behavior similarly unpredictable and hard to control.

Picture 6 shows two clay figures that Grace made to keep herself company in the segregation cell, and which evolved to become concrete, external representations of internal parts of herself. She named them Jenny and Mandy, and has used them to disclose, to reflect on coping strategies and to self-soothe. In reference to the rounded mouths, Grace said "they give blow jobs," which may be indicative of her own experience. The arms of both figures are crossed in front, which suggests a need to protect personal boundaries. Grace also used Jenny and Mandy to reflect on her own experience of being isolated in segregation, and gave them each unique characteristics to represent different ways of coping. Jenny is shy, good, cooperative, and sensitive to others' needs. Indeed, Grace, too, has these qualities much of the time. Mandy, on the other hand, is easily bored, sneaks out of the box and gets into all kinds of mischief, like overflowing

PICTURE 6

the toilets and setting off the fire alarm. Grace is similarly impulsive. Grace worried about how Jenny and Mandy felt when they witnessed her acts of self-injury, and compensated by making the box they sat in more comfortable and safe. This became a self-soothing activity for Grace as she reflected on her own fear and confusion at those times. Art therapy has provided an opportunity for Grace to reflect on the emotional upheavals she experiences and to practice self-soothing.

Susan

Susan is a 24-year-old woman serving a ten-year sentence for second degree murder in the death of her two-year-old son. She denies any responsibility for his death. She is extremely thin and likely engages in some restrictive eating, but has been unable to acknowledge this. Susan was placed in segregation for her own protection from the general population because of her charge. She was referred to art therapy to receive additional support. The goal of art therapy has been to assist Susan in coping with the sources of psychological pain she is experiencing. When I first met Susan she was four months pregnant with her third child and anticipating loss of custody immediately following the birth.

Susan has had a need to discuss her first son who died, and her second son who has been adopted, and ruminates a great deal on her ability to be a good mother. Much of her art work reflects this, with images of children and food juxtaposed as in Picture 7. Susan speaks lovingly of her children and it is clear that losing them has resulted in intense anguish for her. Restricting her eating is a metaphor for restricting her acceptance of the irreversibility of these losses.

Susan has been uncomfortable discussing her own childhood and her anxiety increases dramatically when she does. There were numerous problems at home that revolved around her mother's alcoholism and Susan has recounted, verbally and pictorially, the frequent verbal and physical altercations between them. Taking her mother's prescription drugs at age eight "to calm myself down," and drinking alcohol at age ten, set the stage for her own alcoholism and substance abuse that began in grade seven. She admits reluctantly that she is like her own mother in some ways.

Picture 8 is a painting of two figures in which Susan was able to express and reflect on an inner conflict that leaves her feeling divided or "like two people." The stick figure on the right she referred to as "Happy go Lightly, who just wants to forget everything and have fun and ignore all the dark clouds above." The rounder figure on the left is "Sadness" on top, and "Alright" in the stomach. They "dwell in self pity and are heavy with sadness." Susan was able to acknowledge how difficult it is for her to

PICTURE 7

maintain a happy-go-lucky state, but that the alternative of being fuller and sad is just too foreboding.

In Picture 9, Susan elaborates on this fear and has painted herself hanging by a thread, about to fall into "water that is misty and with dangerous waves." She doesn't know how deep the water is and fears that sharks await her. Susan has metaphorically expressed how she fears the depth of her depression. "If I stay Happy go Lightly, I can float and not drop." Certainly she feels herself to be in a precarious position as she awaits the custody decision regarding her recently born son. Susan also has a history of suicide attempts which the sharks may represent.

Art therapy has allowed Susan to communicate very complex material and has been a good indicator of the issues and conflicts that trouble her.

Sally

Sally was a 22-year-old woman serving a three-year sentence for aggravated assault. She was a prostitute at the time of the offense, when she stabbed a male client who became violent. Sally was in segregation voluntarily due to her concerns for her personal safety from other inmates. She was referred for art therapy when her psychologist noted that Sally was

PICTURE 8

drawing pictures that depicted images of abuse. Sally had a positive attitude and desire to change her lifestyle, but had emotional difficulties
related to an abusive pimp. This was manifested in nightmares, insomnia
and somatic complaints. She had low self-esteem and was very self-criti-
cal. The goal of art therapy was to assist Sally in healing from the toxic
images of abuse.

Picture 10 is a self-portrait in which Sally placed a tape over the mouth
and wrote the words "No comment" underneath. She described this as the
prostitute, who did not speak up for herself. I wondered if Sally was also
giving me a message that she would not be commenting too much in art
therapy. She did describe in detail, however, the physical and emotional
abuse she experienced at the hands of her pimp, but showed very little
affect. When I noted this, Sally replied that she had always worn masks to
hide herself.

This prompted her to make the mask in Picture 11, which both revealed
and concealed. Tears fall from one eye. The mouth is revealed, but pursed
lips are covered in lipstick suggesting an air of festivity. It is closed and
makes no sound to go with the tears. Sally admitted to her stubborness in
never showing hurt feelings. This was in reference not only to her pimp,

PICTURE 9

but to her adoptive mother. She did many drawings after that which were incongruent with reports that indicated Sally's life with her adoptive parents as being "prosocial." Sally described her adoptive mother as emotionally and physically abusive, and I wondered if this was what she could "not comment" on in Picture 10.

Picture 12 is a teddy bear with a scarred face and bleeding nose. The mouth is starting to smile, but the line is quivering, suggesting that tears have fallen. Sally called this her "brave little teddy bear" and saw it as a remnant from her childhood, and how she now felt after reviewing images of her childhood. Sally's next project was to make a cloth teddy bear to

PICTURE 10

self-soothe. Art therapy enabled Sally to gain insight into her past history that may have led to her current situation.

CONCLUSION

The women presented in these case studies were provided a direct and rich encounter with their inner world and feelings through art therapy. The information gained through this non-verbal process allowed them to reach a more complete understanding of themselves without feeling that they had been utterly exposed. Their art work became a container for powerful, potentially destructive emotions and began to clarify for these women who they are and why.

Art therapy provides many benefits for incarcerated women by offering autonomy, strengthening self-esteem and providing a safe and acceptable way of releasing feelings such as anger and aggression. Art therapy as a non-verbal form of communication and expression can be important for this population of highly traumatized women whose unspeakable feelings often lead to emotional withdrawal and isolation, or the practice of de-structive, tension-releasing activities.

PICTURE 11

PICTURE 12

REFERENCES

Cox, C., & Cohen, B. (1995). *Telling without talking*. New York: W.W. Norton & Company.

Estep, M. (1995). To soothe oneself: Art therapy with a woman recovering from incest. *American Journal of Art Therapy, 34*, 9-18.

Haskell, L., & Randall, M. (1993). *The women's safety project: Summary of key statistical findings*. (Ottawa: Canadian Panel on Violence Against Women).

Herman, J. L. (1992). *Trauma and recovery*. New York: Basic Books.

Howard, R. (1992). Art therapy as an isomorphic intervention in the treatment of a client with posttraumatic stress disorder. *American Journal of Art Therapy, 28*, 79-86.

Liebmann, M. (Ed.). (1994). *Art therapy with offenders*. London: Jessica Kingsley Publishers.

Peacock, M. (1991). A personal construct approach to art therapy in the treatment of post sexual abuse trauma. *American Journal of Art Therapy, 29*, 100-108.

Rubin, J. (1984). *The art of art therapy*. New York: Brunner/Mazel.

Sgroi, S. (Ed). (1988). *Vulnerable Populations: Evaluation and Treatment of Sexually Abused Children and Adult Survivors* (Vol. I). Lexington, MA: Lexington Books.

Spring, D. (1985). Symbolic language of sexually abused, chemically dependent women. *American Journal of Art Therapy, 24*, 13-21.

Strait Day, E., & Onorato, G.T. (1989). Making art in a jail setting. In *Advances in Art Therapy*. Wadeson, H. (Ed.). New York: John Wiley & Sons.

Task Force on Federally Sentenced Women. (1990). *Creating choices: Report of the task force on federally sentenced women*. Ottawa: Correctional Services of Canada.

Walker, C. (1992). Art therapy with adult female incest survivors. *Art Therapy, 9 (3)*, 135-138.

Yates, M., & Pawley, K. (1987). Utilizing imagery and the unconscious to explore and resolve trauma of sexual abuse. *Art Therapy (4)*, 1, 36-41.

A Feminist Examination
of Boot Camp Prison Programs
for Women

Susan T. Marcus-Mendoza
Jody Klein-Saffran
Faith Lutze

SUMMARY. Penal law in the United States reflects a strict moral ideology. This moral philosophy has dictated the laws that govern women and the punishments that they receive. Therefore, correctional programming for women has been focused on punishment and has not addressed the needs and problems of women inmates. Boot camp programs (shock incarceration), a low-cost, short-term alternative to traditional prison programming, are one example of such program-

Susan Marcus-Mendoza, PhD, is Assistant Professor of Human Relations and Women's Studies at the University of Oklahoma. Previously, Dr. Marcus-Mendoza was the chief psychologist at a federal prison camp for women. Jody Klein-Saffran, PhD, is a research analyst for the Federal Bureau of Prisons. Her research interests include community corrections, alternative sanctions, and recidivism. Faith Lutze, PhD, is Assistant Professor in the Department of Political Science/Criminal Justice Program at Washington State University. Her current research interests include the rehabilitative nature of shock incarceration programs, inmate motivation to enter treatment programs, and violence toward women.

Opinions expressed here are the authors' own, and do not necessarily reflect policies or procedures of the Federal Bureau of Prisons.

Address correspondence to: Susan Marcus-Mendoza, Department of Human Relations, University of Oklahoma, Norman, OK 73019 (smmendoza@ou.edu).

[Haworth co-indexing entry note]: "A Feminist Examination of Boot Camp Prison Programs for Women." Marcus-Mendoza, Susan T., Jody Klein-Saffran, and Faith Lutze. Co-published simultaneously in *Women & Therapy* (The Haworth Press, Inc.) Vol. 21, No. 1, 1998, pp. 173-185; and: *Breaking the Rules: Women in Prison and Feminist Therapy* (ed: Judy Harden, and Marcia Hill) The Haworth Press, Inc., 1998, pp. 173-185; and: *Breaking the Rules: Women in Prison and Feminist Therapy* (ed: Judy Harden, and Marcia Hill) The Harrington Park Press, an imprint of The Haworth Press, Inc., 1998, pp. 173-185. Single or multiple copies of this article are available for a fee from The Haworth Document Delivery Service [1-800-342-9678, 9:00 a.m. - 5:00 p.m. (EST). E-mail address: getinfo@haworth.com].

173

ming. Correctional boot camps teach discipline and responsibility by "breaking down and building up" inmates so that they will no longer commit crimes. However, the assumption that female offenders commit crimes because they are lacking in discipline and responsibility has not been substantiated by research. In addition, feminist therapy theory is not consistent with some boot camp practices. This paper will examine the social context of female criminality and the resulting implications for prison programming for women, and boot camp practices will be examined in the context of feminist therapy practices. *[Article copies available for a fee from The Haworth Document Delivery Service: 1-800-342-9678. E-mail address: getinfo@haworth.com]*

Strict moral ideology has dictated the laws that govern women in the United States, and the punishments that they receive. Consequently, correctional programming for women has reflected a punishment orientation, aimed at punishing the "fallen woman," and has not considered the needs and problems of women inmates. A recent example of such programming is shock incarceration (boot camps), which has been instituted in many states as a low-cost, short-term alternative to traditional prison programming. The purpose of boot camps is to teach discipline and responsibility, to "break down and build up" inmates so that they will no longer commit crimes. The use of a program to instill discipline and responsibility assumes that female offenders are lacking in these areas and that this is the reason for their criminal behavior. The current research on female offenders does not substantiate this assumption. In addition, boot camp practices are not consistent with feminist conceptualizations of effective clinical practice with women. This paper will examine the theoretical basis and clinical implications of boot camps for women. The social context of female criminality and the resulting implications for prison programming for women will be discussed, and boot camp policies will be examined in the context of feminist therapy practices.

THE SOCIAL CONTEXT OF FEMALE CRIMINALITY

The dominant moral codes and gender stereotypes of American society have dictated the laws used to incarcerate women and the correctional programming available to female inmates. Freedman (1981) examined the political climate of the early 1880s and suggested that the rise in female incarceration during that era was related to the increase in urbanization and the resulting moral reforms. Women were incarcerated for such "moral" crimes as disorderly conduct, vagrancy, drunkenness, and prostitution. Many women who were left without means of supporting themselves and their families during the wars of the 1800s were incarcerated for prostitution and stealing. Society considered them "fallen women," abnormal and unworthy of attention due to their deviance from the strict moral standards of the time. In prison, women were subjected to miserable living conditions and were largely ignored. What little programming was offered was just an adaptation of male-oriented programs. Most of society continued to shun these women upon release from prison.

Even the theories of criminality focused on men, ignoring criminal women as being unworthy of notice (Belknap, 1996). The notable exception was the work of Lombroso and Ferrero (1900), who developed a theory of criminology based on Social Darwinism. Lombroso theorized that women, nonwhites, and the poorer classes were less evolved than white, upper-class men. Therefore, they were more likely to commit crimes. Further, he stated that for a woman to commit crime and stray from the "normal" path of "maternity, piety, and weakness, . . . her wickedness must have been enormous . . . " (Lombroso & Ferrero, 1900, p. 150). This theory is reflective of the madonna/whore duality (Feinman, 1986) by which women of that era were judged; the good woman (madonna) is loyal and submissive and knows her place, and the bad woman (whore) steps out of prescribed roles and must be punished for being evil.

At the end of the nineteenth century, social reformers, who rejected the idea that women who committed crimes were moral deviants, began to explore such correlates of female criminality as mental ability, poverty, and lack of education (Freedman, 1981). These reformers espoused the idea of such preventative services as education and training to keep economically marginalized women from committing crimes. Prison staff began "to retrain women through sympathetic female staff, prayer, education, and domesticity" (Freedman, 1981, p. 90). However, women's prisons still valued discipline. Consequently, " . . . the tension between domesticity and discipline pervaded the internal life of the women's prison" (Freedman, 1981, p. 90).

Ultimately, reformers, who brought about the inclusion of programming for women, only partially met their goals of making women self-supporting. Women inmates were taught to be submissive and feminine, and received training in such domestic skills as cooking and ironing. However, the training they received in domestic skills did not prepare them to be financially self-supporting. They found few jobs that required these skills upon release from prison. Therefore, they often found themselves back in prison (Freedman, 1981).

Female Inmates in the 1990s

By focusing on moral reform and using male correctional programming for women inmates, prison programming often fails to address the real problems and needs of women. Recent research on female inmates has helped to dispel the myth of the fallen woman, and increased our understanding of women in prison. Studies suggest that female inmates are typically young women (mid-twenties to mid-thirties) who have experienced many social, environmental, and personal problems (American Correctional Association, 1990; Belknap, 1996; Eaton, 1993; Marcus-Mendoza & Briody, 1996; Pollock-Byrne, 1990; Rafter, 1990; Sommers, 1995).

Although the incidence of violence against women is high in the United States, rates of sexual and physical abuse are even higher for female inmates. In a study of the incidence of sexual abuse of women in the general population, Russell (1984) found that 25% had been raped and one-third had been sexually abused as children. In her comprehensive review of the literature, Walker (1994) reported that approximately one out of every four adult women had been battered by a partner. Overall, she found that about 50% of women had experienced some form of physical, sexual, or psychological abuse. Research on psychiatric patients revealed that 50% to 80% of hospitalized male and female patients had experienced some form of physical, sexual, or psychological abuse, and 68% of female outpatients had experienced physical or sexual abuse (Walker, 1994). However, research on female inmates indicates that 80%-88% have experienced at least one type of physical, sexual, or emotional abuse (Gilfus, 1988; Marcus-Mendoza, Sargent, & Chong Ho, 1994; Owen & Bloom, 1995). Although statistics on abuse often vary due to differences in definitions of abuse and the types of measurements used, this demonstrates a high, consistent rate of abuse. The high percentage of abuse perpetrated against women in the United States is alarming. However, the fact that there is a higher incidence of abuse among psychiatric populations and inmates than among the general population of women clearly demonstrates the debilitating effects of violence against women.

Female inmates frequently report substance abuse, which is common among survivors of trauma (Herman, 1992). According to the Bureau of Justice Statistics (BJS), 41% of female inmates reported daily drug use in the month before their arrest (Bureau of Justice Statistics, 1991). Overall, according to BJS, the majority of female inmates have used drugs and alcohol, and close to half the inmates report having a drug or alcohol problem. In contrast, in a survey of women in the United States in 1995, only 8.7% reported using drugs within the past year, and 4.5% reported using drugs within the past month (U.S. Department of Health and Human Services, 1996).

Female inmates often face economic problems as well as personal and interpersonal problems. Many female inmates have children and are the sole providers for their families. As many as 70%-80% of female inmates have children, the majority of whom are under the age of 18 (American Correctional Association, 1990; Bureau of Justice Statistics, 1994; Gilfus, 1988; Marcus-Mendoza & Briody, 1996; Owen & Bloom, 1995). Gilfus (1988) found that of those inmates with children, 46.7% were single mothers. Nationwide, only 22% of families with children are headed by single mothers (U.S. Department of Commerce, 1995). And, in their study of female inmates in Oklahoma, Marcus-Mendoza and Briody (1996) found that 73% of the inmates who were mothers were not receiving any child support from their children's fathers.

Research reveals that just over half of female inmates were unemployed prior to their arrest (Bureau of Justice Statistics [BJS], 1991; Marcus-Mendoza & Briody, 1996; Owen & Bloom, 1995). The BJS (1991) study found that 53% of female inmates were unemployed prior to incarceration, as opposed to only 32% of male inmates. This statistic is particularly alarming given the high percentages of women inmates who, prior to their incarceration, were single mothers and received little or no child support. Fletcher, Shaver, and Moon (1993) reported that female inmates are also concerned about job prospects upon release. When asked about what they needed to be successful upon release, 80% of the female inmates wanted more education and training to get jobs.

Although the problems commonly faced by women before incarceration are being studied, researchers have largely neglected to study women's motivations for committing crimes, and have instead adapted theories from research on men (Belknap, 1996). The theories of male criminality include social control theory which suggests that the strength of a person's social bonds and the degree of their belief in society's rules determines whether a person will commit a crime, and power-control theory which posits that power dynamics in the home and workplace determine risk-taking, and therefore, criminal behaviors. However, Sommers (1995), in her qualitative study of 14 female inmates in Canada, found that women commit crimes for reasons unrelated to control theories or gender stereotypes. Some women commit crimes to maintain an adequate standard of living for their families, and others are looking for acceptance by trying to buy expensive gifts for others. Several women committed crimes as an expression of the pain that had been inflicted upon them. This study found that relational and economic needs were the pervasive primary motivators of women's crime, and that power was not generally a factor. Sommers concluded that researchers and therapists must consider the societal context of crime, and the individual experience of each woman in order to understand the motivation for crime.

The work of reformers has led to current programming that more accurately reflects some of the needs of female inmates. Many prisons offer education, vocational programs, life skills training, and psychological services. Despite recent progress, however, Morash, Haarr, and Rucker (1994) argued that programming for female inmates still reflects gender stereotyping. They point out that women learn horticulture, typing, and food preparation, while men learn more marketable skills. This still puts women at a disadvantage when they enter the job market. The skills they acquire in prison are more appropriate for full-time homemakers, whereas the majority of women in prison are single mothers. The gender-stereotyped vocational training also reinforces the attitude of the "fallen woman." By training inmates to be better at "women's work," correctional administrators are perpetuating the notion that if inmates can learn to assume gender-stereotyped roles, they will stay out of trouble. This is contrary to feminist therapy theory which encourages women to resist dominant role expectations so that they can formulate their own life goals. Prison administrators still set therapeutic goals rather than encouraging women to formulate their own.

Hannah-Moffat (1995) suggested that although changes have "softened some of the rough edges of incarceration" (p. 159), women's prisons do not empower women in the feminist sense of the word. For instance, the Canadian program, *Creating Choices,* was designed to empower women by offering programming designed to meet women's specific needs, rather than just adapting male programming for women. However, programs were not created by consultation with prisoners as originally intended, but by the government. In essence, as Hannah-Moffat commented, *Creating Choices* dictates certain programs designed to increase individual responsibility of the inmates, and "disregards feminist analysis of the social, economic, and political barriers experienced by women–and, in particular, by marginalized women" (p. 159).

BOOT CAMPS

A relatively recent addition to prison programming for men, and subsequently for women, is the correctional boot camp. Since the first prison boot camp was started in 1983, more than 50 boot camps have opened in prisons and jails around the country. Prison and jail boot camps, modeled after military boot camps, are typically short-term programs which emphasize military drill and ceremony, discipline, physical training, and daily work assignments (MacKenzie, 1991; Parent, 1989). Some boot camps also offer educational programming, psychological services, substance abuse counseling and education, and life skills training. Inmates who are sentenced to boot camps are generally non-violent first offenders and non-violent juveniles.

The rationales for the development of boot camp programs vary from camp to camp. Parent (1989), in his study of the advent of shock programs, found that personal experience with the military and success stories by other prison administrators were the basis for most of the boot camps, and that there was little empirical data to support the utilization of boot camps. Prison administrators most often cited the goals of boot camps as improved discipline of offenders during and after incarceration, punishment, deterrence, incapacitation, reduction in recidivism, reduction in cost of housing inmates, and rehabilitation (Austin, Jones, & Bolyard 1993; Osler, 1991; Parent, 1989).

The results of research on boot camps are mixed. Some studies have found positive results, such as reduction in recidivism (Marcus-Mendoza, 1995), and positive changes in attitude (Burton, Marquart, Cuvelier, Alarid, & Hunter, 1993). Women in one study reported that learning discipline would be helpful to them in negotiating life after prison (MacKenzie, Elis, Simpson, & Skroban, 1994). Others have found that the goals cited above are not being met or the results differ across camps (MacKenzie, 1991; MacKenzie, 1994; MacKenzie & Brame, 1995; MacKenzie, Brame, McDowall, & Souryal, 1995; MacKenzie, Shaw, & Gowdy, 1993; MacKenzie, Shaw, & Souryal, 1992; MacKenzie & Souryal, 1994). The short duration of the programs may help to reduce costs and relieve overcrowding, but this is only the case when programs are well designed (MacKenzie, 1994; Parent, 1994).

Questions have also been raised about the possible detrimental effects of boot camps. Critics claim boot camps are demeaning, poorly implemented, and a "quick-fix" (Morash & Rucker, 1990; Osler, 1991; Parent, 1989; Sechrest, 1989). They argue that the strict discipline and drilling is abusive in some instances (Osler, 1991), and may be traumatic for inmates who are survivors of abuse (MacKenzie et al., 1994; Marcus-Mendoza, 1995).

Currently, there are only six boot camps for female offenders in the United States, and several which are co-correctional–for men and women. Both the stated goals of the boot camps and the programming differ across camps for women. The common theme that seems to define the boot camp concept is the goal of improving self-concept and instilling discipline, which was given as a goal by all six camps. Some camps also have more pragmatic goals such as reducing overcrowding and protecting the public. Two camps list reducing recidivism as a goal. Only one program lists the seemingly conflicting goals of punishment and improved self-concept/discipline. Although they all have one goal in common (instilling discipline), the intents of the camps still seem to differ.

Differences in programming at the camps are reflective of the divergent beliefs about the purpose of the correctional boot camp. The programs are similar in that they are short-term programs that have a military drilling component, work, and physical fitness. However, they differ in the inclusion of educational, psychological, religious, vocational and life skills programming. More extensive programming tends to be used in institutions where "reducing recidivism" is listed as a goal. To date, the most comprehensive camp for women is the six-month program at the Federal Prison Camp in Bryan, Texas, in which drilling is minimal, and a full range of programming exists. Inmates participate in programming three days a week, and most evenings.

Feminist Theory and Boot Camp Ideology

The goals and methods of the boot camp as described previously are very different from the goals and methods of feminist therapy. In fact, feminist therapy emerged as a reaction to similar ideas and practices in the fields of psychology and psychiatry. Many volumes have emerged to dispel the myths of women's frailty, incompetence, and dependence, and have put forth new, more accurate ideas about women and feminist therapy with women. In her synthesis of work on feminist therapy to date, *Subversive Dialogues,* Laura Brown (1996) describes a vision of therapy which is grounded in feminist political philosophy. Brown suggests that a therapist aids the client in resisting dominant cultural norms and attending to her own voice. Resistance is a positive and healthy endeavor given the social and political context, rather than a form of denial or misconduct. The therapist and client work "toward strategies and solutions advancing feminist resistance, transformation, and social change in daily personal life, and in relationships with the social, emotional, and political environment" (p. 22).

Such works as Brown's have created alternatives for women therapists and women clients. Women who are dealing with the issues that the female inmates are dealing with–poverty, abuse, domestic violence, and addiction–can seek out feminist therapy that will help them address such problems as low self-esteem, inability to trust others, and anger (Herman,

1992). The therapist and client address problems in the context in which they were created, and solutions provide movement toward personal and social change. Women can receive help in an environment that fosters resistance and personal integrity rather than infantilization, self-directedness rather than conformity, and self-esteem rather than self-doubt.

However, boot camps for women reflect a curious mixture of ideologies, goals, and programs which do not necessarily consider the problems and needs of female inmates. Utilization of boot camp programs presumes that all women offenders who qualify for boot camp have the same difficulties and need the same "treatment." The boot camp conceptualization of female offenders assumes that women who have committed crimes need a stronger sense of discipline and responsibility. This doctrine is reminiscent of the "fallen woman" ideology that feminists and reformers have been fighting for the last two centuries, and ignores our current knowledge about female offenders. As a form of social control, boot camps attempt literally to drill these missing attributes into the "fallen women" in an attempt to make them "disciplined," "respectable," or "socially acceptable."

This form of "treatment" is contrary to feminist therapy practice as conceptualized by Brown (1996). In boot camps, women are dressed alike, drilled, and worked in a regimented manner. Prison administrators assume that drilling and work (with no other programming in some cases) will instill discipline, thereby producing the desired positive changes in women. This is contradictory to Brown's conceptualization of feminist therapy in which women learn to attend to their own voice and resist dominant role expectations if these expectations conflict with their own goals. Although MacKenzie et al. (1994) found that some female inmates felt that learning discipline might help them better to negotiate life after prison, this premise has not been empirically validated. Further, the notion that improved discipline and responsibility are the proper therapeutic goals for all women in boot camps is inconsistent with the existing research on female inmates, especially Sommers' (1995) findings on women's motivation for committing crime. It ignores such social contexts of women's crime as poverty, violence, and substance abuse. Indeed, prison programs will probably best address social problems by helping women to confront prescribed social norms rather than drilling them into conformity.

Boot camp programs also set up a very definite and unhealthy power structure which may be detrimental to the female inmates, especially those who have been survivors of incest, acquaintance rape, and domestic violence. Such abuse, which occurs in the context of an "intimate" relationship, leaves the victim confused and traumatized (Herman, 1992). This confusing dynamic is the core of boot camps which try to habilitate but may further traumatize by sending conflicting messages to women. Boot camps in which a woman is marching and being inspected by a powerful other one minute, and in therapy with that same powerful other the next, may create a similarly warped environment to the one in which the woman was abused. This strategy institutionalizes and further sanctions the abuse dynamic, in which a parent or spouse is both a caring confidante and an abuser. It would be less confusing (to both inmates and staff) if the jailer and the counselor were different people, in different settings. Female inmates could learn that, contrary to much of their prior experience, intimidation and intimacy do not have to coexist in all relationships.

Finally, boot camps are first, and maybe foremost, punishment. The drilling and yelling that take place in all boot camps to a greater or lesser extent are punishment. In addition, Hannah-Moffat (1995) points out that in a society as liberal as ours, depriving a person of numerous rights by incarceration is a serious penalty. Since boot camp programs are housed in prisons, the assumption that female offenders should be punished is inherent to boot camps and any other prison-based programs. And this is, again, contrary to feminist and most other forms of therapy. It creates the same unhealthy tension that Freedman (1981) referred to in the nineteenth century prisons, where "fallen women" were being punished and taught to be domestic.

CONCLUSIONS

Feminist therapists employed in a boot camp must learn to work in a difficult environment. The therapist in a boot camp, as in other prison settings, has the difficult assignment of earning the trust and respect of the inmates in a context in which it is advisable for inmates to be cautious. Therapists must also find a way to separate themselves sufficiently from the power structure of the prison so that they do not engage in confusing dual relationships that would undermine the process of feminist therapy (i.e., acting as both therapist and disciplinarian). Maintaining confidentiality, acting as an advocate for the inmates, and treating the inmates with respect in an environment where others may treat the inmates with contempt may help the therapists' efforts. Negotiating clear boundaries with prison administrators that are conducive to providing a safe and respectful environment is also imperative.

In their practice with female inmates, whether in boot camps or in other prison settings, therapists face the challenge of working in a punishing environment. This poses a difficult balancing act for the feminist therapist who must somehow nurture personal growth in a situation where resistance may be punished by expulsion from the boot camp program and a longer and more unpleasant incarceration. The feminist therapist working in the boot camp or other prison must aid the clients in identifying and asserting their own needs while their clients are being denied their freedom in an environment that demands conformity. In addition, the therapist must find a way to help women identify and express their feelings, including those about their incarceration, in a way that will not be punished. It is incumbent upon the therapist to face these challenges successfully in order to help to counter the negative messages of the boot camp and prison, support the women and foster growth, and help their clients survive the confusion and trauma they are experiencing.

Unfortunately, it is not possible to separate punishment and habilitation of offenders as long as they are being sentenced to prison. It is important to try to find alternative methods of sentencing offenders, especially the non-violent first offenders who are typically sentenced to boot camps. The advent of the boot camp is an important one in that it does represent a willingness to institute short-term habilitative correctional programming as opposed to long-term warehousing of offenders. However, departments of corrections should institute short-term programs conducted on a community or "out-patient" basis, and without the punishment. Therapists who work in such programs could orient interventions toward helping women to identify and attain their own objectives rather than imposing other people's ideals upon them. Punishment need not be the focus of corrections. After leaving the bench when ordered by the Supreme Court of Pennsylvania to impose a mandatory five-year sentence that she felt was unjust, Judge Lois Forer (1994) observed, "The rage to punish is a costly American obsession. Punishment is defined as 'subjecting a person to pain for an offense or fault.' In any other context the desire to cause pain is considered sadism, a psychiatric disorder" (p. 10).

REFERENCES

American Correctional Association. (1990). *The female offender: What does the future hold?* Arlington, VA: Kirby Lithographic Company, Inc.

Austin, J., Jones, M., & Bolyard, M. (1993). *The growing use of jail boot camps: The current state of the art.* Washington, DC: National Institute of Justice, U.S. Department of Justice, Office of Justice Programs.

Belknap, J. (1996). *The invisible woman: Gender, crime, and justice.* Belmont, CA: Wadsworth Publishing Co.

Brown, L. S. (1996). *Subversive dialogues: Theory in feminist therapy.* New York, New York: Basic Books.

Bureau of Justice Statistics. (1991, March). *Special report: Women in prison* (Report No. NCJ-127855). Washington, DC: U.S. Government Printing Office.

Bureau of Justice Statistics. (1994, March). *Special report: Women in prison: Survey of state prison inmates* (Report No. NCJ-145321). Washington, DC: U.S. Government Printing Office.

Burton, V. S., Marquart, J. W., Cuvelier, S. J., Alarid, L. F., & Hunter, R. J. (1993). A study of attitudinal change among boot camp participants. *Federal Probation, 57* (3), 46-52.

Eaton, M. (1993). *Women after prison*. Buckingham, England: Open University Press.

Feinman, C. (1986). *Women in the criminal justice system* (2nd ed.). New York: Praeger Publishers.

Fletcher, B. R., Shaver, L. D., & Moon, D. G. (Eds.). (1993). *Women offenders in Oklahoma: A forgotten population*. New York: Praeger Press.

Forer, L. G. (1994). *A rage to punish: The unintended consequences of mandatory sentencing*. New York: W. W. Norton & Company.

Freedman, E. B. (1981). *Their sisters' keepers*. Ann Arbor: The University of Michigan Press.

Gilfus, M. (1988). *Seasoned by love/tempered by violence: A qualitative study of women and crime*. Unpublished doctoral dissertation, Brandeis University.

Hannah-Moffat, K. (1995). Feminine fortresses: Woman-centered prisons? *The Prison Journal, 75* (2), 135-164.

Herman, J. L. (1992). *Trauma and recovery*. New York: Basic Books.

Lombroso, C., & Ferrero, W. (1900). *The female offender*. New York: Appleton.

MacKenzie, D. L. (1991). The parole performance of offenders released from shock incarceration (boot camp prisons): A survival time analysis. *Journal of Quantitative Criminology, 7* (3), 213-236.

MacKenzie, D. L. (1994). Boot camps: A national assessment. *Overcrowded Times, 5* (4), pp. 1, 14-18.

MacKenzie, D. L., & Brame, R. (1995). Shock incarceration and positive adjustment during community supervision. *Journal of Quantitative Criminology, 11* (2), 111-142.

MacKenzie, D. L., Brame, R., McDowall, D., & Souryal, C. (1995). Boot camp prisons and recidivism in eight states. *Criminology, 33* (3), 327-357.

MacKenzie, D. L., Elis, L. A., Simpson, S. S., & Skroban, S. B. (1994). *Female offenders in boot camp prisons*. Washington DC: National Institute of Justice, U.S. Department of Justice, Office of Justice Programs.

MacKenzie, D. L., Shaw, J. W., & Gowdy, V. B. (1993). *An evaluation of shock incarceration in Louisiana* (NCJ no. 140567). Washington DC: National Institute of Justice, U.S. Department of Justice, Office of Justice Programs.

MacKenzie, D. L., Shaw, J. W., & Souryal, C. (1992). Characteristics associated with successful adjustment to supervision: A comparison of parolees, probationers, shock participants, and shock dropouts. *Criminal Justice and Behavior, 19* (4), 437-454.

MacKenzie, D. L., & Souryal, C. (1994). *Multisite evaluation of shock incarceration* (NCJ no. 142462). Washington DC: National Institute of Justice, U.S. Department of Justice, Office of Justice Programs.

Marcus-Mendoza, S. T. (1995). A preliminary analysis of Oklahoma's Shock Incarceration Program. *Journal of the Oklahoma Criminal Justice Research Consortium, 2,* 1-6.

Marcus-Mendoza, & Briody. (in press). Female inmates in Oklahoma: An updated profile and programming assessment.

Marcus-Mendoza, S. T., Sargent, E., & Chong Ho, Y. (1994). Changing perceptions of the etiology of crime: The relationship between abuse and female criminology. *Journal of the Oklahoma Criminal Justice Research Consortium, 1,* 13-23.

Morash, M., Haarr, R. N., & Rucker, L. (1994). A comparison of programming for women and men in U.S. prisons in the 1980s. *Crime & Delinquency, 40* (2), 197-221.

Morash, M., & Rucker, L. (1990). A critical look at the idea of boot camp as a correctional reform. *Crime & Delinquency, 36* (2), 204-222.

Osler, M. (1991). Shock incarceration: Hard realities and real possibilities. *Federal Probation, 55* (1), 34-42.

Owen, B., & Bloom, B. (1995). Profiling women prisoners: Findings from national surveys and a California sample. *The Prison Journal, 72* (2), 165-185.

Parent, D. G. (1989). *Shock incarceration: An overview of existing programs.* Washington DC: National Institute of Justice, U.S. Department of Justice, Office of Justice Programs.

Parent, D. G. (1994). Boot camps failing to achieve goals. *Overcrowded Times, 5* (4), 8-11.

Pollock-Byrne, J. M. (1990). *Women, prison, and crime.* Pacific Grove, CA: Brooks/Cole Publishing.

Rafter, N. H. (1990). *Partial justice: Women, prisons, and social control* (2nd ed.). New Brunswick, NJ: Transaction Publishers.

Russell, D. E. H. (1984). *Sexual exploitation: Rape, child sexual abuse, and sexual harassment.* Beverly Hills, CA: Sage.

Sechrest, D. K. (1989). Prison "boot camps" do not measure up. *Federal Probation, 53* (3), 15-20.

Sommers, E. K. (1995). *Voices from within: Women who have broken the law.* Toronto: University of Toronto Press.

U.S. Department of Commerce. (1995). *Statistical abstract of the United States 1995* (115 ed.). Washington, DC: U.S. Government Printing Office.

U.S. Department of Health and Human Services. (1996). *National household survey on drug abuse: Population estimates 1995* (DHHS No. SMA 96-3095). Rockville, MD: Author.

Walker, L. E. A. (1994). *Abused women and survivor therapy.* Washington, DC: American Psychological Association.

Index

Abortion, as a moral crime, 2
Addiction. *See* Treatment
  approaches: for addiction
African American prisoners
  childcare patterns of, 60-63,
    66-69,73*table*
  with children, 21,24-25
  in services and prevention study
    children relationships and, 21,
      24-25
    demographics of, 16,16*table*
    housing needs and, 23
    job training need and, 23
    outside relationships and,
      19-20
    physical and sexual abuse
      incidence and, 18-19
    prison relationships and, 20
    substance abuse incidence and,
      18,19
  statistics on, 14,58,144
Art therapy
  case studies in, 159-169
  communication by, 158,169
  conclusions regarding, 169
  empowerment through, 159,169
  image focus of, 158,159
  protective environment of, 158
  repressed information and, 158
  self-injurious behavior and,
    159-161,162-165,169
  summary regarding, 157
  trauma experiences and, 157-158,
    160-161,162-165,167-169

Battered women. *See* Murderers of
  abusive partners

Battered women's movement,
  empowerment from, 7
Boot camp prison program: feminist
  examination of
  boot camp development and,
    178-179
  conclusions regarding, 182-183
  detrimental effects of, 179
  female inmates of 1990s and,
    176-178
  feminist theory and, 180-182
  gender stereotyping and, 175,178
  goals of, 177-180
  historical perspective on, 174-175
  male criminology theories and,
    175,177
  moral crime concept and, 2,175,
    181
  moral ideology of penal code and,
    173,174
  power structure and, 181-182
  summary regarding, 173-174
Borderline personality disorder, of
  childhood sexual abuse
  survivors, 39-40
Bureau of Justice Statistics, 3

Case examples
  of art therapy, 159-169
  of internalized sexism of female
    adolescent offenders,
    136-137
  of interventions for female
    adolescent offenders,
    86-87,94-95
  of motherhood in prison, 104,109,
    110-113,115-121

Center for Substance Abuse
    Treatment, 149
Childhood sexual abuse survivors
    betrayal and, 34-35,37
    Borderline Personality Disorder
        and, 39-40
    conclusions regarding, 42
    criminal behavior correlation and,
        30
    inmate code and, 36
    learned helplessness concept and,
        33
    peer support teams and, 39
    Posttraumatic Stress Disorder
        and, 40
    powerlessness and, 32-34,37,38
    prevalence of, 29,37
    reentering society and, 36-37,42
    research implications of, 41-42
    self-blame and, 33
    self-injury coping strategy of, 30,
        36,37,39
    staffing policy implications of,
        40-41
    stigmatization of, 35-37
    substance abuse coping strategy
        of, 30,35,36,37,38-39
    suicide coping strategy of, 30,34,
        36,37,39
    summary regarding, 29-30
    therapy implications of, 38-40
    traumatic sexualization and,
        31-32,37
    violence coping strategy of, 30,
        34,35,37,38
Children in Custody census, of
        Office of Juvenile Justice
        and Delinquency
        Prevention, 90
Children of women prisoners
    affordable housing for, 7
    extended family caregivers of,
        4-5,20-21,60-61,63,66,
        73*table*
    trauma of, 5,24-25

welfare reform and, 6-7
    See also Motherhood in prison:
        specific subject
Complex Posttraumatic Stress
        Disorder, 40
Criminal justice policy, male/female
        parity in, 2-3
Criminalization of abortion, 2

Developmental framework, of
        women prisoners of color,
        18-19
Disorder of Extreme Stress Not
        Otherwise Specified, 40
Dissociative Identity Disorder, 158,
        161
Domestic violence. *See* Murderers of
        abusive partners

Educational needs, of women
        prisoners of color, 22,25-26
Extended family, as children
        caregivers, 4-5,20-21,
        60-61,63,66,67-68,73*table*

Family Unity Demonstration Project,
        6
Female adolescent offenders:
        feminist intervention
        strategy for
    case examples of, 86-87,94-95
    conclusions regarding, 99-100
    increase in, 85
    juvenile justice system framework
        and
        developmental needs and,
            92-94
        gender bias and, 85,90-92
        gender-specific needs and, 85,
            92-94
        mental health treatment
            resources and, 86,94-96,100

social/political attitudes and,
  88-90
restorative justice movement and,
  86,96-100
retributive justice response and,
  86,89-90,97
runaway offenses and, 89,91
self-advocacy issues and, 85,93,
  94-96
self-identity issues and, 85,93,99
status offender concept and, 89,
  90-91,127
summary regarding, 85-86
systems intervention model use
  and, 87,93,94-96,99-100
Twelve Step programs and, 152
See also Female adolescent
  offenders: internalized
  sexism and
Female adolescent offenders:
  internalized sexism and
adultism tendency and, 135
ageism weapon and, 135-136
conclusions regarding, 138-139
goals and, 138
group demographics and, 129-130
group development history and,
  128-130
group process and
  father issues, 132
  first effects, 130-131
  mother issues, 131
  sex issues, 132-133
  violence, 132
learning process and, 133-135
  other mistakes, 135-136
listening importance and, 131,
  135,138
personal statements and, 136-137
"role strain" concept, 127
self-identity and, 130
status offender concept and, 127
successful topics and, 137-138
summary regarding, 127
therapist limitations and, 134-135

traditional roles and, 134
Feminist viewpoint. *See* Boot camp
  prison program: feminist
  examination of; Female
  adolescent offenders:
  feminist intervention
  strategy
Fostercare of children of inmates,
  patterns of, 60,62-67,69,
  73*table*

Gay relationships. *See* Lesbian
  relationships
Gender bias, toward female
  adolescent offenders, 85,
  90-92
Gender roles. *See* Female adolescent
  offenders: internalized
  sexism and
Girls Incorporated, 128
Girls in jail. *See* Female adolescent
  offenders: *specific subject*
Glover v. Johnson (MI), 2
Grandparents as parents
  problems encountered by, 4-5
  racial and ethnic patterns of, 65,
    67-68,69,73*table*
  statistics on, 4,20-21,60
Guilt, of mothers in prison, 104,
  105-106,114-118,145

Hispanic American prisoners
  childcare patterns of, 60-62,68,
    73*table*
  in services and prevention study
    children relationships and, 21
    demographics of, 16,16*table*
    housing needs and, 23
    language needs and, 23,26
    outside relationships and,
      19-20
    prison relationships and, 20

substance abuse incidence and,
    18,19
statistics on, 14,58,144
Homosexuality. *See* Lesbian
    relationships
Human Kindness Foundation, 153
Human Rights Watch Women's
    Rights Project, 145

Illegitimacy, moral crime of, 2
Internalized sexism. *See* Female
    adolescent offenders:
    internalized sexism and

Job training, for women prisoners of
    color, 23
JusticeWorks Community, 6

Kinship. *See* Extended family

Lesbian relationships
    conformity and, 81
    counseling implications and,
        82-84
    experience of, 79-81
    manipulation targets and, 80
    outside relationships and, 81-82,
        83-84
    prison approaches to, 78-79
    prison therapy and, 82
    self-esteem and, 76-77,82
    "serious" vs. "players"
        relationships and, 79
    sexuality discovery and, 78
    social standing and, 77,80-81
    summary regarding, 75
    therapy sincerity necessity and,
        83
    "turned out" terminology and,
        77-78
    violence myth of, 75,77

Male prisoners
    criminal justice policy parity and,
        2-3
    criminology theories of, 175,177
    fatherhood statistics of, 4
    vs. female profile, 13-14
    services for, 12,142
    statistics on, 2
Motherhood in prison
    childhood trauma and, 5
    public assistance policies and, 6-7
    statistics on, 1,4-5,144-145,177
    See also Motherhood in prison:
        specific subject
Motherhood in prison: child
        placement factors and
    conclusions regarding,
        70-71
    family crime networks and, 59
    family elasticity concept and,
        61-62
    family embeddedness and, 58-59
    introduction regarding, 57-59
    kinship networks and, 61
    parental fitness issue and, 63,67
    paying back child-caring
        obligation and, 64
    placement options and patterns
        and, 59-62,73*table*
    policy implications and, 71
    racial and ethnic placement
        factors and, 60-62,65,
        67-68,69,73*table*
    research needs and, 70
    study aims and, 62
    summary regarding, 57
Motherhood in prison: psychosocial
        approach to
    active role importance and,
        107-108
    assessment regarding, 121-122
    case examples of, 104,109,
        110-113,115-121
    grief/loss focus of, 106,118-121

group psychotherapy impact of,
  108-109,122-123
guilt and shame focus of, 104,
  105-106,114-118,145
inmate background and, 106-108
mothers need to be mothered
  focus of, 109-114
peer vs. professional therapist
  and, 122-123
powerlessness and, 106-107,124
program background and,
  104-105
reflections regarding, 123-124
social or group process impact
  and, 106,109-114
summary regarding, 103-104
theoretical framework regarding,
  108-109
trauma recovery process and, 105,
  106,109-114,141,142,
  148-149,176-177
*Mothers in Prison, Children in Crisis
  Campaign*, 6
MPDQ (Mutual Psychological
  Development
  Questionnaire), 18
Murderers of abusive partners
  battered women myths and, 46
  battered women strategies and, 47
  domestic violence cycle and,
    45-46
  help-seeking behavior and, 46-47,
    48
  self-defense homicide and, 47-48
  vs. shelter-assisted women, 45-46
  social isolation factor and, 46,48,
    54
  study discussion and, 52-54
  study intent and, 46,52
  study limitations and, 53
  study method and
    measures, 49
    participants, 49
    procedures, 49-50
  study results and, 50

help-seeking behavior, 51-52,
  53
helpfulness of resources, 52,53
judicial system response, 51
police response, 51,53,54
study summary regarding, 45
suicide attempts and, 48
Mutual Psychological Development
  Questionnaire (MPDQ), 18

Native women prisoners (Canada),
  child abuse background
  of, 30

Office of Juvenile Justice and
  Delinquency Prevention
  (OJJDP), 90,128
OJJDP (Office of Juvenile Justice
  and Delinquency
  Prevention), 90,128

Parenting From a Distance program.
  See Motherhood in prison:
  psychosocial approach to
Personal Responsibility and Work
  Opportunity Reconciliation
  Act (1996), 6,88
Physical abuse
  drug treatment implications and,
    8, 145,150
  inmate history of, 3,13,18-19,26,
    109-114,145,148-149,
    157-158,167-169,176
Posttraumatic stress disorder, 40
Prison population statistics, 1-2
Progressive Era, "moral" crimes of,
  2,175
Psychological counseling
  addiction treatment and, 141,142,
    148
  of women prisoners of color,
    22-23

See also Motherhood in prison:
    psychosocial approach to

Racial and ethnic factors
    in child placement, 65,67-68,
       69,73*table*
    in prisoners, 12,144
    in services, 15
Reagonomics, 88
Relational framework
    addiction treatment and, 142,148,
       150-151
    MPDQ questionnaire and, 18
    outside relationships and, 19-20
    of women prisoners of color,
       14-15,19-20,24-25
    See also Lesbian relationships;
       Motherhood in prison:
       specific subject
Restorative justice movement, for
    female adolescent
    offenders, 86,96-100
Restricted love. *See* Lesbian
    relationships
Retributive justice response, to
    female adolescent
    offenders, 86,89-90,97

Self-advocacy, of female adolescent
    offenders, 85,93,94-96
Self-esteem
    of childhood sexual abuse
       survivors, 35
    of mothers in prison, 118-119,123
    of prison lesbians, 76-77,82
    sexuality and, 141
    of women prisoners of color,
       21-22
Self-identity
    in addiction treatment, 150
    of female adolescent offenders,
       85,93,99,130
    in female boot camps, 180

Self-injury
    art therapy and, 162-165
    as coping strategy, 30,36,37,39
Services and prevention for women
    prisoners
    developmental and preventive
       framework of, 15
    male vs. female prisoner profile
       and, 13-14
    male prisoner perspective on, 12
    racial discrimination and, 15
    relational theory framework of,
       14-15,24
    study discussion, 23-26
    study method
       measures, 17-18
       procedure, 17
       sample, 15-16,16*table*
       setting, 15
    study needs assessment
       additional prison resources, 23
       counseling-self knowledge,
         22-23
       education requirements, 22, 25
       employment and job training,
         23,25-26
       motivation sources, 22
       respect from correctional
         officers, 21-22
    study results
       children, 20-21,24-25
       developmental histories, 18-19
       relational context, 19-20,24-25
    summary regarding, 11-12
Sexual abuse
    art therapy and, 167-169
    drug treatment implications and,
       8,145,150
    inmate history of, 3,13,18-19,26,
       109-114,145,148-149,
       157-158,162,176
    See also Childhood sexual abuse
Sexuality, addiction treatment and,
    151

Shock incarceration. *See* Boot camp prison program: feminist examination of

Spirituality, addiction treatment and, 151-152

Status offender concept, of female adolescent offenders, 89, 90-91,127

Stigmatization, of childhood sexual abuse survivors, 35-37

Substance abuse
as coping strategy, 30,35,36,37, 38-39
counseling for, 23
crime statistics and, 3-4
incidence of, 18,19,176-177
treatment of, 4,8
See also Treatment approaches: for addiction

Subversive Dialogues (Brown), 180

Suicidal behavior
of murderers of abusive partners, 48
as sexual abuse coping strategy, 34,36,37,39

Systems theory. *See* Female adolescent offenders

Trauma
addiction treatment model and, 141,142,148-149,176-177
of mothers in prison, 105,106, 109-114,141,142,148-149
See also Art therapy; Childhood sexual abuse survivors

Traumagenic Model of Child Sexual Abuse, 31,34,35

Treatment approaches
adolescent mental health and, 86,94-96,100
battered women's movement and, 7
to childhood sexual abuse survivors, 38-40

family-centered interventions and, 8
See also Treatment approaches: for addiction

Treatment approaches: for addiction, 4,8
AIDS and, 144
conclusions regarding, 153
integrated model of, 146-147
addiction theory and, 141,142, 147-148
psychological development theory and, 141,142,148
trauma theory and, 141,142, 148-149,176-177
lack of, 141,142,143,145-146
motherhood and, 144-145
prisoner demographics and, 143-145
recovery and
comprehensive model of, 142, 149-150
relationships and, 142,148, 150-151
the self and, 142,150
sexuality and, 142,151
spirituality and, 142,151-152
summary regarding, 141
Twelve Step programs and, 141,149,150,152-153
war on drugs and, 142,143
women prisoners increase and, 143
women's vs. men's needs, 142
See also Art therapy; Services and prevention

Twelve Step programs, 141,149,150, 152-153

Violent crime
physical/sexual abuse and, 3,26
women vs. men's victims of, 3

Violent Crime Control and Law
    Enforcement Act (1994),
    6,89

Welfare reform, 6-7
Welfare Reform Bill of 1996, 88
Women prisoners
    battered women's movement and,
        7
    community-based sanctioned
        alternatives for, 5-6
    drug treatment for, 8
    drug-related crime statistics and,
        3-4
    family-centered interventions and,
        8
    increase in, 1-2,11-13,57-58
    racial and ethnic composition of,
        12
    rehabilitation equality and, 2
    violent crime statistics and, 3
    welfare reform and, 6-7
    See also Art therapy; Boot camp
        prison programs; Childhood
        sexual abuse survivors;

Female adolescent
    offenders; Lesbian
    relationships; Motherhood
    in prison: *specific subject*;
    Murderers of abusive
    partners; Services and
    prevention for women
    prisoners; Treatment
    approaches: *specific
    subject*; Women prisoners
    of color
Women prisoners of color
    abuse incidence of, 18-19
    children demographics and,
        20-21,24-25
    developmental histories of, 18-19
    discrimination and, 15,144
    identity and behavior of, 14
    needs assessment of, 21-23,25-26
    relational framework of, 14-15,
        18,19-20,24
    substance abuse incidence and, 19
    See also Services and prevention
        for women prisoners
Women's voices. *See* Art therapy

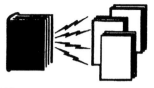

Haworth
DOCUMENT DELIVERY
SERVICE

This valuable service provides a single-article order form for any article from a Haworth journal.

- *Time Saving:* No running around from library to library to find a specific article.
- *Cost Effective:* All costs are kept down to a minimum.
- *Fast Delivery:* Choose from several options, including same-day FAX.
- *No Copyright Hassles:* You will be supplied by the original publisher.
- *Easy Payment:* Choose from several easy payment methods.

Open Accounts Welcome for . . .
- Library Interlibrary Loan Departments
- Library Network/Consortia Wishing to Provide Single-Article Services
- Indexing/Abstracting Services with Single Article Provision Services
- Document Provision Brokers and Freelance Information Service Providers

---

MAIL or *FAX* THIS ENTIRE ORDER FORM TO:

Haworth Document Delivery Service | **or FAX:** 1-800-895-0582
The Haworth Press, Inc. | **or CALL:** 1-800-342-9678
10 Alice Street | 9am-5pm EST
Binghamton, NY 13904-1580 |

PLEASE SEND ME PHOTOCOPIES OF THE FOLLOWING SINGLE ARTICLES:

1) Journal Title: _____

   Vol/Issue/Year: _____ Starting & Ending Pages: _____

Article Title: _____

_____

2) Journal Title: _____

   Vol/Issue/Year: _____ Starting & Ending Pages: _____

Article Title: _____

_____

3) Journal Title: _____

   Vol/Issue/Year: _____ Starting & Ending Pages: _____

Article Title: _____

_____

4) Journal Title: _____

   Vol/Issue/Year: _____ Starting & Ending Pages: _____

Article Title: _____

_____

(See other side for Costs and Payment Information)

COSTS: Please figure your cost to order quality copies of an article.

1. Set-up charge per article: $8.00
        ($8.00 × number of separate articles)   _____

2. Photocopying charge for each article:
       1-10 pages: $1.00   _____

       11-19 pages: $3.00   _____

       20-29 pages: $5.00   _____

       30+ pages: $2.00/10 pages   _____

3. Flexicover (optional): $2.00/article   _____

4. Postage & Handling: US: $1.00 for the first article/
        $.50 each additional article   _____

        Federal Express: $25.00   _____

        Outside US: $2.00 for first article/
         $.50 each additional article_____

5. Same-day FAX service: $.35 per page   _____

       GRAND TOTAL: _____

METHOD OF PAYMENT: (please check one)

❑ Check enclosed ❑ Please ship and bill. PO # _____
    (sorry we can ship and bill to bookstores only! All others must pre-pay)

❑ Charge to my credit card: ❑ Visa; ❑ MasterCard; ❑ Discover;
      ❑ American Express;

Account Number:_____ Expiration date:_____

Signature: ✗_____

Name: _____ Institution: _____

Address: _____

_____

City: _____ State:_____ Zip:_____

Phone Number: _____ FAX Number: _____

MAIL or *FAX* THIS ENTIRE ORDER FORM TO:

Haworth Document Delivery Service	**or FAX:** 1-800-895-0582
The Haworth Press, Inc.	**or CALL:** 1-800-342-9678
10 Alice Street	9am-5pm EST)
Binghamton, NY 13904-1580	

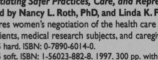

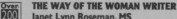